In praise of *The On*

"Writer and photographer Heacox delivers a genuine, deeply moving account of the past twenty-five years he has spent living in Glacier Bay, Alaska. . . . Heacox's ability to use this tension—between the beauty of the Alaskan wilderness and the creeping encroachment of modern life—is the thread that unites his varied observations, and it's what gives the book its uniqueness and keeps it from being another pale imitation of *Coming into the Country*, John McPhee's late-1970s classic on Alaska."

—Publishers Weekly

"A long-time resident of Alaska's Glacier Bay reflects on and explores human accountability toward the area. . . . [It is a] tender chronicle of a miracle in process, with glints of its rarity thrown by the handful from these pages."

—Kirkus Reviews

"'Make access easy, and a place dies,' is his motto, and therein lies the paradox that Heacox tries to resolve in this book. . . . As he wrestles with such conundrums, Heacox creates a nicely balanced environmental portrait of Alaska's ice-cut coast."

—Booklist

"Heacox is a poet, a scholar, a naturalist and a wild man who, in this great book, weaves together the story of the land and the people. *The Only Kayak* helps us reconnect what the Lakota call the sacred hoop of life. I want to give this book to a dozen friends and, dear reader, I want to share it with you. Bravo, Kim Heacox."

—Mary Pipher, author of Reviving Ophelia and
The Shelter of Each Other

"Few have wandered more deeply and thoughtfully through the wilds of Alaska than Kim Heacox. Those who know him best through his extraordinary photographs now have the chance to accompany him in words through some of the wildest and most beautiful country anywhere on earth. *The Only Kayak* is a delight."

—William Cronon, Frederick Jackson Turner and Vilas Research
Professor of History, Geography, and Environmental Studies,
University of Wisconsin-Madison

"With this powerful book, Kim Heacox enters the first rank of writers on the wild, the human, and the mix between the two. It's set in one of America's most spectacular landscapes, but it's also set in one of its kindest, most open hearts. A real triumph."
—Bill McKibben, author *The End of Nature*, and *Wandering Home: A Long Walk Through America's Most Hopeful Region*

"Perhaps more than ever before, we need passionate, eloquent voices speaking out for the American land. . . . Kim Heacox's writing evokes the fundamental paradox of our times: the vast, beauty of Alaska shining brilliantly against the dark, encroaching peril of industrial America. Anyone who cares about our remaining wild places, and about the conscience of those who stand in defense of our natural heritage, should read this extraordinary book."
—Richard Nelson, author of *The Island Within* and *Make Prayers to the Raven*

"*The Only Kayak* is an important and beautiful book about what it means to fall in love with a place—not just any place, but the wild, dangerous, breath-catching, gorgeous Glacier Bay. And not just any love, but a wistful, sometimes desperate yearning to protect a wilderness even as it melts away. Kim Heacox is what this world needs—a defender of the land as fierce and funny as Abbey or Thoreau."
–Kathleen Dean Moore, author of *Riverwalking* and *The Pine Island Paradox*

"Heacox's book is both a coming-of-(middle)age memoir and a love story, with Alaska serving as both the journey's end and the beloved. While Heacox writes passionately about his home in Glacier Bay, he also acknowledges the inevitability of change there. In prose that is both lyrical and powerful, he gives the reader a complete picture of the beauty of that wilderness and what will be lost in its deterioration." —*Book News*

"...this book is about learning to walk with purpose. It's about a lot of things, actually—love, community, heartbreak, hope for people and place. It's about how living an unexamined life is far riskier than sleeping on a beach with bears."
—*Anchorage Daily News*

"The naturalist expert for National Geographic Expeditions is a talented writer, a good storyteller, and passionate about his state; and he takes [us] through his journey of falling in love, aging and learning when to let go." —*Everett Herald* (Washington)

the ONLY KAYAK

the ONLY KAYAK

A Journey into the Heart of Alaska

KIM HEACOX

THE LYONS PRESS

Guilford, Connecticut

An imprint of The Globe Pequot Press

All photos by Kim Heacox except where otherwise noted.

"Geotheomorphology" and "Pioneers" first appeared in slightly different form in the
literary journal *Connotations*, published by the Island Institute, Sitka, Alaska.

Paperback ISBN 1-59228-894-4

The Library of Congress has previously cataloged an earlier (hardcover) edition as follows:
Heacox, Kim.
  The only kayak : a journey into the heart of Alaska / Kim Heacox.
    p. cm.
  Includes bibliographical references.
  ISBN 1-59228-715-8
  1. Glacier Bay Region (Alaska)—Description and travel. 2. Glacier Bay Region
(Alaska)—Social life and customs. 3. Community life—Alaska—Glacier Bay Region.
4. Outdoor life—Alaska—Glacier Bay Region. 5. Glacier Bay Region (Alaska)—
Environmental conditions. 6. Environmentalism—Alaska—Glacier Bay Region. 7.
Glacier Bay Region (Alaska)—Biography. 8. Heacox, Kim—Travel—Alaska—Glacier
Bay Region. 9. Kayaking—Alaska—Glacier Bay. I. Title.
F912.G5H43 2005
917.98'2—dc22   2004063302

For my mother and father, Virginia and Bill Heacox,
who taught me when to hold on and when to let go.

Contents

※

※

And now I understand. I understand all the old attempts at description. I understand why they were written and why they failed.

—Dave Bohn, *GLACIER BAY: The Land and the Silence*

LETTING GO

Prologue

I LIVE IN THE SUNLIGHT OF FRIENDS and the shadows of glaciers. I suppose I will die there too, if all goes well. No hurry, though. The hardness of water, the ebb and flow of ice, the once and future glaciers of America—they created my home and they will destroy it. My winter is only a heartbeat to them.

Don't get me wrong. I wasn't born in a cave or raised by wolves. I grew up on pavement and the soft seat of a Schwinn Red Racer, gripping the handlebars with everything I had. Then somewhere along the way I let go and found something new, but also something ancient. I moved to Glacier Bay, Alaska, the last wild shore, nine hundred miles north of Seattle and nine hundred years in the past, and I never came back.

An hour ago I left Melanie in the tent, curled deep in her sleeping bag, dreaming her finger-twitching dreams. I swear she's a coyote out here. Give her a tail, and she'd wrap it over her nose. A September gale blows as I walk the rocky beach. Waves pound the shore. Spokes of sunlight stab the cross-grained sea and stir it into a running scrim of hypothermic blue and glaucous gray. Bonaparte's gulls pinwheel into the gusts, if not impervious to the storm, then certainly defiant of it. A flock of crows, sixty black birds previously raucous at the mouth of a stream, is quiet now, mute in the forest, waiting to return, like the ice.

By the light of two teachers, three friends, and one lover (the coyote back in the tent), I came to this wild shore when I was twenty-five, and stayed. Now I'm fifty, dear God. A man is expected to have achieved something in half a century. Cure cancer. Conquer Asia. Find a face in a raindrop. We joke about cheating death until a friend dies. After that, the Earth wobbles more than it spins. The weather itself becomes a wild animal. The glaciers stir.

Life is precious here because it can end suddenly. Planes go down. Boats disappear. A hiker goes into the winter woods in tennis shoes, a cotton shirt, and blue jeans, and never comes out.

In Lituya Bay, on the Outer Coast of Glacier Bay where the Fairweather Range catches storms off the Gulf of Alaska, disasters are legendary. The French explorer Jean-François LaPerouse anchored his ships there and gave written instructions to one of his officers to take three longboats to map the area and avoid the treacherous shoal at the mouth of the bay. The officer replied, "Do you take me for a child? I have commanded ships of war." Sure enough, he approached the shoal and got caught in a riptide. Two boats went down, with all hands lost.

LaPerouse buried an account of the tragedy in a bottle. "At the entrance of this harbour perished twenty-one brave seamen. Reader, whoever thou art, mingle thy tears with ours."

FROM WHERE I stand at Tlingit Point, I can see a wide fetch of the lower bay running thirty miles south to Icy Strait. To the north, the upper bay branches into a dendritic pattern of smaller inlets that reach talon-like into tall mountains and bedrock cliffs. The inlets aren't visible from here, but after twenty-five years I can trace them in the bones in my hand.

Standing guard at the heads of these inlets are blue tidewater glaciers that in winter are as silent as falling snow, and in summer calve massive shards of ice into the sea with a sound the Native Tlingit people called "white thunder." They make a strong impression, yet are mere vestiges of the great glacier—one hundred miles long, five thousand feet thick—that filled the entire bay just two hundred years ago. It was an icy sarcophagus, brittle, cold, entombing, but also alive, pulsing to a metronome nobody understood then or understands now, not fully, not yet.

When the ice did retreat, it did so rapidly. In little more than one hundred years it pulled back seventy miles to unveil a naked, ice-chafed land, yet one remarkably resilient. A thousand habitats were born—and are *being born* every day—above sea level and below, homes for whale and wolf, merganser and mountain goat, sea urchin and Sitka spruce, brown bear and bufflehead, halibut and hermit thrush. Total destruction has become a tabula rasa for total rebirth; a dark ages followed by a renaissance.

People are reborn here, too. This place is that powerful. In Glacier Bay you don't inherit, you create. You practice resurrection because the land and sea show you that anything is possible. Moose swim across fjords. Bears traverse glaciers. Flowers emerge from granite boulders. Inlets fill with glacial silt. Shorelines shift and nautical charts become obsolete as the land—the actual crust of the Earth—rebounds after the immense weight of glacial ice has been lifted. As the land rises, islands merge with the mainland to become peninsulas. Tideflats become meadows. Meadows become forests. Travel this country and you move through more than geography, you move through time. Trace your finger over glacial striations in metamorphic rock. Stare into the fractured blue walls of the Ice Age, and you'll find they're not walls at all. They're windows.

I swear, sometimes I find myself wondering if glaciers, like crows, will once again fold an indigo wing over the land and steal the light.

THE STORM CALMS. I feel the wind catching its breath. The crows fly by, silent now, a shifting constellation of black on gray, a positive negative going wherever it is crows go. I scan the water and see a single little boat, impossibly small and alone, balanced fore and aft. I can't quite make it out, if it's coming or going. It may be a mirage, a chimera, a strange and foolish fantasy lingering on the thin filament of my hopes. I want it to go on forever, youthful in a young land, paddling into a sacred space where the best friends are made and glaciers have the last word and wild Alaska will never die. It's easy, I suppose, to want too much.

Karen Blixen once asked Denys Finch-Hatton about Africa, "Did you really think it would stay the way it was?"

"I thought it might," he answered, wistfully.

I did too. I thought Alaska—the Africa of America—might stay the way it was. Yet change is the only constant. Nature is anything but static. On the last wild shore, it's not the shadows of glaciers that worry me. It's the darker shadow of something Alaska has never seen before. It's saying the long good-bye and learning to say it gracefully, holding on and letting go amid what novelist Wallace Stegner would call my unbroken doublesong of love and lamentation.

I love this ice-cut coast. I love it for its storm-tossed, salt-bitten manners, and its resilience, how it puts on a dress of hemlock and spruce after glaciers have scoured it down to bedrock. I love it for how it sleeps in winter and pulses in summer and invites me to do the same. I love it for the chill of infinity it blows through me; how the rain fills my cup and I drink the sky. I love it the way a kid on a bicycle lets go of those handlebars and throws back his head, riding on faith.

I came here for the place, but stayed for the people. I stayed for the friendships, the warmth we find in the cold, the closeness we feel in the distance. I stayed because my friends stayed, and together we formed a community, a blanket, a family held together by stories about love and loss, risk and hope.

A story, for example, that begins in a little boat.

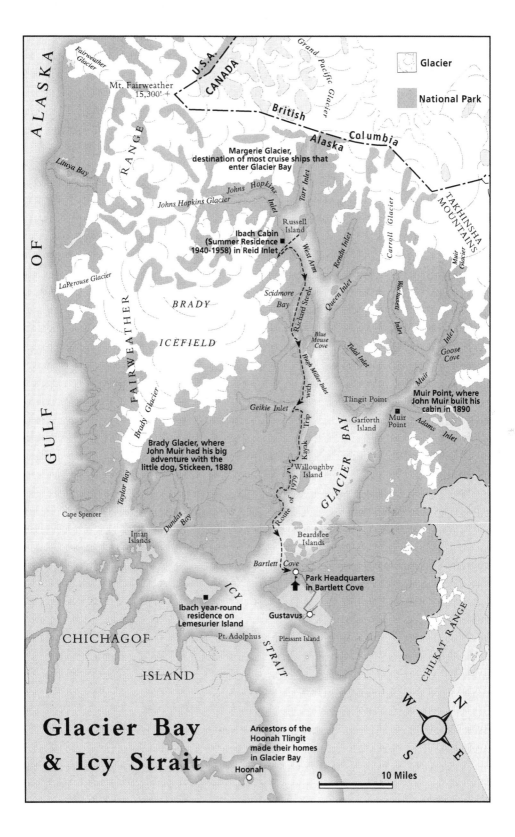

Glacier

National Park

Fairweather
Glacier

ALASKA

Mt. Fairweather
15,300' +

RANGE

Lituya Bay

U.S.A.

CANADA

British

Alaska Columbia

Grand Pacific Glacier

TAKHINSHA
MOUNTAINS

Margerie Glacier,
destination of most cruise ships that
enter Glacier Bay

OF

Johns Hopkins
Johns Hopkins Glacier

Carroll Glacier

Tarr Inlet

Russell
Island

Ibach Cabin
(Summer Residence
1940-1958) in Reid Inlet

West Arm

Rendu Inlet

Wachusett Inlet

Muir Glacier

LaPerouse Glacier

BRADY

FAIRWEATHER

Scidmore
Bay

Richard Steele

Queen Inlet

Inlet

ICEFIELD

Blue
Mouse
Cove

Tidal Inlet

Goose
Cove

Rush Miller Inlet

with

Muir

GULF

Brady Glacier

Geikie Inlet

Tlingit Point

Muir Point, where
John Muir built his
cabin in 1890

GLACIER BAY

Garforth
Island

Muir
Point

Adams Inlet

Kayak Trip

Brady Glacier, where
John Muir had his big
adventure with the
little dog, Stickeen, 1880

Taylor Bay

Willoughby
Island

Route of 1979

Cape Spencer

Inian
Islands

Dundas Bay

Beardslee
Islands

Bartlett Cove

Park Headquarters
in Bartlett Cove

ICY

Ibach year-round
residence on
Lemesurier Island

Gustavus

CHICHAGOF

Pt. Adolphus

Pleasant Island

STRAIT

ISLAND

CHILKAT RANGE

Glacier Bay
& Icy Strait

Ancestors of the
Hoonah Tlingit
made their homes
in Glacier Bay

Hoonah

W   N
   E
S

0   10 Miles

PART ONE

COMING HOME

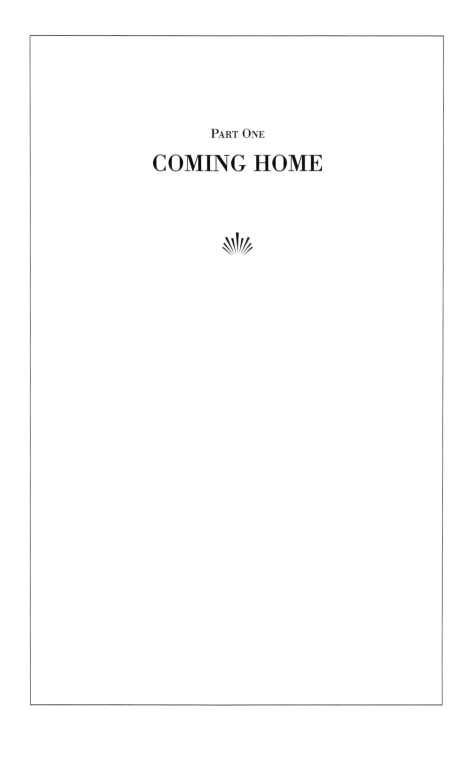

GEOTHEOMORPHOLOGY

Chapter One

———

YOU PADDLE A CANOE; you *wear* a kayak.

I sat at the waterline with my legs outstretched before me, trying to remember who said that . . . *You wear a kayak.* It was my first day in wild Alaska. Rudder down. Life vest on. The whereabouts of my tide tables, map, and compass escaped me. I couldn't find them and didn't care as I approached the luminous tidewater face of Reid Glacier.

Blue minarets of ice tipped away at precarious angles. Others stood as fractured fins and flying buttresses two hundred feet tall, certain to fall any day. Any minute. A light rain washed the ice and rock, the kayak and me. Delicate streams dripped off my hat into Reid Inlet where each droplet beaded diamond-like before joining the great whole of the silt-laden sea. Birds called in dialects of kittiwake and tern. A harbor seal watched me with obsidian eyes, only its head above the water, its whiskered face a cipher of mistrust. Long memory, no doubt, from when Tlingit Indians hunted them in boats of similar design to mine.

Icebergs surrounded me, this one a castle, that one a swan, each a corridor into the magic we know as children but lose as adults. Each capable of rolling over at any time, like innocence.

My knees were braced against the inside of the kayak. My gear was packed in plastic garbage bags stuffed into compartments forward and aft. Not much room to maneuver. My feet operated pedals connected to thin cables that controlled the rudder. Push on the left pedal and the kayak went left; push on the right and it went right. Sit still and it obeyed the higher calling of wind and tides.

I glided forward, thinking that a kayaker's passage through Glacier Bay is more like that of light through water, a refraction, a silent process of changing—*and being changed*—with each pull of the paddle and chant of the rain, each soft landing of snowflake on icefield. You hear the idioms of ice, the crystals cracking, the glacier groaning. You brace for the icefall that doesn't come because the glacier has more patience than you. You think about geologic time, the depth of an epoch, the tiny tenure of a single human life.

I stopped paddling yet continued moving forward as I shared my fate with Richard Steele, a boatman of mysterious pedigree and questionable nautical skill, who managed to torque our two-man kayak with each exuberant stroke. A big-shouldered, deep-chested fellow, Richard, when he paddled, didn't pull himself forward so much as he pushed the ocean behind. As best as I could tell he didn't intend to stop until we rammed the glacier. I wondered if he had his boots on the wrong feet, or if he flossed with twine. Three hundred yards from the blue ice wall. Two hundred and fifty, maybe two hundred. Hard to tell in an uncalibrated place.

"Uh, Richard . . . ," I said, "you think we're close enough?"

He stopped paddling.

We drifted among icebergs like so many stars in the sky. Constellations of ice. I scooped one up in my hand. Shaped like an awl, with a sharp tip and a smooth rounded grasp, it appeared as clear and delicate as glass.

From his sinking shoulders I could read Richard's disappointment. He wanted an icefall. He wanted the glacier to perform. His head twitched, and he seemed to pace even when seated. The rain drummed steady as Ravel's *Bolero* as the sea chewed away at the glacial underpinnings, yet everything was eerily still. I remembered a cartoon of a glacier with a bubble above holding its thoughts: "I may be slow," it said, "but I'm inexorable."

Our map told us the surrounding mountains were six thousand feet high. But the mapmakers were city fellows who didn't come out here. They offered no corrections for the imagination, which itself is a wild place. So with the ridges rising into the mist we made the mountains as high as we wished. Their Anglo-Saxon names cluttered our map like too many pages from an Ivy League phone book and reminded me of a geologist who after many years of fieldwork was to be honored by having a glacier named after him. "Please take that glacier and leave my name off it," he replied, "and promise me it will remain unnamed."

We paddled to shore, if it could be called paddling. Our broad-beamed kayak was a boat with hips. In our attempt to slalom through the icebergs we swaggered and hit every other one. The smaller bergs we glided over. Their percussive music tapped our hull. Hundreds of bergs bejeweled the shore where the receding tide had abandoned them. Holy bergs, they seemed to glow from within, each with its own lambent light. We extricated ourselves from our kayak and walked among them. Richard estimated they weighed tens of tons.

He took off for the glacier, half a mile away; said he wanted to "investigate" an ice cave in its flank. Perhaps walk into it. He was tired of living sensibly. He came from Indiana and had never seen a glacier firsthand. Shopping malls and aggravated assaults, yes. Black and white, bread and butter, rich and poor, issues central to civilized America, Indiana had them all. But no glaciers. After carving the Great Lakes ten millennia ago and pushing the Ohio River south to its present position, they disappeared from Indiana and Richard had been missing them ever since. He moved over the rocky, mossy slope like a fullback and called to me over his shoulder, "I'll be right back."

For a moment he reminded me of Tom Buchanan, Daisy's husband in *The Great Gatsby*, the urban creature whose actions mimicked his darting eyes and suggested he was ready to rebuff any on-comer, real or imagined. Why this image came to mind might be explained by the fact that I carried with me a tattered copy of F. Scott Fitzgerald's masterpiece. For the twentieth time, maybe the thirtieth, I was drawn to the lovely tragedy. I couldn't say why, other than the notion that transience itself is also tragic, and lovely. What water may bring, water may take away.

When I considered that I might not see Richard again, I found myself committing his face to memory—his dishwater hair that fell incorrigibly across his brow, his honest eyes and husky laughter and sweet moments of quiet reflection. I realized that I hardly knew him, yet in country like this—far from Gatsby's mansions and gilded deceits—he seemed excellent company. He seemed authentic. His powerful chest and arms were those of an eagle, a great soaring bird that by comparison made a hardworking heron of me. While I ended each day with Fitzgerald, Richard ended his with *Travels in Alaska* by John Muir.

It was May 1979, ten years after Woodstock, ten years before the *Exxon Valdez*, and one hundred years since Muir had made his first trip to Alaska. We told ourselves this had special significance for us, but what exactly, we didn't know.

I HAD MET Richard a week before when our National Park Service supervisor introduced us in a grocery store in Juneau and told us we'd be roommates in Glacier Bay for the summer. Richard squared up to me and shook my hand gently, a surprising gesture from the big-shouldered man. He pushed his cart down the aisle and threw in boxes and bags as if shopping for the Franklin Expedition to the Northwest Passage, the expedition that never returned. Every man froze to death. Twenty pounds of popcorn, ten pounds of spaghetti, a weightlifter's bag of flour, a vat of yogurt, a tub of honey, four large jars of peanut butter. Richard said, "I'm going kayaking for a week before our season begins. You want to come along?"

I hesitated.

He talked about kayaks and how Native Alaskans had been per-fecting them for *five thousand years*. Swift and silent, the Native Kayaker was the seal hunter his wife made him. He wore a hat made of wood with a long visor to shed the rain. Believing that seals loved beauty, the wife made the hat ornate so her husband could approach the seals closely. He used a sea lion bladder for a canteen, and filled it with air as a buoyancy bag. He used a small gaff to haul in fish, and a large gaff to haul himself onto ice floes. When a storm blew, the hunter would take refuge in a bed of kelp, the forest of the sea, and wrap the long fronds around his little boat. Snuggle deep into the hull to wait for the waters to lie down.

THE WORD ITSELF is a palindrome: *kayak*. It reads the same forward as backward, just as the boat is balanced fore and aft. As Richard spoke he seemed to lift off the ground to become a hunter himself, though he had no wife and no wooden hat, and the kayak he intended to use was an old fiberglass hog patched with duct tape and glue.

"Still," he said, "a kayak is special. It's something you . . ."

"Something you wear?" I said.

"Right, it's something you wear. How much beer should we get?" He loaded four cases into the bulging cart, and a bottle of whiskey, and headed for the checkout stand.

Only three years before, John McPhee's book on Alaska, *Coming into the Country*, had been published. Like many young men seeking adventure then, I had consumed it. Somewhere in those pages McPhee talked about the size of Alaska. Rather than use acres or square miles or a cliché comparison with Texas, he said that if anybody could figure out a way to steal Italy, Alaska would be the place to hide it. It was that big, that vast.

"Okay," I said to Richard, "I'll go on your kayak trip."

He gleamed at me like a madman—something I would see again and again—and told me a National Park Service patrol boat would drop us off in Reid Inlet, fifty miles northwest of headquarters, in

Bartlett Cove, and leave us there. We'd paddle our way back. Have a great time. "I may not know karate," he said, imitating the black soul singer James Brown, "but I know craaaa-zy."

I thought, *I'm a dead man.*

"If we're careful, the kayak will be our cocoon," Richard added. "If we're stupid, it'll be our coffin."

I tossed him a look of alarm. He laughed and said, "Don't worry. We'll be fine."

IN REID INLET we were two men in a little boat, rookie park rangers in Alaska, model GS-4 employees who had no idea what we were doing. Richard had come from the Everglades; I from Death Valley. To say we were naïve would have been generous. From reading our embellished NPS summer seasonal park ranger applications you'd have thought we were Leatherstocking and Black Elk, brother hunters in the wilderness, sons of the Earth. Richard liked John Lennon, I liked Paul McCartney, and together we agreed there was no beating the Beatles. Alone in the big quiet, we pulled on our paddles and shared passages of Fitzgerald and Muir while dimly aware that this prism called Glacier Bay was about to bend every beam of light within us. Our lives would never again be what they had been.

I WAS BORN in the Bitterroot Mountains of Idaho and named Kim after the street urchin in the Kipling novel. Dad bartended a tavern and was his own best customer. Mom worked as an accountant for the railroad and smoked her Lucky Strikes as she pulled the handle of an old gum-stuck adding machine. She liked to say that Bitterroot country was the only place that threatened to starve Lewis and Clark. It nearly turned them back. They learned respect in these mountains, and we would too, by God.

On days with no school Mom would drive the rusty Buick up logging roads and set my two teenaged older brothers free amid the clearcuts and slash. That was their daycare center, the place William Clark described as "the most turrible mountains ever beheld."

"Be home by nightfall," Mom would tell them. They knocked over outhouses and threw them into the river and ran rapids sitting on the peaked roofs with the half-moon cutouts between their legs and .22 rifles across their laps and the whole sky to shoot at.

I was much younger. At two, while walking backward and pulling one of those little toy trains on a string, I flipped into a large laundry tub of hot water and scalded myself. Mom peeled off my clothes, taking my skin with them as I screamed and passed out. Wrapped in sterile gauze, I was put in a hospital burn unit and tended by a team of specialists insofar as was available in northern Idaho back then. They told my parents to call a priest. My family had never been very religious, let alone Catholic. We went to church on Christmas Eve and Easter just to cover our bets. Yet my brothers sat by my bed and wrapped a rosary around my bandaged hand. An intravenous line fed me through my ankle, the only spot on my body that wasn't burned. Dad smoked his pipe and said small words to console Mom. I lived for a day. A week.

"It looks like he's going to make it," the chief doctor conceded after ten days, "but prepare yourself—he'll be badly scarred."

They unwrapped the gauze and my mother cried with relief. My skin was fine. My hair had begun to grow back. I even managed a weak smile, so I was told.

I never walked backward after that. If I were going to fall, I'd fall forward.

We moved to the dryland wheat country of eastern Washington State and I faced north with vigorous determination, always welcoming winter. The heat of the sun held little appeal for me. I loved skiing and splitting wood at ten below, and throwing frozen eggs that bounced off trees. We visited Seattle, and while I liked the rain I recoiled at the flood of headlights on wet pavement, the neurotic windshield wipers struggling to keep up, the fragments of forest flashing by on I-5, everybody in a hurry to be somewhere else. So many people going, going, going . . .

En route back home, Dad got off I-90 and followed a blue line on the map past Mount Rainier. We stopped on a bridge over a river and listened to its steady voice of snowmelt and seabound travel. Dad pointed up the valley to a glacier. I told him I wanted to live there.

"On the ice?" he said.

"Yup."

"Like a dead fish?"

"Like a poked pig."

We laughed. Later, when I learned what actually *did* live on a glacier—algae, fungal spores, dormant seeds, and in some places entire forests on stagnant ice, plus water pipits, snow buntings, gray-crowned rosy finches, and the occasional odyssey-bound mountain goat, bear, wolverine and wolf, all crossing crevasses with Homeric resolve—I was thrilled.

Mom said I was a "miracle boy" to be alive. Dad wasn't so sure. In his sidelong glance at life he regarded miracles as the handmaidens of religion; Jesus was remarkable enough without having to turn water to wine, was he not?

We lived in Spokane, where I did poorly in school. I was told that a person's skin changes every seven years or so, and that the cellular memory of my burn would disappear. I remember wondering if nerve endings changed too. The only thing that occasionally hurt was the scar on my ankle where the intravenous line had kept me alive.

I often skipped school and rode my bike along Hangman Creek and missed the rivers of Idaho. Captured and reincarcerated, I would sit in the back row of the overheated classroom and rub my ankle. I was a ferocious speller who plowed from one mistake to another. Mom reminded me that William Clark (she liked him more than Lewis) also had problems spelling. He wrote about tracking "bearfooted Indians," and how he was proud to serve the "Untied States."

Regardless of Clark's company, my grades sank. I had no interest in books and seemed to learn only one thing: to hate school. Then I received a gift. Two teachers—one when I was ten, the other when I was twenty—changed my life in ways I could not anticipate. They showed me the way to Glacier Bay and taught me to *see* as I had never seen before.

SHE WROTE on the blackboard as most fourth grade teachers do, enthralled by numbers that held nothing for me. The arithmetic may as well have been hieroglyphics. My eyes would drift away and land on a large nature mural on the opposite wall. She had put it there at the beginning of the school year and said nothing about it, as if it could speak for itself, which for me it did. It showed a landscape in primary colors, of mountains tumbling into the sea, and above each geographical feature a one-word label written in bold, black type: **peak, ridge, glacier, valley, marsh,** and **beach.** Dozens of common names, and some uncommon ones too: **arête, isthmus, estuary.** The mural showed no sign of humankind, and that must have appealed to me as I felt the sensation of flying over it, falling into it, of Robinson Crusoe alone yet not lonely in all that vastness. Day after day I stared at it and found it staring back at me, working its slow osmosis.

"You like that mural, don't you?" she asked one day as she suddenly stood beside my desk, catching me in a daydream when I should have been working on my arithmetic.

"Yes," I said, startled.

"You know why I put it there?"

I shook my head. Words and pictures intrigued me more than numbers.

"I put it there for you."

"For me?" I couldn't believe it. The mural was so big and I felt so small. I searched her eyes for honesty, uncertain what it would look like. To this day I can't remember her face or name, and I regret that. But I remember the mural, and I appreciate estuaries.

Ten years later I signed up for a college class in geomorphology, the study of landforms. My professor was Dr. Michael Folsom, a dynamic man who taught earth sciences as if every day were a geological epoch. He would mimic the physical power of a raindrop by throwing chalk at the board. He would ribbon wet soil between his forefinger and thumb to test its composition. If that weren't good enough, he'd chew it, rolling the particles between his teeth and tongue to taste the ratio of sand, silt, and clay. "A fine silt loam," he would say, spitting it out.

On a field trip in Montana he drove the university van with utter indifference to the road, half on the pavement, half on the shoulder, gravel spraying the chassis as he pointed out the window and said, "See that over there? That's a young mountain composed of old rocks. And see that?"—he would swing his arm and the van— "That's an old mountain composed of young rocks."

I tightened my seat belt and studied his inscrutable expression in the rearview mirror; his thinning wheat-colored hair compensated by a robust beard, his bright eyes dancing with mirth.

"Is that clear?" he asked my classmates and me.

He explained that to understand geomorphology was to see the Earth as clay in a potter's hands, wet, formative, spinning. He spoke of plate tectonics and granite continents as if they were clipper ships that traveled the floors of the seas with their sails trimmed, making only a few inches per year, but floating nonetheless. Lighter rock on heavier rock. Erosion and deposition weren't just processes; they were ceaseless crusades wherein water sought to smooth the surface of the Earth while tectonics and volcanics conspired to wrinkle it. Life wasn't just respiration and reproduction; it was friction and force, frost and rain, stream piracy and misfit rivers, intrinsic thresholds and laminar flows. He spoke past midnight until I thought my head would explode. Like a medieval peasant bent over his dirty potatoes, I had bumbled through the years unaware of the long past and future, never seeing the world as anything other than fixed, unchanging, unchangeable. To accept change in my own family and town, in me, my friends, and that girl down the street who was never very pretty but look at her now, I could do that. But to see the Earth as something on a potter's wheel would require some convincing.

"We shape the clay into a pot," Folsom quoted Lao-Tsu, "but it is the emptiness inside that holds whatever we want."

I told him about a vacant lot where I used to play as a kid. For me it wasn't vacant as everybody said it was. It was full. It had mystery, dirt, grasshoppers, and birds. It offered an escape from the rows of mansions built around it. It accommodated me best on my hands and knees where seeds and burrs would stick to my pants and require my inspection. Others said the lot was "vacant" because it didn't have a house or a baseball diamond or a mall. Such was the vacancy that filled me.

Dr. Folsom asked if it was still there.

"No," I said. "It's filled with big homes now."

Folsom nodded with wrinkles around his eyes. He spoke wistfully about the reign of the automobile, the loss of open space, the pervasive fear of crime. It seemed to take the wind out of him. He had been born in Skagway, Alaska, beneath tall coastal mountains, the grandson of a Klondike gold-rusher who sharpened his teeth on uncertainty. Nowadays, he said, kids don't play pickup games in sandlots or find grasshoppers in fields. They belong to a nation that systematizes everything, where gated communities teach seminars on how to make friends and walk your pets, and the once elegant act of spontaneous play is regimented into teams and leagues and schedules and rule books and box scores and rankings and coaches and referees paid for by parents who build résumés for their children.

I told him about the mural from fourth grade, with the absence of any human element.

"Think about it," he said, his face brightening. "All the high-elevation features—peak, ridge, and so on—are erosional. They remain after the surrounding material has been carried away by water and ice. The low-elevation features—valley, marsh, beach—are depositional. They're composed of the materials taken from above: rocks plucked off mountains and pounded into gravel, sand, and silt."

"So the river carries them from one place to the other?" I asked.

"So does the glacier. Ice creates and ice destroys."

When speaking of landforms, Dr. Folsom often used the verb *composed*. To him the Earth was a Beethoven symphony, a Chopin étude, something spherical, divine. All the better that it was an unfinished symphony, a work in progress. All you had to do was go out there and see it. He would quote his fellow Scot, John Muir: "I only went out for a walk, and finally concluded to stay out till sundown, for going out, I found, was really going in."

I was twenty years old, in my second year of college, a product of twelve years of public education in Spokane, Washington, and I had never heard of John Muir. I was too busy playing my guitar and chasing girls. Sophomoric, yes, but I was a sophomore.

EARLY THE NEXT MORNING, still in Montana, Folsom followed a dirt road through an open gate behind a farmhouse and a yard full of chickens. He parked the van facing a horse pasture and the foothills of the Rocky Mountains. "Look at that," he said, pointing. "This is textbook stuff. Notice the escarpment along the . . ."

The back door of the farmhouse creaked open and a woman appeared on the porch, her hand at her brow, shading her eyes from the morning sun. She padded along the footpath with little clouds of dust billowing at her feet. Didn't even stop to check her planted irises and lilies. She opened the wooden gate and let it slam behind her. A matriarch on a mission, she wore a bathrobe and curlers in her hair, and aimed a squint of utmost skepticism at the university insignia on the van door. Put a shotgun in her hands, and she would have made a perfect character from a Clint Eastwood Western. We students saw her, and wondered about the impropriety of being on her land. Only Dr. Folsom remained unaware as he dissertated on catchment basins and alluvial terraces and Glacial Lake Missoula that thirteen thousand years ago broke through an ice dam and flooded west to scour the channeled scablands of eastern Washington State, slicing through the windblown material called loess that formed the Palouse Hills and . . .

"Can I help you?" she asked him, suddenly standing at his arm where it folded out the van window.

"Oh, good morning," Folsom said. "We're just admiring the landforms here, if that's okay."

"Landforms?"

"Yes"—Folsom pointed—"you see that pair of alluvial terraces over there, flanking that stream? Two terraces of equal size and height, each a mirror of the other on opposite sides of a stream. They're the only angular features in a topography dominated by rounded foothills. Fascinating, don't you think?"

She wrinkled her nose.

"We're wondering how they got there."

"Easy," she said, "God put them there."

"Of course he did," Folsom said, not missing a beat. "There's no disputing that. But *how* did God do it?" He raised a finger as if he were Sherlock Holmes and the woman Doctor Watson. She chewed her lip.

"Water," Folsom whispered. "He did it with water."

"The Great Flood," she said, her face aglow.

"There you go. The great flood. Only water could make a flat-topped landform like that."

Folsom declined to tell her that while her flood was the famous one with rain and an ark and an old bearded guy with so many animals two by two, his flood involved a glacier, not rain, and was largely unknown outside academic circles. By then it didn't matter. He did explain a little yin/yang, however: that while running water erodes, quiet water makes things level. It deposits suspended sediments in stratified layers at the bottom of a lake. Then much later, after the lake has dried up and the sediments become exposed, running water, seeking a deeper level, cuts into the very strata it deposited, leaving only shadows of what once was.

"That's how each terrace became a mirror of the other," Folsom said. "They were once connected, born together."

"Like twins," the woman said. "Yes, I see."

She looked us over. "College kids?"

"Yes, ma'am."

"Have you had breakfast?"

We shook our heads.

"Well then, come inside for some muffins and milk."

We left our boots at the door. I can't remember what we spoke about, something like "geotheomorphology," a careful blend of science and spirituality, matters of fact and matters of faith. Her husband had died long ago, she said. He was her best friend. Cancer got him when he was only thirty. She spoke with such tenderness, her words should have hit me harder than they did. Not for another five years, when my mother drove off an icy December road and left my father alone and I heard him crying in the night, would I remember what the Montana woman said. Live now. Every day with a friend is a gift. Nothing lasts forever. Even mountains wash to the sea.

She had weathered hands and skin, and a voice like a summer breeze through riparian willows. As we drove away in the college van, kicking up dust, I watched her wave from her porch, knowing I would never see her again.

DR. FOLSOM HEADED to a broad valley where a gigantic boulder rested in silent testimony miles from the nearest mountains. I walked to it and placed my hands on its cool roughness and immovability. It stood twenty feet high, all by itself, shaped like a great trapezoidal monolith. Folsom called it an erratic. He explained that glaciers had deposited it seventeen thousand years ago when they filled the valley. The great boulder was a traveler, a foreigner of different composition than the bedrock far below. Ripped from its mountain home by glacial ice and carried here, it was as vocal as any rock could be.

We camped that night and built a fire. Folsom told stories until our conversation spiraled onto glaciers. He said that during the last great hurrah of the Ice Age—what geologists call the LGM (the Last Glacial Maximum of the Wisconsin Period of the Pleistocene Epoch, twenty-five thousand to ten thousand years ago)—a continental ice sheet buried most of Canada and pushed south to carve the Great Lakes. One ice lobe dropped its overburden of sediment and rock into a perfect hook-shaped terminal moraine we today call Cape Cod. Another glacier, the same one that sculpted the Hudson River Valley, deposited parts of Manhattan Island. With firelight in his eyes he described glaciers as if they were no less alive than ravens.

What a time to live back then, hunting mammoths and mastodons when glaciers swallowed entire valleys and people ate and slept in tribal unity under the same skins and furs, when granddaughters picked berries with their grandmothers and learned the stories that held them together. Folsom reminded us that it wasn't that long ago, just minutes on the geologic clock.

A fellow student lamented that it was a pity none of these grand icy processes existed on a human scale today; that within a single lifetime no landscape was born or lost to ice.

"There is such a place," Folsom said. "It's a bay in Alaska, near Juneau, a bay reborn from the icy tomb of a great glacier that buried it just two hundred years ago. When the ice retreated it unveiled a new home for wolves and whales, a world in transition from bare rock to bears, a magical place, a miracle place . . . if you believe in miracles."

MIRACLES

Chapter Two

———————

STANDING IN THE COLD RAIN in Glacier Bay, I felt a sense of doom come over me. We had forgotten our tent. Twice in Bartlett Cove, fifty miles to the south, Richard and I had inventoried our gear before loading it onto the National Park Service patrol boat that carried us and our duct-taped kayak to Reid Inlet. Now a knot of panic tightened in my throat. Again I searched every bag. Again I checked the kayak from bow to stern. Again I found no tent.

We had no GPS either, no VHF radio, no cell phone (they weren't around then), no palm pilot (they weren't around either), no Get-Out-of-Jail-Free cards. We had only a 1:250,000 USGS topographic map that showed Reid Inlet as a tiny blue smudge on a vast arc of the wildest coast in North America, a tectonic jumble of mountains, glaciers, rivers, inlets, and coves without a single trail or road. Our rain gear had lasted ten minutes before it started to leak. A wind blew off the glacier with no hint of sympathy. The air temperature may have been five or ten degrees above freezing, but the wind and rain made it feel much colder. We had no thermometer, other than our red and runny noses. We had forgotten our tent, and Richard had cracked our only compass.

"Don't worry," he said as he barreled off to explore an ice cave in Reid Glacier, "We don't always want to know where we're going."

I suppose there's an elegance to that. Robert Frost wrote about the beauty of being lost, didn't he? And Fitzgerald? Once you get over your own softness and smallness you can work at finding yourself. You might find parts of yourself you never wanted to find. Awash in my own vulnerability, it never occurred to me then—I'm glad it didn't—that a place like Glacier Bay could be vulnerable as well.

As I watched Richard hurry off toward the ice cave, his arms pumping to and fro, his shoulders rocking, I could see that he wasn't a burdened Tom Buchanan or a Gatsby at all. He was buoyant with his own being, floating over the mossy rocks, buteo-winged, infused with every element of wildness around him. Crazy yes, but crazy like John Muir, rapturous, pulled to the glacier like a moth to a flame.

Rivers of ice do that. They have their own gravity, their own light.

"WHY DOES MUIR climb mountains in gathering storms?" four Tlingit Indians asked in October 1879 as they huddled around a campfire near what is today Hugh Miller Inlet, not far from Reid Inlet, in the West Arm of Glacier Bay. It was a cold and dreary time.

"To seek knowledge," answered Samuel Hall Young, a Presbyterian minister who shared their fire. The Tlingits shook their heads and mumbled that Muir must be a witch.

By way of Scotland, Wisconsin, and the mountains of California, Muir had finally come to Alaska to see glaciers at work on a grand scale. He traveled by canoe into Glacier Bay, where the Hoonah Tlingit had lived long ago, before the advancing ice evicted them. The Tlingit spoke of how the land and sea had been rich with forests, salmon, and seals back then; how every meadow and cove was a memory place alive with stories and legends. But now it seemed only a shadow of that, so raw and ice-chafed. It offered no gifts, except to Muir.

"Man, man, you ought to have been with me," Muir would tell Minister Young after a solo exploit on a glacier. "You'll never make up what you lost today. I've been wandering through a thousand rooms of God's crystal temple. I've been a thousand feet down in the crevasses, with matchless domes and sculpted figures and carved ice-work all about me. Solomon's marble and ivory palaces were nothing to it. Such purity, such color, such delicate beauty! I was tempted to stay there and feast my soul, and softly freeze, until I would become part of the glacier. What a great death that would be."

I scanned Reid Glacier for Richard, hoping to find him still alive. I had a premonition of him softly frozen. The blue escarpment of ancient ice appeared as a looking glass that Alice might step through, what Muir called a "startling, chilling, almost shrieking vitriol blue," a portal into another world, another time.

One year later, in 1880, Muir was back in Glacier Bay with Minister Young and a little black terrier named Stickeen. "I like dogs," Muir wrote, "but this one seemed so small and worthless that I objected to his going and asked the missionary why he was taking him."

Young said he would be no trouble, and "that he was a perfect wonder of a dog, could endure cold and hunger like a bear, swim like a seal, and was wondrous wise and cunning, etc., making out a list of virtues to show he might be the most interesting member of the party."

In due time Muir found himself on the Brady Glacier, attempting to cross a skein of crevasses as daylight faded and a storm descended. There at his heels was little Stickeen. They negotiated several ice bridges across crevasses, while Muir cut foot notches with his ice axe. Stickeen followed, each time with more trepidation as the bridges narrowed and the crevasses deepened. Finally, man and dog found themselves on an island of ice surrounded by deep chasms with only two routes off—the way they had come (which was opposite the way they needed to go), and the other route, what Muir described as "an almost inaccessible sliver-bridge."

As Muir worked his way across the sliver, cutting one foothold after another, Stickeen began to whimper and cry. Gaining the opposite side, Muir turned to face him, but the little dog screamed louder than ever. Muir could have walked away. Instead, he got onto his knees and gestured the dog to come to him. It was then that he spoke words I knew the moment I read them I would never forget: "Hush your fears, my boy, we will get across safe, though it is not going to be easy. No right way is easy in this rough world. We must risk our lives in order to save them."

RICHARD RETURNED, his life risked and saved, his face aglow. He had walked into the Ice Age and back. I told him we had no tent, and he threw his head back and laughed.

I expected him to say, "Tent? We don't need no stinking tent."

Instead he said, "We'll sleep in the kayak. We'll turn it over and crawl inside just like Aleut otter hunters. We'll be fine."

Okay, I thought, *we'll be fine.*

An hour later the National Park Service patrol boat returned and brought us our tent. We had left it on board. We paddled out to meet the boat. The two rangers, Rick and Dave, handed us the tent, their eyes filled with doubt.

"You guys going to be okay?" Dave asked.

"Yeah," Richard said, "we'll be fine."

We pitched camp, and all that night Reid Glacier calved columns of ice into the sea. Pleistocene thunder filled our dreams until sometime before dawn, unable to sleep, we climbed from our tent and sat on the ground with our legs crossed and our backs against the cold. Like two monks before Heaven we watched one ice-fall after another, each more illuminated than the one before in the emerging light of day. No two icebergs were the same. With only their upper parts visible it occurred to us that they were human, in a way—the visible conscious above, the invisible subconscious below, each unique and yet like every other. I kept hearing Dr. Folsom's voice. I kept seeing his eyes in the firelight as he spoke about a bay reborn. Mystery is not always in the invisible, he said. It's in the visible too.

Richard seemed to drink the texture of the air, his thirst boundless. He jumped to his feet and without a word lumbered down to the kayak. When he returned, a question arose in my throat (it must have come from my heart). "Richard," I asked, "do you believe in miracles?"

He stopped and said nothing. He didn't meet my gaze. For a moment I was embarrassed at my inquiry, uncertain if our young friendship permitted a question not easily asked between men. He looked at a button of moss anchored on the bedrock, impossibly alone in the shadow of the glacier.

"I believe in this," he said, pointing at the moss. "This is a miracle."

He sat next to me with his wool hat askew on his wet head, his raincoat misbuttoned so one side ended higher than the other. He wore a splotch of mud on his chin and a wild-eyed look as if he were searching for Sigmund Freud's sofa, or his cigar. At a deeper level he appeared so relaxed as to be indifferent to the rain. If a fastidious kayaking and camping partner was what I wanted, Richard was the wrong guy. But I could tell that he was right in many other ways. He never complained. He found humor everywhere and told stories at his own expense. He had an oblique view of the human condition and reveled in the double entendre. He spoke fluent French. As the rain fell and he became wetter and wetter, he behaved as though it were no more serious than an April shower in the flowered fields of Arles.

He pulled out a bag of popcorn and the bottle of whiskey. I stared at him.

He laughed and said, "Our kayak is a floating pantry. I've got lots of surprises."

We ate and drank as one icefall after another sent concentric rings down Reid Inlet and I felt the layers peel away, the shell of my own existence letting go, releasing me to a wildness that cannot be packaged.

"The more you package places like this," Richard said, "the more they vanish."

"There are no more places like this."

" 'Nothing dollarable is safe'—that's what John Muir said." Richard fell silent for a moment, then added, "People have lost their way. They count their money to find out what they're *worth*. They trade *futures* on Wall Street."

We talked on and on as if we were the only two philosophers in the world. Richard poured me another whiskey. When I said it was too strong, he added rainwater by squeezing it from his smelly wool hat. It occurred to me then, that while we had come out here to learn, we had also come to forget.

I told Richard, "Somebody once said that we travel down the road of mystery not to gain knowledge, but to deepen the mystery."

"That Somebody, he's a smart guy."

"Like that other guy, Anonymous."

As the whiskey hit, I wondered to what degree our reverence would absolve our transgression. Unlike the steps of sandal-footed monks who walked the smooth stones of their monastery and made them smoother, here in Glacier Bay one footfall could destroy an entire community of moss. I thought about the man from New York City who came to Alaska and couldn't sleep. He said the silence was too deep, the land too empty. He missed the vigilant sound of sirens, the pitch and wail that comforted him and told him the people of his great city were being looked after, even saved, in moments of terror and loss.

The night before, until the icefalls awakened me, I had slept like a trouble-free child on the hard earth, innocent of fear. With our tent on a slope and me curled into a corner of it, I had breathed the glacial air and felt my heart slow . . . way . . . down. Perhaps then in my sleep, I decided that what we needed in Glacier Bay wasn't safety but danger, not convenience but inconvenience, not order but chaos. Throw away the guidebooks and glossy magazines with their Best-Bets, Don't-Miss, Gotta See, Top Ten, Off-the-Beaten-Path packaging that sell predictability like Big Gulp soda pop, good to the last drop. In a rush to create a stable environment, we put ourselves in stables. The beauty of chaos is that beyond a certain point we cannot predict things for the pure and lovely reason they cannot be predicted. Chaos gives us mystery, and mystery gives us wonder— those little epiphanies when people find what they didn't even know they were looking for. Don't tell me where the next good camping spot is, and I won't sing for you the song of the hermit thrush.

True, I had yet to determine the meaning of determinism. Perhaps Richard and I were disillusioned utopians searching for a place where life was celebrated and not scheduled. Had we been younger we would have known everything. This I was certain: Glacier Bay offered a clarity more profound than any book; an original text, a reminder that our language evolved as we moved *away* from places like this, not *into* them. Some people might call it timeless. I felt that way to a degree. But in another way I found Glacier Bay ripe with time. Not conventional time with its clocks and calendars and other metaphors from technology, but time written in the blue crevasses of the ice itself, deep enough to frighten a little dog.

MUIR SHOUTED words of encouragement while Stickeen cowered on the opposite side of the ice bridge, paralyzed with fear, unable to cross. *"Hush your fears, my boy. . . . We must risk our lives in order to save them. . . ."*

Stickeen lowered his trembling legs onto the first notch that Muir had cut with the ice axe. Step by cautious step he worked his way down to the narrow ice bridge, then the treacherous crossing, placing one foot before the other as gusts of wind rocked his little body. Muir struggled to watch through the blinding snow and dying light. Stickeen inched across the bridge and was about ten feet below Muir, facing a series of notched steps he needed to ascend to safety. "Here he halted in dead silence," Muir said, "and it was here I feared he might fail, for dogs are poor climbers." Muir was on his knees, arms outreached. Stickeen made no motion but remained transfixed on the notched steps as if memorizing their exact number and distance. "Then suddenly up he came in a springy rush," Muir said, "hooking his paws into the steps and notches so quickly that I could not see how it was done."

He zipped past Muir and ran in wild circles. "He flashed and darted hither and thither as if fairly demented, screaming and shouting, swirling around and around in giddy loops and circles like a leaf in a whirlwind, lying down and rolling over and over, sidewise and heels over head, and pouring forth a tumultuous flood of hysterical cries and sobs and gasping mutterings. . . . Moses' stately song of triumph after escaping the Egyptians and the Red Sea was nothing to it."

Man and dog made it across the glacier and reached camp in darkness to find a large fire with roasting porpoise meat, a gift Minister Young had received from visiting Hoonah Tlingits. Thereafter little Stickeen, previously aloof, never left Muir's side. One year later he was stolen by a tourist off a dock in Fort Wrangell, and wasn't seen in Alaska again.

Muir returned to California to work in his father-in-law's orchard, an enterprise that nearly killed him more from heartbreak than from physical exercise. His hands became too round from picking fruit. He missed the angular grasp of ice-cut rock. He called this ranch-time his "seven lost years." In June 1890, with full blessings from his wife to go heal himself, he sailed for Glacier Bay "like a Crusader," he said, "bound for the Holy Land." A wisp of a man, worn thin from a bronchial cough and a tyranny of consumerism that threatened his beloved Yosemite and the ancient forests of California, Muir, now fifty-two, prescribed for himself time on the glaciers of Glacier Bay. A steamship disembarked him near his namesake glacier, where he built a tent platform and commenced to hike in the rain. Two weeks later Harry Fielding Reid, a professor of geology at the Case School of Applied Sciences in Cleveland, arrived with four graduate students and roughly seven tons of gear, including a theodolite, logarithmic tables, camp stools, tents, a gasoline stove, a small library, and a pile of lumber.

"We now have quite a village," exclaimed Muir.

Steamships visited that summer and disembarked tourists in their Victorian tweed suits, velvet dresses, and broad-brimmed hats. Muir greeted them with mixed emotions. Having written about Glacier Bay in national magazines, he was largely responsible for them being there, and he knew it. Like Thoreau at Walden Pond, he suffered the sins of eloquence. He was the brightly colored bird who sang so beautifully that he drew the attention of thousands who came to listen, see, and trample.

While Harry Fielding Reid set about to make the first accurate maps of the region, Muir took off across the glacier for ten days, pulling a wooden sled loaded with hardtack, cocoa, and tea. Twice he nearly killed himself, first by glissading onto a talus slope, then by plunging into a crevasse filled with icy water, an experience, he said, "no lowland microbe could survive." He crawled into his sleeping bag and wrote with numb fingers, "I am cozy and comfortable here resting in the midst of glorious icy scenery." His cough disappeared. He warmed his tea in tin cans over little fires built with wood splinters shaved from his sled. He attempted to sketch, but snow blindness rendered everything double. Miserable at times with his feet half-frozen and his eyes bandaged, he would trade it for nothing. He was fifty-two going on twenty-five, rapturous that a man could still live in counterpoint to a culture enamored with too many clever devices, all those unnecessary things that removed us from the everyday miracles of the Earth. He heard wolves, and called their home Howling Valley. He felt the glacier rumble below. Most often, though, he heard nothing save himself. He concluded, "A man who neither believes in God nor in glaciers must be very bad, indeed the worst kind of all unbelievers."

"WHERE IS THIS HOWLING VALLEY?" Richard asked. He wanted to see a wolf, that most persecuted of wild animals (whose treatment by the State of Alaska, we would learn, was one more chapter in the ongoing story of extermination by poisoning, trapping, and shooting).

"Must be somewhere in lower Muir Inlet," I told him.

We were back in the kayak, under the influence of a thousand things we couldn't control. Richard asked if I had a totem animal in Glacier Bay. His was the wolf. Was there something out there that for me filled more space than its actual being?

"A whale," I said. "That's what I want to see. A humpback whale." *Megaptera novaeangliae*, forty feet long, forty years old, forty tons. I imagined it rising up from below our kayak like the lump in my throat. Every summer humpbacks arrived in Glacier Bay to feed on krill and small schooling fish—sand lance, capelin, and herring—that were rich in fats and oils. Each whale would eat

up to a ton of fish per day for a hundred days or so before returning to winter waters off Hawaii where it would fast and mate and
give birth. Researchers knew many of the whales individually by the
distinct patterns on the undersides of their flukes. They had names
for them: Snow, Barnacle, Sam, Tic-Tac-Toe, Garfunkel . . .

Garfunkel? This name intrigued me. I had thought singing was
restricted to humpback males in their warmer winter waters. Was
this one different? Raised on Simon and Garfunkel's folk music of
the 1960s and '70s, I liked the idea of a great male whale somewhere
beneath me in Glacier Bay, humming softly as Art Garfunkel's
angelic voice filled my head.

For hours we paddled without a word, then drifted, then paddled and drifted again. We talked about what we wanted to be when
we grew up. As seasonal employees with the NPS we had the freedom to move from park to park, but no benefits or retirement.
Always a consideration was a permanent career with the NPS.
Graduate school might work, the lure of science. I enjoyed photography but doubted I could make a living at it. I told Richard my
greatest dream was to be a writer. It just came out. Riding the swell
of the sea, pushed along by winds and tides, you say things you
would never say under the common pull of gravity.

"You can be Jack Kerouac," Richard said. "I'll be the hobo he
admired, the tramp on the train riding the open horizon with no
agenda, just a spore on the wind with a bedroll and a banjo, free as
any man can be."

Dr. Folsom had given me a B+ in geomorphology and told me I
could do better. After a few days in Glacier Bay I began to think that
it wasn't the *doing* that mattered, it was the *being*. Rick and Dave,
the two rangers who had brought us our tent, told us we'd be the
only kayak in the bay this time of year. The only kayak in 3.3 million acres of wilderness.

I told Richard that maybe like John Muir we'd also find God in
a glacier.

"Maybe," he said.

I remembered a story from Dr. Folsom. It involved a professor from Wisconsin who in the 1940s noticed a little cemetery on the outskirts of his town. Like many cemeteries it had a fence in need of painting, a rabble of headstones, a few bouquets of fading flowers. What was unusual, this professor noticed, was the cemetery's triangular shape, with one corner at such an acute angle it couldn't be cut or mowed. So it grew wild and free. A little corner of a little cemetery held the last remnants of a tall grass prairie that one hundred years before had filled the entire heart of a continent. A prairie that had appeared to early pioneers as vast and unconquerable as an ocean. Now conquered, it was reduced to a tiny fenced-in island.

If an ocean can be vanquished, Folsom asked, is any place safe? He let the question rise with the smoke of our campfire, hanging there for each of us to answer in our own time and way.

Five years after that college field trip, as a new ranger in Glacier Bay, I still hadn't answered it. My pie-in-the-sky-Rocky-Mountain-High world made no room for new conquests. I wanted Alaska to be exempt from the common greed of elsewhere. That too, I would find, would take a miracle.

It begins with just one cabin, Folsom had told us. That pioneering spirit that turns prairies into parking lots and meadows into strip malls begins with just one cabin.

As it turned out, there *was* a cabin in Reid Inlet. It belonged to Joe and Muz Ibach, who had used it as a summer home for nearly twenty years as they prospected for gold. Richard and I were determined to find it.

A timpani of rain played on our kayak. In the presence of seals we signed with our hands so as not to alarm them. We heard the puff and blow of a harbor porpoise; the muted music of birds. We sensed something descended through the ages, and contrary, as if other places existed when Glacier Bay did not, and Glacier Bay did when others did not. Richard said something about with so many landscapes having been shaped by man the past ten thousand years, it was nice to find one that could still shape us.

On shore that night, near the Ibach cabin, we found a plover that walked away when we approached. But once we sat still it came to within a couple feet and issued a thin peeping call. We might have picked it up and cupped it in our hands. The temptation was there. If ice could carve rock, could the soft down of a bird's belly shape our morality?

The following day, back in our kayak, Richard found a feather on the sea, a gift from a gull. He reached for it and it stuck to his wet finger. As he set it on a new course and watched it drift away, I was reminded of a young boy who found a leaf on a stream bank, and believing it a boat set it on the water to watch it go. For hours he played with that leaf in his make-believe world. His mother commented that kids didn't need bedrooms filled with plastic toys. All they needed was nature and an imagination. All they needed was nature to *give* them an imagination.

Richard said he liked it out here. In the wilderness you learned what was authentic and what was not. To "boot up" meant to put on your boots, not turn on your computer. A mouse was still a mouse. Software was warm socks. Hardware was your kayak. You slept on the ground until you were uncomfortable in a bed. You breathed fresh air until you suffocated indoors. You laughed from your toes and flew in your dreams. You found that you could sing the high notes; that true wealth was not a matter of adding to your possessions but of subtracting from the sum of your desires. You understood what was enough and what was too much, and why the prophets went into the desert alone. You accepted impermanence, or at least you thought about it. You navigated without numbers. You regarded the powerful and the large, but also the small and unheralded. You thought about relationships more than names; stories more than statistics. You remembered that gifts are not taken, they are received, and best of all, given. You made a new friend. You learned an economy of motion in each synchronous stroke, watching the paddles rise and fall, the blades up and down, the droplets dripping away with unspeakable grace. You found that every tool had a simple yet profound value: map, knife, tide table, tent, tarp.

Ah yes, tent and tarp, to create the illusion that we would stay dry in the rain. Day four, and we had had rain from everywhere and nowhere; a maelstrom and a mist; a reign of rain and a find-every-leak-in-the-tent rain; rain as a renaissance and rainessence to texture a leaf and make a flower nod, to make a glacier grow, to make rainbows and rainarrows that shot through the sky and back again; rain on the rocks, a rain of tears for the lost and wounded beneath a clamshell sky, the water cycle forever giving, taking, eroding, depositing, anointing us within and without.

"It is now about half-past nine and raining pretty hard," wrote Harry Fielding Reid when he returned to Glacier Bay in 1892. "We have concluded that there are many infallible signs of rain in this region. If the sun shines, if the stars appear, if there are clouds or if there are none; these are all sure indications. If the barometer falls, it will rain; if the barometer rises, it will rain; if the barometer remains steady, it will continue to rain."

With the barometer steady, Richard and I paddled out of Reid Inlet into the West Arm of Glacier Bay. Shawls of fog rendered the mountains into an impressionist's view. Every point was a vanishing point. I thought, *It should always be like this.* No painting would be right in Glacier Bay were it not a watercolor, and no photograph true were it not a black and white. Looking south toward Icy Strait, then north beyond Russell Island, we breathed the distance and attempted to grasp the full history of glacial advance and retreat.

When Harry Fielding Reid did his work here, a great tidewater glacier commanded this view, six miles across, broken in the middle by Russell Island as it emerged from the retreating ice. Reid lost his boat to the tides three times that summer of 1892. Each time he had to swim for it. Once he nearly drowned. John Muir stayed in California and founded the Sierra Club. Walt Whitman died that year, and Rudolf Diesel, a German inventor, patented the internal-combustion engine. A century later America would have ten thousand exhaust pipes for every one poet, and people would wonder why the climate was changing.

I MADE DINNER. Last night beans and rice. Tonight rice and beans. I garnished it with intertidal mud and received a grunt from Richard. He washed it down with a beer and read aloud from *Travels in Alaska*, John Muir's last book. The evening turned through a wheel of blue, green, and gray as icebergs patrolled the brooding waters. A few days earlier I had compared them to castles and swans, which now seemed absurd. *Wasn't it enough*, I wrote in my journal, *that an iceberg was an iceberg, spared of the simile shock of each one having to be* like *something else?*

The next morning we rounded an islet off Russell Island and flushed thirty scoters that circled back to see what had frightened them, their wings beating a complaint.

"Maybe our only kayak is one too many," I said.

After a moment Richard replied, "Do we have to tame ourselves to keep this place wild?"

I mentioned something about regretting my own birth. Too many people in the world. Extinctions everywhere. More dogs in Juneau than wolves in Alaska. Our chocolate running low. No more whiskey. The Beatles breaking up.

Richard said, "Let's go find a cliff and jump off it."

We talked about the lives we left behind and the source of our restlessness. We wondered how far we must travel before we arrived at where we belonged. I mentioned a movie I saw once about strife in a large city. It had a single scene, not a minute long, that showed a small stark park at night, with naked trees and leaves on the ground, and a group of thugs burying the body of a small boy they had kidnapped and killed. That was nature to them: a place to dispose of bodies.

This is what fascinated me—I think even haunted me—about *The Great Gatsby*. I told Richard that at the end of the story, after so many lives have been ruined, Fitzgerald widens the arc of loss to America-at-large. He describes the protagonist, Nick, who stands on his porch on Long Island and sees the land not as it is then, but as it once was. He notices a green light from the dock, the same light that Gatsby would have seen from his house, and Daisy from hers. Yet for Nick the light reflected in moon-bathed waters represents another green. It is the green of Long Island long gone. I read from the last page, how "the inessential houses began to melt away until gradually I [Nick] became aware of the old island here that flowered once for Dutch sailors' eyes—a fresh green breast of the new world. Its vanished trees, the trees that had made way for Gatsby's house, had once pandered in whispers to the last and greatest of all human dreams; for a transitory enchanted moment man must have held his breath in the presence of this continent . . . face-to-face for the last time in history with something commensurate with his capacity for wonder."

Richard nodded. He'd earned a master's degree in creative writing and American literature from Indiana University. He told me it was a central doctrine of human experience that every ideal finds itself yoked to its opposite ideal. "Think about it. How opposites are bound together: Nick and Gatsby, Muir and Fitzgerald, hippies and hawks, wilderness and civilization . . . rice and beans."

"The inessential houses," I said quietly. "I like that."

"You need therapy."

"I need wilderness."

"If everybody needed what you need, the wilderness would die."

"They do need it, but nobody's telling them."

"You are, with your writing."

"Nobody reads my writing."

"Good thing."

Here I confess that Richard and I each carried a second book. Mine was a softcover copy of *Moby-Dick*, which I brought along as ballast but also to feed my fascination about whales. Richard's was a ribald romp by Charles Bukowski about a postman and a big-breasted woman who are sitting naked at the breakfast table when they see a man free-fall past their apartment window, late for his own suicide. Richard howled when he read this. Of course he shared passages with me. First Kerouac, now Bukowski. It wasn't the writing that made me laugh so much as Richard's own laughter.

Then he saw *Moby-Dick*.

"Great book," he said. "No two characters are more emblematic of polarized ideals than Ishmael and Captain Ahab." There's Ishmael, Richard explained, innocent, wise, yoked to the madman Ahab and his lust for revenge. Ahab drives his entire crew to their watery graves, all save Ishmael who survives by clinging to a coffin. Most wild places left today, what few remain, are themselves remnants and survivors, like that Wisconsin cemetery, barely afloat in a sea of sprawl.

We sat in the silence, centuries of silence. Whatever itinerary Richard and I had begun with was forgotten. The urgency that once choreographed us was gone. Having lived by minutes most of our lives, we now lived by tides, traveling the laminar bare back of the sea before everybody else arrived, before the cruise ships, tour boats, and other kayakers whose hunger would be like ours. Escapees and emissaries of humankind, we were the perpetrators and victims of our own paradox. Perhaps like little Stickeen, we had our own crevasse to cross. We had to risk ourselves not in some counting-coup stunt adventure, but by walking a thin sliver of ice that bridged one way of thinking to another.

Having fallen in love with Glacier Bay, would we spend the rest of our lives saying the long good-bye? In a bay of rebirth, could we be reborn too?

The night was moonless when the rain stopped and the stars had their way and we slept on shore with the sea-tossed shells and the tangled kelp and nothing seemed urgent because nothing was. Whales swam into our dreams then. I heard a spouting in the distance, a deep breathing through the fog.

"Was that a whale?" I asked Richard the next morning. "Or was it a dream?"

He whispered an echo from Ishmael, "And I alone am escaped to tell thee . . ."

The only kayak in Glacier Bay, we too were alone, and escaped, left to wonder how long it could last, this wildness and grace. Not forever. But at that moment it was the most beautiful place on Earth. The ice, the sea, the rain. In that transitory, enchanted moment, it was perfect.

It was a miracle.

PIONEERS

Chapter Three

———

"THE OLD IBACH CABIN," is what everybody called it. It waited ahead as Richard and I approached, still as any cabin can be, facing north toward the promise of Alaska. We knew only this: One of three brothers who left western New York in the late 1800s for adventure in Alaska, Joe Ibach was the only one who found it. A trapper, fox farmer, prospector, boatman, builder, and big game guide, he embodied the frontier. To cross a frozen lake in winter he'd use a hunting knife to fashion a pair of skis from an alder. Then he'd stash the skis on shore should he pass that way again. If he came upon another frozen lake he'd simply make another pair of skis. He hid dynamite in the hollows of trees and sent his finest silver-tipped fox furs to London. He rowed boats across dangerous inlets with only his wits for navigation, his suspenders tight over his shoulders, his feet snug in hip-waders, his face turned squint-eyed at the sea and sky. He lived most of each year with his wife Muz (Shirley) on Lemesurier Island, in Icy Strait, not far from the entrance to Glacier Bay. It seemed no place was too remote for them, yet they had many friends and visitors, among them novelist Rex Beach, mountaineer/photographer Bradford Washburn, and Hollywood screen star John Barrymore, who said Joe and Muz were the only "real people" he ever met. They were the only ones who made him feel like a regular guy, a normal human being.

When I first arrived in Glacier Bay, prior to my kayak trip with Richard, I had found a photograph of Joe and Muz on the NPS office wall in Bartlett Cove. How genuine they appeared in that old black-and-white, framed in their cabin doorway on Lemesurier Island. No vacant hunger glazed Joe's eyes as it does other gold hounds. He stood like a fencepost in a prairie wind, with Muz to his leeward, bright as a wild strawberry from her garden. I wanted to tell them everything was fine, that Lemesurier Island was still filled with deer, that their summer cabin in Reid Inlet was rotting and falling apart but the country they loved around it—the country now working its magic on Richard and me—was still wild, for now.

No doubt the legendary status that embroidered their names in Icy Strait and Glacier Bay would make them uncomfortable. Muz would hear nothing of it as she brushed garden dirt off her hands and invited you inside for berry pie. Joe would listen and let others do the talking, unless the subject was politics or gold.

In 1924, one year before Glacier Bay became a national monument, Joe staked a mining claim up Ptarmigan Creek and prepared to do battle with the federal government. Some fifteen years later in Reid Inlet, not far from Ptarmigan Creek, he and Muz off-loaded lumber and a dozen ore sacks filled with garden soil and commenced to build a cabin, a home-away-from-home on an outwash fan near the tidewater face of Reid Glacier. They might have built there sooner, but as recently as 1930 the glacier occupied the site.

Joe actually built one cabin and two outbuildings. Muz terraced up her garden and planted strawberries, carrots, lettuce, and flowers, plus three spruce saplings as a windbreak. To help fertilize the deglaciated earth she hauled in kelp from Icy Strait. "Make no mistake about it," wrote Dave Bohn in his acclaimed book, *Glacier Bay: The Land and the Silence*, "an immense amount of personality was invested in that tiny plot of land in the wilderness."

That statement took my breath away when I first read it. I don't know why. Maybe in my own way I wanted to be a pioneer, embraced by a world still new and wet with dew. Maybe I wanted a wife like Muz, a love unbounded, unbroken, unbreakable.

RICHARD'S PACE was faster than mine. He accelerated ahead with his arms swinging and legs pumping as if he didn't get there soon the cabin would fly away. That's how it appeared, wing-like with its steep roof folded into the wind, improbable in the middle of the wildest place Richard and I had ever experienced—the wildest place we could *ever* imagine. Here was this gold prospector's cabin. Here was Enterprising Man.

It would have been less noteworthy had it not been alone and framed by such wild geography, protected in a vast piece of public land that permitted the construction of no other cabins. The National Park Service had decreed that it remain in a state of "benign neglect," left alone to rot and fall as nature commanded. Nobody was to tear it down or shore it up. All those years and storms after Joe built it, four decades and counting, it was still on its feet but a bit aslant, braced by large timbers at forty-five degrees and backdropped by an impartial glacier and ice-cut mountains that held the promise of gold.

I stopped to study the ground where pioneering mosses, lichens, avens, and willows patterned beds of gravel and silt. Soon I was on my knees, then on my belly to inspect rain droplets on the leaves.

"Kim," Richard called from inside the cabin, "you gotta come look at this. This is incredible."

I pulled out my camera and macro lens and hovered over a cluster of willow catkins. An image presented itself and I squeezed off a shot. I moved to the dryas, a small, ground-hugging member of the rose family that grows in circular mats.

"Kim, you gotta see this. . . ."

I squeezed off another shot.

". . . These people were real pioneers."

So are these little plants, I thought. *Just as tough and unlikely, yet here they are in the shadow of a glacier, growing where nothing else can.*

"Kim . . . ?"

I walked toward the cabin door, stepping over old cables and empty barrels that Joe had hauled up there God-knows-how and neglected to haul out. Maybe he liked the looks of it, the industry of his own work. The barrels had rusted into the earth beneath a thin skin of dryas and moss. I weaved through Muz's transplanted spruce, grown fifteen feet in forty years. I peeked into an outbuilding and found wrenches, hammers, pliers, saws, a pick, an axe. On the rotting wooden floor were a dozen bottles of colored fluid, perhaps mercury and cyanide and other toxins to separate gold from quartz, the chemistry lab of a hard rock prospector.

I pulled away and walked to the cabin. Even before entering I could see that it had been neglected—benignly, though, I wasn't so sure. How long since Joe and Muz had been there? The late 1950s was my best guess—more than twenty years ago.

I removed my daypack and had to turn sideways to get through the door. It was long and narrow, by today's standards more of a closet than a cabin. Richard sat in a small chair at a small table, his large frame bent over a 1935 copy of *LIFE* magazine, his fingers slowly turning the pages. On the back cover was an opera diva, white-faced and ruby-lipped with long blonde hair. An advertisement announced that she had the finest voice in America only because she smoked smooth-flavored Camels, the cigarette for the modern woman.

I was still for a moment, waiting for a voice from the back room, Muz telling us to make ourselves at home; she'd be right out.

Richard looked up, the *LIFE* magazine in his lap.

"Can you believe this?" he said. "It's like they just left. Like they intended to come back and never did."

Everything was small—the stove, bed, counter, and shelves—everything except Richard and me. Joe had built this place but Muz gave it life, the touch of a woman so distinct from that of a man, the flowered curtains versus the rusting barrels, the embroidered aprons versus the bottles of mercury.

Decorative dishes and metal cutlery sat on the counter. A red-and-white-checkered tablecloth, the kind you would use on a wine-and-cheese Sunday picnic, adorned the table. Richard stroked it with his big hand. He grabbed a deck of cards, shuffled them, and eyed me with poker temptation, one-eyed jacks wild, winner takes all. I knew that look. He let it go and put the deck back where he found it, on a counter next to a Rex Beach novel and a book by Henry Nash Smith called *Virgin Land*. I opened it to a marked passage: "God made this earth to be free to all, and whoever takes wild land, and clears it, and cultivates it, makes it his own—he's a right to it!"

Back outside, I took a deep breath.

Richard walked around the cabin and found somebody's initials carved into the wall.

"That's too bad," he said. For him the cabin was a shrine and the initials graffiti.

For me it was different. The landscape of Glacier Bay was the shrine and the cabin graffiti. I couldn't say that to Richard then, or to myself. In fact, it's taken me many years until I could write it down right here, right now.

WE SET UP our camp and commented on how futuristic our tent looked beside the cabin, with its dome-shaped yellow fabric and exoskeleton of flexible aluminum poles.

"What would old Joe think of that?" I asked.

"The past is a funny thing," Richard said. "We either romanticize it or run away from it."

"Was the West won or lost?" I asked him.

"Won." He looked at me with a grin.

"Lost," I said.

He laughed.

"Adam picked the apple in the Garden," I said. "We can't leave anything alone—the human race, I mean. That's all. No big deal."

"Whiner."

"I guess I am."

"Whining makes you angry, and anger makes you bitter."

I looked at the mountains and thought of the mural from fourth grade.

"Go take photographs," Richard said. "I'll make dinner."

As I hovered over those little plants and lost myself in their intricate beauty, it occurred to me—you could say it was an epiphany—that like Joe and Muz, the mosses and willows were tough pioneers. They arrived in the wake of glacial retreat and built a thin soil, and so contributed to their own demise by making the area hospitable for other plants to displace them. Call it the pioneer's paradox, the act of destroying what you love, the beginning of the end of open space. It's Daniel Boone bringing settlers over the Cumberland Gap into Kentucky, and later leaving when he can see smoke from his nearest neighbor's chimney. It's Jessie Fremont, wife of John C. Fremont, writing with pride fifty years after his expeditions that "cities have arisen on the ashes of his lonely campfires." Did her vision of progress leave no room for preserving the original America her husband had enjoyed as an ambitious young man? Denver, Sacramento, Kansas City, Salt Lake City—what would John Fremont do there today? Sell cars?

I'd been there. Those cities had many nice things, but no room for lonely campfires.

Spaghetti night. Richard cooked in the intertidal zone, the area on shore between the lowest low tide and the highest high tide. The rising water would then erase any evidence of our occupation, and reduce the chances of our food attracting bears, wolves, lions, tigers, and the great winged pterodactyl of Jurassic Alaska. We didn't want that. Did we?

With the pasta boiling, Richard stirred up the sauce. He added oregano and minced bay leaves from small plastic containers. His movements were awkward, but it was a practiced awkwardness.

"I hope you're hungry," he said.

The rain had stopped. After four wet days in Glacier Bay the sky had run dry and we could spread out our gear. Climbing into my sleeping bag that night would for once be drier than rolling into a wet flour tortilla. Wisps of clouds pirouetted against the faulted mountains where ancient rocks looked down on us with distant indifference. The old felt new and the cold felt warm and the air turned from gray to blue. The last limbs of daylight embraced the clouds. A raft of surf scoters paddled past, cutting the water with neat chevrons. Two arctic terns worked a lagoon behind us, diving for small fish and chattering their success. Seated on the rocky shore, I saw the calm sea catch my reflection and throw it back as a thousand ideas came and went and came back again, different than before.

Richard served me a mountain of pasta buried in thick sauce that filled my plate. He used a ladle but could have used a shovel. He handed me a bag of Parmesan cheese he called "paramecium cheese." I ate a few mouthfuls and felt the warmth course through the cold cave of my body.

"This is good, Richard. Thanks."

"There's more."

I looked back at the cabin and thought about the simple burro and blanket prospectors of the American West for whom no mountains were too big or horizons too far. The romantic in me imagined them sitting around their campfires eating flapjacks and dreaming of prospecting the night sky to find a Jupiter carved of copper or a Saturn gilded in gold. The realist in me knew otherwise. Skipping a year of college after studying geotheomorphology, I tumbleweeded through Mexico and the American West and ski-bummed in Aspen until my money ran out (it didn't take long). Landing in California, I found lives and landscapes turned inside out by gold. I learned of wars fought over it. I camped in state parks where children and their parents panned for gold. I wondered if one day those same children, now grown, might test for contaminated water, or treat mercury-caused madness, or survey for vanishing wildlife.

In Mexico I visited where Cortez's men had looted the riches of Montezuma and loaded their pockets with silver and gold before fleeing across the canals of a great Aztec island city.

"The Spaniards who had taken the most were the first to sink upon falling into the lake," a historian wrote. "So those who died, died rich."

A few years later I read about a young writer from the dust-in-your-throat Texas ranching country who was working on a screenplay for three Hollywood superstars: John Wayne, James Stewart, and Henry Fonda. The story, he said, was "a bittersweet, end-of-the-West Western in which no scalps were taken and no victories were won." He described the three actors as "horrified, genuinely and touchingly horrified" that the Old West was over. "They couldn't quite articulate it, but what they were struggling to say . . . was that the only point of the movies, and thus, more or less, of their lives, was that the Old West need never be over. You might as well say that America could be over, a notion so high-concept as to be, at the time, unthinkable, or at least, unproduceable."

The writer was Larry McMurtry. The story, which he later shaped into a novel, was *Lonesome Dove*.

Thundering out of Yale and Harvard about this time was a new Wild Bunch of historians who produced what came to be called "revisionist criticism." They announced that Manifest Destiny had been nothing more than a white man's irresponsible adventure—a conquest of sorts—that destroyed habitats and cultures by the hundreds and left America ecologically, ethnically, and morally destitute. As a result, they said, the West was a mosaic of failure. It was time to dismantle some myths. Their ideas went through me like high voltage. I read about their disciples, the so-called "New Writers of the Purple Sage," and decided I wanted to be one.

"Failure Studies," I said to Richard. "That's what McMurtry called it. 'Maybe Buffalo Bill was right: winning the West was in the end just a form of entertainment, something the nation did while it was waiting for television to be invented. Bugles in the afternoon, 7th Cavalry, Custer, the Alamo, amber waves of grain, all the rest were just brief and engaging white man's lies. Little wonder that it's only as a form of entertainment—the Western—that it now survives.' "

"Big cars, big bellies, big egos," Richard said. "Americans don't like being told there's no more of anything."

As W. H. Auden said, "The lights must never go out, the music must always play."

I suppose my deepest sentiments belonged to another pioneer, one different from Joe Ibach. He was William Cooper, a bespectacled plant ecologist who understood the paradox. In 1916 he arrived in Glacier Bay and established nine vegetation plots, then over many years returned, often on hands and knees with a magnifying glass, to study the progression of plant communities in the aftermath of glacial retreat. Before a mature forest of Sitka spruce and western hemlock could establish itself, he said, "The way must be prepared by humbler types of vegetation. Alders and willows must enrich the soil and provide shade. Under them spring up the seedlings of spruce, which ultimately grow into tall trees and, through the shade they cast, ungratefully bring about the death of the shrubs, which nursed their tender youth. . . ."

During a presentation at the Ecological Society of America, Cooper was encouraged by colleagues to seek permanent protection of the Glacier Bay region, so its scenic and scientific value would remain undiminished by commercial enterprises.

A MONSTROUS PROPOSITION, cried the *Juneau Daily Empire*. "The suggestion that a reserve be established to protect a glacier that none could disturb if he wanted and none would want to disturb if he could, or to permit the study of plant and insect life, is the quintessence of silliness."

When President Coolidge signed the proclamation creating Glacier Bay National Monument in 1925, Joe Ibach was not happy. He had staked his Ptarmigan Creek claims the year before and wanted things reworded so he could continue prospecting. Rex Beach wrote many letters (including one to President Franklin D. Roosevelt) that said prospecting had no deleterious effects on Glacier Bay. Congress voted. Roosevelt signed, and Rex Beach, to his astonishment, won. Over the next couple of decades the pesky scientists succeeded in doubling the size of Glacier Bay National Monument while old Joe pulled out his ore and Muz hauled it down to their boat on a barrel stave go-devil, one sack at a time. What a gal.

THE NIGHT pulled itself over us. The tide began to rise. Sounds became strange the way they do on unfamiliar ground. I told Richard that all the gold ever mined would form a sixty-foot cube, and eighty percent of it was in bank vaults, jewelry stores, and personal jewelry boxes.

"That's what we should mine," he said, "people's jewelry boxes."

I spoke critically about Enterprising Man and Richard reminded me that I too, as a photographer, even as an aspiring photographer, was Enterprising Man. I made one thing out of another. Forty percent of the silver consumed in the United States went into photographic film (this was before digital cameras).

"The minute I finish this meal," I said, "I'm throwing my camera into the sea."

"Tie a rock to it," Richard said. "Make sure it sinks."

I said that Pascal was right when he said all of man's problems stemmed from his inability to sit alone quietly in a room. But then I realized that *somebody had to build the room.* . . . "Somebody less fortunate than Pascal," I said, "somebody who had to roll up his sleeves and pound nails for a living."

"Every philosopher needs a carpenter," Richard added.

"Every carpenter needs a berry pie."

"A pie needs a tin to bake in."

"A tin made of metal, mined by a miner."

"Given to his wife."

"The love of his life."

Richard grinned. "Paradox, dirty socks, glacier rocks, Goldilocks."

I laughed while he made instant cheesecake from a box, just add water.

"How is it," I asked, "that the General Mining Law of 1872 that allowed men to poison fresh water across the American West was passed the same year we got our first national park, Yellowstone? How could Congress be so blind and visionary at the same time?" At a deeper level I was asking how could we value gold over water, something we lock up over that which we are made of, which connects all things?

"Pretty easy to pass judgment on those who aren't around to defend themselves," Richard said.

"So as a writer, if I'm not a catalyst for change, I'm a servant of the established order."

Richard shrugged. The dangerous thing, he said, was to live the unexamined life, to judge others without judging yourself. I admired him for his grasp of history, his compassion for people on a road different than his own. He said that half the years from 1866 to 1900 (in the U.S.) were in economic depression. Two-thirds of all families that homesteaded then failed. By 1900 two percent of the population owned sixty percent of the nation's wealth. The average annual family income was five hundred dollars. The average man lived forty-seven years. "With those odds," he said, "why work for a dollar a day and stand frozen-footed in a Chicago soup-and-bread line when Alaska was calling? Why die in an ash can when you could fall off a cliff and break your neck and feed a wolf?" He looked at me from beneath his disheveled hair, a wry grin on his unshaved face.

"There's more of Joe Ibach in you and me than we think," he said. "That's why we're sitting here on these hard rocks by this glacier, with nobody else around, eating funky food."

"Still, all that gold . . . just for jewelry."

"So Liz Taylor can look good on Oscar night."

"She wears diamonds."

"And gobs of mascara. . . . Hey, you think Muz wore jewelry?"

"No."

"I'll bet she wore a wedding ring."

"Yep," I found myself smiling. "I'll bet she wore a wedding ring."

It was my turn to do the dishes but Richard beat me to it. He trundled down to the shore while I walked to the cabin and sat with my back against the weathered timbers. This is what I wrote:

> Reid Inlet, May 1979, kayaking with Richard Steele, student of literature, John Lennon, history, and pasta. William Cooper studied primary succession in plants here, and arrested that same process in people. Were it not for him and the creation of Glacier Bay National Monument (now a national park), how many other cabins—or lodges, hotels, ports, or towns—would be in Glacier Bay today? Juneau is a gold town, and it started with just one cabin.

I could see Richard down by the water, writing as well, sitting on the rocks with the spaghetti pots at his feet. My admiration for him was growing every day. He was more forgiving than I, less judgmental. I wanted to learn from him; to laugh in the face of my own pride and shallow reflections. It wasn't the Ibachs I wanted to emulate, it was Richard. When he returned to the cabin he told me that poetry was a fine truth, but as Auden said, "It makes nothing happen; it survives in the valley of its saying." Then he handed me his poem:

> *This year I cruised a fair*
> *swam the sea*
> *ate for free*
> *Cuban restaurant; Chinese fare:*
> *Whatever, ever should I wear?*
> *I heap the experiences around me*
> *Like a miser with his millions*
> *A Getty with his billions*
> *A tyrant with his trillions*
> *Gold coins, speckling, spoiling the bed.*

EARLY THE NEXT MORNING we paddled south. The Ibach cabin disappeared over my shoulder and I didn't look back. I let it slip away as a life slips away. We hit high tide and glided through a shallow cut between the mainland and the Gilbert Peninsula. The water, opaque with suspended glacial silts in Reid Inlet, shone gemstone blue in Scidmore Bay, where no glaciers reached tideline. In Hugh Miller Inlet we saw a brown bear, and I felt Richard go straight-backed and stiff-legged in the kayak, as if trying to stand on his toes for a better look.

The next two days we crossed the entrance to Geikie Inlet and bucked a nasty chop down Whidbey Passage past Willoughby Island, paddling as if our lives depended on it, which they did. In the calm waters of Finger Bay we found dozens of commercial crab pots, their red buoys swept in a wide tide arc.

The following morning, the last of our journey, we awoke in teal light to see a cruise ship passing by, a great floating city with its industrial hum and bright lights framed by mountains as bold as God's soldiers.

"Welcome to the promised land," Richard yelled. Then we mooned it.

In another two days we would board a ship like that. Dressed in our National Park Service class-A uniforms, we would regale passengers with our infinite knowledge while of course being polite, patient, well-groomed, provocative, and brilliant, giving commentary and programs with clear themes, goals, and objectives. What Richard called "dreams, shoals, and objections."

Not unlike Lennon and McCartney singing for the queen, we told ourselves with a laugh.

"He has too many of the wrong ambitions and his energy is too often misplaced," a teacher once wrote of John Lennon. It could have easily been Richard, or Joe Ibach, or John Muir. Heaven save us from a world where everybody conforms. Jesus himself was a radical.

So we paddled through the rain and the waves to be the only kayak, to prove to ourselves (more than to anybody else) that we could do it. We were ready for it to end, for the hot showers and chocolate ice cream waiting in Bartlett Cove. We also wanted it to last forever, the lean living and cherished illusions, the rhythm of the paddles, the music of water, the feeling of coming home to a home we'd never known before. We wanted to be the pioneer who never runs out of wild country, the dreamer who dances on the mirror of paradise with his inverted reflection, paradox.

On a slack tide we crossed the wide lower bay and worked our way through the Beardslee Islands. Then we sighted another boat, a kayak like our own but with one paddler. Astonished, we glassed him with binoculars. He wore a knit cap with tassels, like the Greenland Inuit wear, and paddled a steady beat to the north. As he did, the entire bay seemed to open up and take him in.

"Who is that guy?" Richard said. "I couldn't do that. Could you do that?"

"I couldn't do that."

"Neither could I. . . . Who is that guy?"

Later we would find out. He was a photographer from Japan, a quiet soul the same age as Richard, a year younger than I. With a gentle handshake and a slight bow he would accept our hospitality and roll his name off his tongue like water over stones: Michio Hoshino.

Richard would call him "the man from Japan."

Did I understand then? Did I comprehend how a bay shaped by glaciers would in turn shape me? No. I was young. I was the only kayak. Despite all I had learned from Dr. Folsom about mountains and glaciers, how they can and will change, I was unprepared to apply a landscape to a life. I would risk falling in love and saying good-bye to something that could never stay the same.

BACK IN BARTLETT COVE, I buried myself in the library to read about the Ibachs. When Muz fell ill in the spring of 1959, Joe took her to the hospital in Juneau thinking he would have her back home soon. She died there. It wasn't right, he told a friend, that she should die in a city with so much traffic and everything worn down by the feet of too many people. They had been married for fifty-one years. One year after her passing, Joe could stand it no more. He left a note on brown parchment: "There's a time to live and a time to die. This is the time." Then he shot himself.

Stepping outside, I watched sunlight dance on the cove where sandpipers flitted about. A blue heron lifted on broad stroking wings that flexed against the sky. I found Richard in the trailer making dinner.

"Did you know that old Joe committed suicide?" I asked.

He turned. "Yeah, didn't you?"

I didn't answer.

"It's part of the deal, Kim. It comes with being born. You live, you die."

For all his toughness, trap lines, and gold mines, Joe couldn't live without the woman he loved. His world was too quiet, his bed too wide. Friends buried him next to Muz on Lemesurier Island, facing Icy Strait. Years later I would learn (from the Internet and Joe's great grand-nephew) that Joe did indeed leave home before age twenty, with two older brothers. All three made it to Chicago and ran out of money. One brother stayed to work the barges of Lake Michigan. Another brother returned home to the family farm, near Buffalo. Joe pushed on. He got to Prince William Sound, excelled at fox farming (made a bundle, some say), and married Caroline Shirley "Muz" Sharpe in the little town of Cordova in 1908. Born in 1885 in Ontario, Muz no doubt got herself to Alaska in a pioneering manner that proved admirable to Joe. The youngest of nine children of Isidor (Charles) and Mary Ibach, Joe was born in 1879, the same year John Muir first came to Glacier Bay.

OUTSIDE, RICHARD AND I watched sandpipers fly by as if the entire flock were a single organism choreographed by a powerful hand. It occurred to me then, as Richard served dinner and we laughed and gave thanks, that God lived within us but also in the spaces between us: husband and wife, friend and friend, bird and bird.

It would have made a good photograph, those sandpipers winging over sun-sparkled water, but my camera was gone. I had pitched it into the sea near the end of our kayak trip.

Ker-plunk. It went straight to the bottom, fast as gold. I'd be lying if I said it felt good. I wasn't sure what I felt anymore, or who I was, or what I was becoming. Crossing crevasses is no easy thing. Neither is being a pioneer. The chasm of uncertainty stares up at you and despite all the warnings, you look right down into it.

Luxury five-star cruise ships. Yachts with names like *Safari Quest, Majestic,* and *Obsession.* Hungry masses looking for the America that used to be. They were coming. Alaska was for sale and they were coming. We would greet them in the shadows of glaciers.

Richard said, "I hope they like poetry."

PART TWO

STAYING PUT

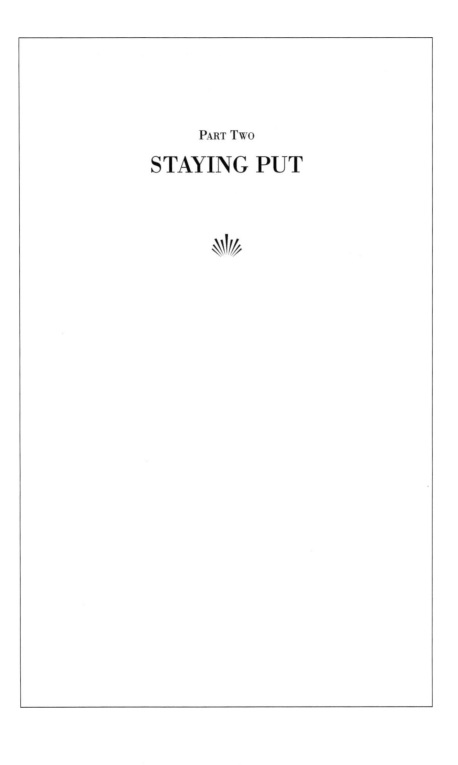

PLANET PRINCESS

Chapter Four

———

OUR BOAT moved slowly through the fog as we huddled over the yellow-green glow of the radar. I rubbed the sleep from my eyes and saw Richard do the same. Next to him, Melanie, a new recruit from Yellowstone, about to begin her first summer as a seasonal ranger in Alaska, looked as if she'd been up for hours. She was wired with anticipation, having never been on a cruise ship before. The radar picked up something ahead.

"Gulls," said Maggie, our skipper.

I stepped out onto the aft deck to scan the horizon. *There was no horizon.* It had disappeared in the fog. Up was down and down up. We might as well have been cloud-bound in an open basket balloon. Then I saw the tight flock of gulls feeding on the water, some hovering and diving for fish. As we parted it, the flock swirled around us like two lobes of a magnetic field that closed in behind. Marbled murrelets paddled away, their heads turned to keep a wary eye on us, nervous with last-minute indecision if they should fly or dive as we drew nearer. Maggie throttled back to give them room.

I joined the others in the wheelhouse, yawning.

"There," Richard said as he pointed to the upper arc of the radar. "What's that?"

"That's it," Maggie said.

"The Love Boat," Richard said with his crazy grin. "It's coming to take us away."

Maggie radioed the cruise ship and identified us as the National Park Service motor vessel *Serac*, one-quarter mile off their starboard beam, ETA five minutes.

A refined British voice (like George Bernard Shaw's Henry Higgins) answered back that the ship would embark us on its port side at five knots, standing by on VHF channels 16 and 12.

It emerged through the fog as an apparition, not so pointed on the bow yet blunt on the stern, with freshly painted flanks rising like palisades into the stratosphere. It didn't look like a ship; it looked like the box the ship came in. A picture of what happens when open deck space is sacrificed for stacked-and-racked staterooms to create a great white *thing* some one hundred feet high, a floating hotel, a five-star milk carton, the world's largest loaf of Wonder Bread. We gawked as we cut through its wake and rounded its stern. It was a Princess ship out of London—the *Sun Princess*, *Island Princess*, *Dream Princess*, *Bride Princess*, *Palace Princess*, *Pamper Princess*— something like that.

"They get bigger every year," Maggie said. "They used to carry hundreds of passengers; now they carry thousands."

"Someday they'll make the *Sphere Princess*," Richard predicted. "It'll be a mile across and a mile high, the largest man-made thing on Earth. It'll hold a million passengers and roll through the sea like a giant ball, with the inner decks on gimbals so there'll be no motion from the waves."

"Everybody on board will meet everybody they ever wanted to meet," I said.

"They'll eat as much food as they want and still lose weight," Richard added.

Melanie looked at us like we were nuts.

We put out the fenders as Maggie sidled us alongside at five knots. A long ladder was lowered by the ship's able-bodied seamen.

Richard went up first, then Melanie and me. We hauled up a large trunk filled with books, and watched the *Serac* pull away. A ship's officer then escorted us through warm passageways up to the bridge.

The captain welcomed us with good cheer, but the Alaskan pilot did not. A stolid authoritarian who chafed under any regulations outside his own, he seemed to resent our presence on his exalted platform. As rangers we had the jurisdiction to tell him where he could and could not go in Glacier Bay, not from a navigational standpoint but from a wildlife standpoint, mostly to protect feeding humpback whales and pupping harbor seals.

The captain offered us tea. We discussed the day's itinerary and met the cruise director, an affable Australian named Mark who wore white shoes, white socks, white slacks, bright white teeth, and a white shirt with huge lapels and an open collar to reveal his down-under tan. While some cruise directors were of the game show host variety—the kind of guy who when you asked who he *really* was would say, "Who do you want me to be?"—Mark seemed more genuine. He invited us to follow him so he could show us the many features of what he called "the most beautiful vessel afloat." We passed potted plants, grand pianos, double-wide stairways, teak trim, and many full-length opportunities to reflect upon ourselves. If mirrors were books, what a library that ship would have been. Mark told us that everything on board was there to *provide enjoyment*. Not entertainment. That wasn't good enough. Enjoyment was the goal, *satisfaction guaranteed*. "Edutainment" is what he expected from us. It was great to have us on board, by the way, "so our passengers might actually learn something."

Unlike Richard, who looked like a captured animal when brought to the zoo, Melanie was on her toes, enchanted. She marveled at everything and I marveled at her. After three seasons as a ranger assigned to the geysers and hot springs of the world's first national park, she would need an escort—two fellow rangers, Richard and me—to instruct her on the wilds of Alaska, the rigors of cruise ship etiquette, and the art of not taking yourself too seriously.

As if on cue it began to rain. Many passengers were already up and about in their perma-press jogging suits and gift shop ball caps. After making calls in the port towns of Ketchikan, Juneau, and Skagway, this was their only day in Glacier Bay—the real Alaska—and they weren't about to miss it. They looked outside with the frustrated expressions of people who could buy anything except good weather.

"When's it gonna clear?" a man asked Richard.

"Any day now."

"Is this as spectacular as it's going to get?"

"Probably not."

"Then you'll let us know when we see something, right?"

"You bet."

Richard and Melanie headed for the breakfast buffet. I found a large table, spread out a map, and began telling stories to an elderly couple. Soon twenty other old-timers were buzzing around me, many with hearing aids. "Where are we?" they asked. "Are you a forestry ranger?" "How'd you get here [on the ship]?" "What elevation are we at?" "Ever seen a wolf?" "The Northern lights?" "Been charged by a bear?" "Does the ocean go all the way around that island?" "You married?" "Why not?" One man said, "On a helicopter ride outta Juneau we saw a glacier that had a dark line right down the middle of it. What was that?"

"That line," I said, "was a medial moraine."

"More rain?" another man exclaimed. "It's raining hard already."

"No, no." I explained that a moraine was a surface feature on a glacier, a ridge of rock and gravel. "But it's true that we do get a lot of rain here."

"Reindeer? Did you hear that Maude? They got reindeer here."

I liked these people. How easy it was to make fun of them, and how wrong. In the haunted eyes and lingering limps of the old men were memories from World War II and Korea. One guy named Pete still carried shrapnel in his hip from Italy. A woman named Josie had worked as a nurse in a triage unit in France, and years later served with the Peace Corps in Africa.

"I got charged by an elephant once," she told me with a wave of her bony hand, "so I just snarled at him and chased him off." But then she went deeper as she wrapped her arthritic fingers around my arm and told me about the ecology of elephants, how they make entire environments (by knocking over trees and feeding on them) and might have contributed to the creation of African savannahs that long ago enticed humans from the forest and into the open; that is, to stand up straight and really have a look around. Elephants may have helped to make us who we are. She asked about humpback whales. Did they communicate over great distances as elephants did? "We have to save the whales," she told me, "just as we have to save the elephants. We owe it to them."

Josie and her friends all volunteered in their communities. They grew up during the Great Depression and knew the taste of real adversity. Many had read Jack London and dreamed of coming north since childhood. This was it, their dream come true. They were too frail to sleep on the ground or paddle a kayak. Yet their sacrifices gave me freedoms that they themselves would never enjoy. I saw my father in them, himself a WWII vet, and Mom, who like Dad grew up in North Dakota and had to follow a rope through hip-deep snow to get from the farmhouse to the barn and back during winter blizzards. Whenever I complained about my Schwinn Red Racer, they reminded me that they walked to school uphill both ways, through famine, flood, and fire.

These scrappy old folks who gathered around me were from Iowa City. They ate in moderation—a little bacon here, a fruit cup there—and told me that they all belonged to the same bowling league. Harriet had just rolled a 240 game. Maude was president of her garden club. Josie drove Meals on Wheels. The men nodded with quiet appreciation. Their wrinkled faces were the maps of their lives.

A woman named Margaret said to me, "You came aboard this ship this morning with a woman ranger didn't you?"

"Yes, I did. Her name's Melanie."

"Good for her. When we were her age"—Margaret waved her hand to encompass her elderly women friends—"all we had for career possibilities was secretary, teacher, and nurse. That's all. To be a park ranger was unthinkable. I hope your friend Melanie realizes how lucky she is."

Josie reminded Margaret of their friend Alice, who'd been a journalist. She'd passed away years ago, bless her soul. She had a wonderful sense of adventure.

I asked them, "Have any of you ever heard of Eliza Scidmore?" They shook their heads no, so I said, "Let me tell you a story. . . ."

The first cruise ship to Glacier Bay arrived in the summer of 1883, less than four years after John Muir had paddled in by canoe. It was a sidewheeler called the *Idaho*, commanded by Captain James Carroll. On the bridge next to him stood Eliza Ruhamah Scidmore, twenty-seven, a journalist who would one day be the first woman writer/editor at a new magazine called *National Geographic*. She would make five trips to Glacier Bay. As Captain Carroll steered the *Idaho* to within an eighth of a mile of the tidewater terminus of a huge glacier, Scidmore wrote, "Words and dry figures can give little idea of the grandeur of this glacial torrent flowing steadily and solidly into the sea, and the beauty of the fantastic ice front, shimmering with all the prismatic hues, is beyond imagery or description. . . . There was something, too, in the consciousness that so few had ever gazed upon the scene before us, and there were neither guides nor guidebooks to tell us which way to go, and what emotions to feel."

No guides or guidebooks? The Iowa City Bowling League liked the sound of that. It reminded them of their untethered youths. An old guy named Arnie said, "There's too much junk in the bookstores nowadays telling you where to go and what to wear and how to feel. No wonder kids are struggling. How can they find themselves and learn to use their wits if they can't get out in the woods and get lost in the first place?"

Eliza Scidmore returned to Glacier Bay the next summer and wrote about sitting on a rock and watching the "wondrous scene." Captain Carroll named the glacier after John Muir, and that year, 1884, Muir Glacier became an official "Wonder of the World."

The cruise ship industry in Glacier Bay came to an abrupt halt in September 1899 when a powerful earthquake rattled the glaciers and filled the bay with so many icebergs that the ships couldn't approach the tidewater ice fronts for years. Not until the 1960s did cruise ships begin to revisit Glacier Bay and grow into the industry it is today.

As I stood to go, Josie stopped me and said, "Thank you for giving us your time. Most young people don't see old people, you know. We're invisible to them. They look right through us. It's nice of you to sit down and ask us about our lives."

I HEADED for fresh air but couldn't find any. I found a stairway. Up and up I went to the stratosphere deck, where the smell of the sea faded and the curve of the Earth appeared. I nodded to joggers doing laps under a large rollout awning. Looking over the rail, I felt divorced from everything below, the patterns of tides, the distant blades of kelp, the murrelets no bigger than specks. Unlike kayaking, cruise ship travel offered little intimacy with the natural world. All that time on the water, and never close to it.

Three middle-aged couples stood at the rail to admire the distant mountains and forested islands. I stood behind them, unseen. One man wore a John Deere cap backward on his big head and said to his wife, "See what I told ya, honey? There ain't nothing here." Not a house or a mall or a farm or a road in sight. All that land going to waste. He wrapped his beefy arm around her as a slice of pink zinfandel light cut through the clouds and a bald eagle flew by. "Whoa, look at that," he said. "That's our national bird. Damn, you don't see that every day."

"They're common here," I said. *The stealth ranger reveals himself.*

The man and woman turned. She smiled. He turned slowly, tractor-like, ready to plow me under. He knew where his tax dollars went. It was time for me to be a portrait of decorum in the National Park Service green and gray, a uniform so starched it could stand up by itself and would get into less trouble if it did. The other two couples also turned.

I introduced myself and said, "I'm with the National Park Service, stationed here in Glacier Bay, if you have any questions."

One of the women asked, "Where'd you come from?"

I pointed to the Beardslee Islands fading off the starboard stern. "Over there, beyond those islands, at a place called Bartlett Cove."

"You live there?"

"Yes, ma'am."

"That seems awfully desolate."

"I like it fine."

"Is where you live inhabited?"

"Yes, when I'm there."

John Deere said, "I'll bet you're one of them back-to-nature types, is that right?"

"That's right."

"Then you must eat biodegradable food."

"Yes, sir." *No more aluminum foil or plastics for me. Too hard on the stomach.*

The three couples sized me up.

"Where are you people from?" I asked.

"Houston," said one man.

"Dallas," said another.

"Houston," said the third.

The wives nodded (dutifully).

I noticed one of the wives, how her manners were practiced to accentuate her slight figure. Her hair fell like gossamer around her face, and she had a way of pushing it back with one finger as if in attendance at her own royal court. She had no smile, at least not a ready one, and I found myself feeling sorry for her. Her husband looked like the former high school quarterback who now gave financial advice, for a price. The other two guys were the former fullback and wide receiver. I got the feeling that all three men had invented their personas in a pickup truck at age fifteen and nothing would change who they were, no epiphany, no midlife crisis, no deathbed conversion. The biggest of them was the kind of guy who looked like he was smoking a cigar even when he wasn't.

"Tell me, ranger," he said, "any of these mountains around here worth anything?"

"Several are important in Tlingit legends and stories."

"I mean minerals."

"Oh . . . There's a large deposit of copper and nickel under the Brady Glacier, and some gold-bearing quartz in the upper West Arm."

"Anybody mining it?" asked the third man, a guy I called Mr. Extraction (there's at least one on every cruise).

"Nope."

"Why not?"

"This is a national park, created by Congress and President Carter when he signed the Alaska National Interest Lands Conservation Act in 1980. Mining isn't permitted. The National Park Service is trying to appropriate enough funds to buy the claims."

The Texans chewed on this for awhile, and then moseyed away. Or ambled or sashayed, I couldn't tell. A minute later a man approached, thin as a stalk of wheat, with cornstarch hair and large, expressive eyes that drank up his face. He made idle chatter, then said, "I imagine, being a park ranger, that you're worried about the environmental crisis and all that." It was more of a statement than a question.

"I am," I said. "But I don't lose sleep over it."

"You don't? You should. For most people in America today there is no environmental crisis. They're too self-absorbed. Or they're at the opposite extreme and they welcome it. They see the end times coming as a salvation—you know, the apocalypse and their own ticket into Heaven. It's been foretold in scripture and no amount of solid science or rational thinking is going to persuade them otherwise. That's all I'm saying. Don't expect them to open their minds and suddenly care about ecology or the environment." He shook my hand vigorously. "My cousin was a park ranger, a seasonal like you. He sells insurance now, in Cleveland. I think our national parks are wonderful, that's all I'm saying. I think you have a noble profession and an impossible job. Like *Mr. Smith Goes to Washington*, remember? 'The best causes are the lost causes.' I hope I haven't depressed you."

"Not at all," I lied.

As he walked away I stood at the rail and listened to the sea groan around me.

The ship passed Tlingit Point and entered the West Arm of the bay. I could see clearing skies ahead, the shoulders of the Fairweather Range disrobing themselves of gray scalloped clouds. The green flank of Gilbert Peninsula threw its reflection into the sea and the sea threw it back. A hundred feet above, a thin wisp of pale blue exhaust lingered from another cruise ship that had passed this way ahead of us, northbound, as were we, for Tarr Inlet and Margerie Glacier.

I found a couple high school boys playing soccer on the ship's bow, kicking a ball with surprising agility. I asked them what they thought of Glacier Bay.

"Cool," one boy said as he bounced the ball on his knee. It came out as ". . . *Kewl.*"

"Yeah," his buddy agreed, "really kewl."

I kicked the ball with them while Melanie began her commentary over the ship's loudspeaker. She spoke in a moderate voice but the volume was fixed to reach hearing-impaired passengers from the bridge to the bilge. Her commentary boomed down the decks and across the water and must have reached every wilderness campsite within miles. She elaborated on predators and prey, about a pack of wolves that had been seen attacking mountain goats on Gloomy Knob, and a pod of killer whales (orca) that had attacked two moose as they attempted to swim across Icy Passage (between Pleasant Island and Gustavus).

"The orca got one moose," Melanie said. "The other moose swam into a bed of kelp, became entangled, and drowned."

A minute later a thin woman dressed in Taos turquoise grabbed my arm and said, "Ranger, this is terrible. Isn't there some way to get all these animals to stop eating each other?"

"I'll see what I can do."

The man with her introduced himself as a political consultant in Washington. He shook my hand and gave me his name but left such an impression I couldn't remember it. I told them about the Tlingits and John Muir, and George Vancouver who had served as a midshipman under James Cook in the 1770s before he captained HMS *Discovery* in Alaska in the 1790s.

"George Vancouver?" The turquoise woman asked. "Is he the one who found the city?"

"Yes," the consultant told her, "but it wasn't as big then as it is now."

THE CLOUDS OPENED and the sun came out and the mountains stood in bold relief against a pardoning sky. We passed the entrance to Reid Inlet, and Melanie announced that the Ibach cabin site could be seen off the port beam.

"Just look for the three spruce trees planted by Muz."

She spoke about the pioneering couple, how they prospected for gold and made a life for themselves in this rough country. Passengers gathered along the rail with hungry eyes.

Mr. Extraction appeared at my elbow and said, "Now that's the kind of pioneering spirit that made America strong."

People nodded.

"This Ibach couple," Mr. Extraction asked, loud enough for everyone to hear, "did they make a living at prospecting?"

"I know of one two-year period when they profited thirteen dollars," I replied. What they really made we'll never know. Prospectors, like fishermen, tend to understate their bounty to keep others away.

"And they were able to live off that?" Mr. Extraction asked.

"Yes, and off the land and sea, the fish they caught, the berries they picked, the garden vegetables they grew."

"Well, good," Mr. Extraction said. "It's good to know that at least *somebody* got *something* out of this place."

I had to agree. There was much to admire about the Ibachs, and many passengers did, their faces aglow, drinking the tonic of open space. One woman in a Red Sox jersey and a wool hat lifted her chin to breathe it all in, her lungs reaching over the mountains. She said, "Thank goodness for public lands." Her comment warmed me until I heard Mr. Extraction boasting about Joe and Muz, how tough they were, the pioneering spirit and all that. Again, I had to agree. But I wondered what Mr. Extraction would say about the pioneering spirit when it grew into a go-for-broke, rape-and-ruin industry. Take Butte, Montana, where two billion dollars in copper was mined in one hundred years. Mom and Dad and I stopped there once en route back home from visiting relatives in North Dakota. Silent and disbelieving, we stared into the massive, toxin-filled open pit that had consumed the homes around it. An impressionable nine-year-old, I never forgot it. Butte became one of the most polluted cities in America, a Superfund site that would require four billion taxpayer dollars to remove heavy metals from the groundwater and rivers. Most of the copper went into transatlantic phone cables that lay useless at the bottom of the ocean in an age of satellite communications. Some went into making coins. The wives of Butte miners whose children were born with birth defects called the coins "pennies from Hell."

From Kennedy's Camelot to Reagan's Want-a-Lot, private gain had become the new path to public good. Mr. Extraction was its living embodiment. Population bomb? It's a dud. Global warming? Turn on the air conditioning. Biodiversity? Bullshit. Forget Teddy Roosevelt and his "legacy of conservation." Forget Richard Nixon and his Clean Air Act, Clean Water Act, National Environmental Policy Act, Marine Mammal Protection Act, and the most remarkable act of all, the Endangered Species Act. Reagan's Republicans were different. They sought every possible device to weaken or circumvent those laws. Under the guise of freedom and family values the party of Lincoln had become the party of greed, God, and guns, and I mourned its passing. I really did.

When I spotted a kayak with two paddlers near the entrance to Reid Inlet and pointed it out, the passengers stared in disbelief.

"My God," said Mr. Extraction's wife, "what are they doing? Are they out there by choice?"

Richard broke in and said, "They were sentenced there by a judge."

Nobody batted an eye.

"Where do they sleep?" the woman asked. "Where do they go to the bathroom?"

Richard said, "They use the letterfly."

"The letterfly?"

"Yep. Just find a place and let 'er fly."

I broke away, looking for a place to hide. As I did, a sadness came over me, a suspicion that few people on that ship envied those paddlers. I hoped I was wrong. I hoped the only kayak wasn't just an aberration to them, a curiosity they could replay on their television screens back in the warmth and comfort of their staterooms. Would technology one day package the wilderness and make it predictable like everything else?

If we lost the wildlands and elegant silence that nurtured our legs, lungs, and hearts for thousands of years, then what—or who— would tell us where we came from and where we should go? The cruise director? The powerful politician? The schoolyard bully? The clever advertiser? They'd try. They do every day. Advertisers were out to convince us of one thing: whatever possessions we had, they weren't enough. Whatever comforts we had, they weren't enough. We needed *more*.

Left with only remnants of the original America that shaped us, Alaska offered a new last chance. That's why I liked the metronome of glaciers, the give-and-take of ice, my dovetail friendship with Richard, point and counterpoint, living with the rain, whispering on the water. We'd been there. We'd gone feral. A part of us wanted the icy rivers to come back and reshape the land, reshape the human race as well. Teach us a thing or two. Moderation amid prosperity; isn't that what made great hearts?

"Don't eat until you're full," my mother would tell me; "eat until you're no longer hungry."

Glacier Bay was here to overwhelm us, not for us to overwhelm it. Restraint and respect, if assiduously adhered to, would keep national parks from becoming amusement parks. Cruise ships and tour boats had collectively become the third largest city in Alaska (exceeded only by Anchorage and Fairbanks) for numbers of people and power produced on any summer day. They did add an arcade element to Glacier Bay, but nothing like Skagway, where they disembarked so many people each summer day it felt like a stampede. Those same ships carried thousands of passengers in and out of Glacier Bay each day without disembarking a soul or disturbing a single flower or bear (unlike most kayakers). They created ambassadors for national parks in particular and for public lands in general, and did it with a smile. I opposed the ships only for their ceaseless growth in numbers and size.

So in the years ahead it would not surprise me when cruise ships were caught discharging black water, gray water, bilge oils, and other toxins (organic and inorganic) into the waters of Icy Strait and Alaska's Inside Passage, with bacteria counts much higher than EPA levels for public safety. Add to that smokestack emissions, the faint aroma of sulfur and oil, the mosquito fleets of helicopters and planes taking passengers on yet a thousand more excursions over the grand majesty of Alaska, keeping the view to themselves but sharing the noise with everybody. It painted a sorry picture.

Some cruise ship companies would attempt cover-ups and be charged with criminal and civil wrongdoing. Of course they would pay their fines and promise to be better corporate citizens. They'd run expensive television ads, and influence the media in every way possible.

After a ship sliced itself open on a reef near Ketchikan, a newspaper headline would read ROCK GOUGES SHIP.

The U.S. Coast Guard never did suspend the license of the rock.

In his landmark book, *The Wealth of Nations*, economist Adam Smith called it the Invisible Hand Theory—the idea that each capitalist out there hustling for himself and making the economy grow will in the end benefit society as a whole through his selfish pursuits, a sort of trickle-down idea, if you don't mind getting trickled on. John Muir watched it destroy the forests and rivers of the American West for fifty years and called it the "Gobble-Gobble School of Economics."

Nothing has changed.

No wonder national parks (and national forests, monuments, and wildlife refuges) are under siege. They belong to everyone and to no one. Islands of socialism in a sea of capitalism, they wash away in the pounding waves of profit becoming our prophet, with each new demand for access and economic growth made in the absence of any deep regard for the land. A uniquely American idea, national parks stand in opposition to much else that is American, which, ironically, makes them even more American. So it is that these dying islands—atolls, if you will, of the-America-that-used-to-be—stand as yet another bold and brilliant pattern in our national quilt of ingenuity, diversity, and original thinking.

At times it seemed impossible to me (then as now) that we could hold onto them in anything more than name.

I found an empty lounge and slipped in behind two men working at a table. Unseen, I stepped behind a curtain. Alone on a stage, I sat on a three-legged stool next to an electric guitar, an electric piano, a set of drums, and a Martin D-28 acoustic guitar. Such temptation came over me. It was the same kind of guitar Arlo Guthrie played when he sang "Alice's Restaurant," and Stephen Stills when he soloed on "Suite: Judy Blue Eyes." Left-handed Paul McCartney used one when he sang "Blackbird," the song that inspired me to learn to play.

I once owned a smaller model of a Martin, but sold it for tuition money. Deep in the university library, having traded my guitar for books, I learned from Dr. Folsom how to be a critical thinker. I read *The Descent of Man* by Darwin, *The Ascent of Man* by Bronowski, and wondered where to go from there. I read about John Muir coming down from the mountains to battle the enormous conceit that everything on this Earth was put here for us. I learned about restoring the West, what writer William Kittredge called "restorying the West." I wondered how to love this world, with its wildness slipping away, and was told to love it in great, good sadness. And how to turn the tide? If not by persuasion then guile, if not guile then force, if not force then poem, prayer, song. I found all the questions without answers frightening, but not as frightening as all the people not asking them. I began to travel, wanting to see things for myself rather than trusting the opinions of TV's conservative talking heads who saw the USA only through the tinted prism of their pride. Whenever I saw a bumper sticker that said PROUD TO BE AN AMERICAN, I thought . . . better to be *grateful* to be an American. Pride is a high horse to fall from.

So I bummed around the world, riding tramp steamers and the Trans-Siberian Railroad. En route across Siberia, my roommate was a retired general from the Soviet Red Army returning home to Irkutsk after heart surgery in Moscow. Whenever we rattled past oil refineries belching black smoke and burning off gas, he would gush with pride and talk about progress ("Just look at it. Isn't it beautiful?"), and how Lenin's Electrification Program would improve the lives of every Soviet citizen. I pointed to the rural scenes instead, the hand-split wooden rail fences and painted window shutters, the babushkas serving tea in their gray, frayed winter wool, and Cossacks on their milk sleds, making their morning deliveries, pulled by shaggy horses like something out of *Doctor Zhivago*.

The general shook his head. Crazy American.

Perhaps. My greatest culture shock came in my own country with its oversized homes, oversized cars, and oversized people with oversized impressions of themselves. I often traveled alone—no Indian went on a vision quest with ten other Indians—and kept a journal. Maybe it was then, traveling alone, that I came to prefer the small mistake over the large precaution, to see myself as a refugee from a sprawling, malling America. The risk I took in the only kayak was not the journey itself, but sharing it with Richard. Glacier Bay was the wildest place we'd ever encountered, and together we did something we wouldn't have done on our own.

I touched the Martin D-28, lightly, on the neck, and thought of Richard. When John Lennon invited Paul McCartney to join his band, he got more than he bargained for. McCartney brought along this other kid, George Harrison, who played brilliant guitar. Together they explored territory new to them and to everyone else. They made great music and became dear friends.

MARGERIE GLACIER offered all the "prismatic hues" and excitement of calving ice that Eliza Scidmore experienced when she visited Muir Glacier in the 1880s. Hundreds of passengers crowded the deck. Some stood atop lounge chairs for a better view. Towers of ice crumbled into the sea. Black-legged kittiwakes flew aerobatics off nearby cliffs. Melanie, Richard, and I moved through the crowd and refrained from using the loudspeaker. The best interpretation now was a careful lack of it. Get the uniform out of the way. Let the ice speak for itself.

A dozen passengers cornered me and asked how glaciers advanced and retreated.

I explained the concept of *deep time*: the notion of the Earth as billions of years old, with geologic epochs lasting for millions of years, some warm, some cold, some violent, some quiet. Then I explained how the glaciologist's terms *advance* and *retreat* referred to the terminus of a glacier only. When the rate of snow accumulation (compacted into ice at high elevations) exceeded the rate of ablation (ice melting, sublimating, and calving at low elevations), the glacier advanced. When the rate of ablation exceeded that of accumulation, the glacier retreated. Simple as that, almost.

One man, a clinical psychologist, looked at me as if to say, "Okay, these glaciers advance and retreat, but are they *in touch* with their advanceness and retreatness?"

A woman wearing a big floppy hat and an anxious expression said, "You spoke about deep time and the geologic calendar, about slowing down and sleeping on the ground and learning to live in country like this. Tell me then, quickly, how does it all work?"

Her unspoken request, I believe, was this: *Teach me patience, but hurry.*

I heard a guffaw and turned around to see Mr. Extraction laughing next to Richard, who had just told a joke, probably at his own expense.

If not prayer, then humor.

As I scanned the herd around me I wondered how travelers became tourists and allowed themselves to be packaged like this. Rich and poor, strong and weak, old and young, everybody fighting a hard battle inside themselves, looking for the big picture . . . what brought so many lives together on this ship, in this place?

Environmental writer David Nicholson-Lord has observed that people "are naturally inquisitive and exploratory, but also that we need the unknown, what historians of religion call 'otherness,' to lend our lives significance. So we conceive of ideal worlds— Paradise, the Golden Age, Heaven, Atlantis, Shangri-la—and dream of attaining them. Modern tourism routinely, and often shamelessly, exploits such myths, as the most casual glance through just about any brochure will attest." Thus every year millions of people launch themselves on their quests for paradise, shoulder-to-shoulder in search of uniqueness and self-discovery, hungry for adventure without adversity.

Long ago travel was full of risk and hard work. The English noun "travel" was born from the word *travail,* which came (by way of France) from the Latin *tripalium,* meaning a three-staked instrument of torture. To travel was to struggle against steep odds and have no guarantees of success. It required a lot of planning and expense, and great physical endurance. By the mid-1800s people began to travel for pleasure. They took tours and came to be known as "tourists." The term "cook's tour" came from Thomas Cooke, an early pioneer in tourism, and was meant to describe "an organized but superficial look at something." While the traveler was active, the tourist was passive. While the traveler was athletic, the tourist was a spectator. While the traveler roughed it, the tourist smoothed it.

"The rise of the tourist was possible, and then inevitable," wrote historian Daniel Boorstin, "when attractive items of travel were wrapped up and sold in packages. By buying a tour you could oblige somebody else to make pleasant and interesting things happen to you."

Jackpot bingo, slot machine, piano bar, golf tips, talent show, dance class, five o'clock funnies, napkin folding, art auction, enjoyment at every turn—these were just a few of the "interesting things" *guaranteed* on most cruise ships.

I knew a young woman in Juneau who was stopped by a cruise ship tourist and asked about her nametag that said NATURALIST.

"What does that mean?" the tourist asked her. "You take your clothes off?"

No; the naturalist explained that it meant she traveled on small tour boats and explained the geology and ecology of Southeast Alaska.

"Oh," the tourist said, "we don't have that on our ship. We have fifteen hundred passengers, seven hundred crew, four dance instructors, three maitre d's, a magician, and a fortune-teller, but no naturalist."

WE SPENT an hour at Margerie Glacier. The captain dispatched a tender to pick up icebergs that would be carved by the galley staff and put on display that night. As the ship turned south, it belched a smear of black smoke onto the sky.

In the dining room I sighted Melanie alone at a table and joined her. A waiter took my order: quiche Lorraine, cherries sublime, a spinach salad, and a blue Alaskan, whatever that was.

Melanie told me about growing up in Los Angeles. Her father was a welder, she said, who loved to drive the freeways and point out every marvel of construction: how one beam buttressed another, how two joints fit, how a weld transferred vertical stress. Overpasses and tall buildings were his icons of ingenuity and progress. Then one spring day they drove east until the freeways became highways, and the highways dirt roads. They stopped and went for a walk past flowering cacti and ocotillos. Wrens called. Lizards darted over sunburned rocks. Her father, typically a talkative fellow, jabbered less with each step. Soon he was by himself—an uncommon event—as the topography pulled him into places and spaces he had never been before. At one point he climbed onto his knees to inspect a flower. He sat on the dusty ground and said nothing as Melanie wordlessly joined him. Driving away that evening, they watched the last rays of sunset glitter off telephone lines that dipped and sliced through their view of the desert.

Her father said, "It's too bad they didn't bury these lines when they put them in."

Amid discussions of where to eat dinner, the comment nearly escaped her. He had made it so casually it seemed insignificant.

"But it wasn't," Melanie said. For a man who loved technology and every new gadget on the market, debunking telephone lines was revolutionary. He had never questioned them before. A walk in the desert had given him new eyes.

She smiled and I smiled too, and somehow her hand ended up in mine. It must have been the cherries sublime.

We talked about welders, how they make many marvelous things but can't make wilderness. Engineers can dam rivers but can't make them meander. I knew an architect, a talented man who designed buildings stronger than oaks. But he would never improve upon a leaf.

I told Melanie about a Dene Indian I had met along the Mackenzie River in Canada's Northwest Territories, where there are no highways. He was traveling alone by skiff when his outboard motor died and he had to row to shore. What to do? He was probably fifty miles from the nearest human being; much farther from his village. No problem. He terraced the rocky slope to make a sleeping spot, erected a lean-to shelter of driftwood, built a fire, and camped under the northern lights with his coffeepot and books. When my boat-mates and I happened upon him we could see he was in no hurry. He knew the country. He said a cousin or a nephew or a friend would come along in a day or two or three and give him a ride. Until then he was fine. By the way, he asked us, you guys want some coffee?

Melanie and I tried to imagine that happening along any freeway in the United States. A guy's car breaks down so he pulls over, builds a fire, and waits for a friend or a relative to come along?

"He'd be arrested," Melanie said.

"Or run over."

It made us wonder who was on the wrong end of civilization.

THAT AFTERNOON Richard offered his formal presentation in a large overheated auditorium. He stood before hundreds of people with his shirt coming untucked and his hair all over his head, as if combed with a firecracker. With his language aimed at retrieving the lost roots of words, he told the audience it was time to put the *Indian* back in Indiana, the *mess* back into Mesoamerica, and the *panic* back into Hispanic. In fact, why not put the glacier back in Glacier Bay? Stir things up. He gesticulated about wolves, eagles, whales, and bears. He showed some slides and read a short poem (more gesticulation), then took questions.

"What's it like living where you do?"

"It's nice," he said.

"How so?"

"It's quiet. Spend a year here, and the rest of America seems like one big Wal-Mart. Consumerism everywhere."

"How cold is the water?"

"Really cold."

"How long would you survive if you fell in?"

"Well, most people would be dead in fifteen minutes. But studies at the University of British Columbia have determined that if you huddle-float and avoid panic to conserve body heat, a small percentage of you might actually survive longer by going into a marine mammal cold-water diving reflex, a kind of physiological stasis. So if you think you're one of those people, and you do fall in, be sure to take along a good book to read."

"Are wolves being killed in Alaska?"

"All the time, even legally."

"Legally? How?"

"In some areas of Alaska wolves are seen as pests that kill caribou and moose. The Alaska Department of Fish and Game kills wolves to provide more caribou and moose as food for people."

"Do you ever get lonely?"

"When I'm by myself."

"How do you get your food?"

"Same way we got you. By boat."

"Are other parts of Alaska as desolate as this?"

"Lots."

"Have you ever been in serious danger?"

"No . . . well, maybe a couple times. I almost fell off a cliff once. Almost rolled my kayak in big seas. Got tangled up with a woman or two. The most dangerous place in the world is in bed, you know. Eighty-five percent of all people die there."

People laughed, and Richard grew serious for a moment. He thanked them for coming to Alaska, the last wild place. He asked them to consider what the world would be like one day if we succeeded in breeding the wildness out of ourselves, as we seemed intent on doing. If we became so enamored with technology that we computer-hacked our DNA and manufactured our children, instead of giving birth to them.

Nobody said a word. I stood in the back and thought, *Remember, when you pull that security blanket up to your chin, don't pull it over your eyes.*

The lights came up and he received a nice applause, thanks in no small part to Mark who reminded everybody "how lucky we are to have these knowledgeable and friendly rangers on board with us today." He pointed to the back where Melanie and I waved sheepishly.

In the ship's library I found a man in a polo sweater writing at a table. I made no motion toward him as I browsed the fiction shelf: Danielle Steel, Anne Rice, Mary Higgins Clark. In the nonfiction area I searched for a book—any book—on the natural history of Southeast Alaska. The man looked up and stopped writing. I had seen him earlier on the stratosphere deck and taken him for the kind of guy who had twenty Porsches in his garage and whose chief occupation was getting number twenty-one. He seemed different now. A sad surrender rimmed his eyes.

"This is quite a place you have here," he said softly.

"Oh?"

"Glacier Bay."

"Oh yes," I said. "It's not mine, though. It belongs to all of us." *And none of us.*

"Thank God." He put down his pen and leaned back. He attempted to take a deep breath and I saw him wince. He was difficult to age, as if it were important, which it was not. "Do you get out much around here?" he asked. "Camping and hiking, that sort of thing?"

"I do a lot of sea kayaking."

"Really? What's that like?"

I told him about the only kayak, the immense quiet, the music of the rain, the paradox and dirty socks. He nodded and invited me to join him at his library table. I declined, saying I had to be going. The *Serac* was on its way out from Bartlett Cove. He watched me organize my daypack, as I prepared to disembark, and told me he was an architect from Atlanta.

"An architect?" I mentioned that I thought ice was the architect in Glacier Bay. "It did a pretty fine job, don't you think?"

"Ice is more than an architect here," he said. "It's a finish carpenter."

A finish carpenter? "Do you mind if I use that in my journal?"

He managed a small smile. "Not at all. Are you a writer?"

"I'd like to be."

"Good. Don't give up on your dreams." He looked out the window at the blue-green Earth, the mountains cutting the sky. "It's more beautiful than I ever imagined it could be," he said. "So much open space and pure air. Now I can go home and let the damn cancer take me."

AS WE CLIMBED down the ladder to the *Serac*, I heard Mark announce over the loudspeaker, "Ladies and gentlemen, our intrepid rangers are leaving us. You can watch them go from the port side."

Passengers lined the rail on the stratosphere deck and waved as we pulled away. I could see John Deere up there, and Mr. Extraction, and between them Josie the Elephant Defender and her Iowa City Bowling Battalion.

"Intrepid rangers?" Maggie asked as she steered the *Serac* into Bartlett Cove.

Richard shook his head and said, "I can't do it anymore."

Neither could I. We joked the way men do when their humor comes from fear. One day the *Planet Princess* will arrive, so large it will block the sun. Every human being inside will be insulated from all that he or she dislikes, satisfaction guaranteed. Bird songs will be piped into staterooms with volumes adjusted for perfect pleasure. Beds will be made without ever seeing who makes them. "Planet Princess" will be written on every bar of soap.

Clean yourselves thoroughly.

Those humans outside will be rolled over and crushed.

We laughed. Perhaps it was for others to enlighten the eager masses of industrial tourism. Melanie, for example, with her ability to stand in one place and parlay a thousand questions without losing her patience or smile.

"How do you do it?" I asked her.

She spoke about the "interpretive moment," of having a thousand people in your hands and being able to change the way they see the world and themselves in it. "Any job that does that is a privilege," she said. "We can't ask them to be where we are. We can only ask them to take the journey. And for some, the first step on that journey is on a cruise ship in Alaska. We need to celebrate that."

I realized then that while it was my nature to question everything, it was Melanie's to answer everything. She wanted passengers to leave Glacier Bay with a new relationship with their homes and neighbors and with every living thing. I did too. But she *actually believed* it was possible, that a day in Glacier Bay could change people's lives. It might even change the world. Her belief had power. I could feel it reaching out, grabbing me. And that smile, the sun-tossed hair, the seashell eyes . . .

"Look," Maggie said, "gulls."

The flock swirled off our starboard beam as Maggie killed the engine. The *Princess* receded in the distance, bound for Sitka. A silence settled over us, broken only by the delicate chatter of birds. Melanie reached over and touched the water. I looked at Richard and he looked at me and we knew one thing: Nature wasn't for us to rise above. It was to sink into; to sleep upon and go bootless, and in silent protest to walk the finest rugs and fanciest tile and leave our naked, muddy footprints as the signatures of new beginnings.

THE MAN FROM JAPAN

Chapter Five

———————

I HEARD HIM before I saw him. He approached from off my shoulder some distance away. I glanced over to make certain he was a man, not a bear or a wolf, then turned back to focus on a ptarmigan perched atop a small spruce tree in Denali National Park.

Interior Alaska, Latitude 64 North, so cold in winter you can hear water freeze. For a short time I had traded the tides of Glacier Bay for the tundra of Denali, that subarctic Serengeti with its caribou, moose, grizzlies, and wolves, its misfit rivers and galloping glaciers, its oceans of land and gale-force mountains, its waves of peaks stacked together like a stormy sea turned to stone, and above it all an icy granite crown making the highest mountain in North America. Not a bad résumé for a national park. A sailor and a forester once visited Denali. The forester found it disturbing. It had no big timber, only small specimens of spruce huddled in river valleys safe from the fiercest winds. It had no naves of hardwoods or chamber-like groves of conifers reaching in supplication to the sky. He felt naked and exposed, as might a man outside his holy land. The sailor loved it. It reminded him of the sea, the open fetch of tundra running to every horizon. What trees he did find were islands to him, little green respites and reefs. He took deep breaths and faced watery-eyed into the wind. So did I. Time in Glacier Bay had made more of a mariner of me than I realized. Now and then the landscape of Denali would roll beneath me and I would wrap myself in my coat as if reefing a sail.

A couple of years had passed since my time with Richard and Melanie on *Planet Princess*. Richard was in Kenya meeting a Luo girl he had supported for many years through the Christian Children's Fund. One of the lucky ten percent of Kenyans who went to high school, she had written to him and invited him to come visit.

I was back from a winter in southern Spain, where I'd worked for the World Wildlife Fund (restoring wetlands) and read so much Hemingway and drunk so many dark spirits (handed to me by dark strangers) that I believed I could be a bullfighter, until I saw my first bullfight.

Now it was spring, or trying to be. Some years it arrives reluctantly in Alaska. At the moment I was on a slope above the Savage River, alone until this other man approached, coming nearer, tripod over his shoulder, his movements more calculated than mine, like smoke through dwarf birch. A cold wind nipped at my neck. Gray, fingerling clouds raced by. I secured Miller-mitts over my hands to leave my fingertips exposed so I could operate my new Nikon camera and once again play the game of nature photography in Alaska, trying to squeeze the essence of a wild subcontinent onto a tiny rectangle of film.

The willow ptarmigan softly clucked atop its tree. Its scientific name, *Lagopus lagopus*, is Latin for "feathered foot." Of the four hundred or so species of birds that occur in Alaska every summer, only a handful stay for the Arctic winter. The willow ptarmigan is one. At fifty degrees below zero it pays to have feathers on your feet.

I had once heard this bird described as "stupid." People said the clever raven, not the willow ptarmigan, should be the state bird of Alaska. Perhaps my photographing it had something to do with wanting to redeem its honor. It did look noble in the crown of that tree, as noble as any chicken-like bird could look. Then again, it might have interested me only because to my eye it made a nice picture. I admit that I enjoyed the power of framing an animal to appear as I thought it should, transposing image and reality. It also felt good to be out in the park in early May, before things got crazy with summer crowds and traffic and dust.

My tripod was affixed to a 500-millimeter lens, with the camera balanced on one end and the heavy lens glass on the other. (The glass was designed to capture maximum light and create the sharpest picture possible; the downside was the weight.) I had wanted a picture like this for a long time: a male ptarmigan in transition plumage, half-white, half-brown, emerging from winter into summer, sitting atop a tree in the mating season, calling its territorial imperative as if every ptarmigan hen for one hundred miles should drop her laundry and come consort with him.

"*goBEK . . . goBEK . . . poDAYoh, poDAYoh, poDAYoh . . . goBEK . . . goBEK . . .* "

I squeezed off a couple shots and turned to check on the other photographer. He had circled around and was on his knees in the dwarf birch, upslope and shooting across at the bird. I was shooting from below, having taken the more convenient position within easy walking distance of my Volkswagen van parked on the road a quarter mile behind me and down the hill. A second VW van was parked near mine, oblique to the road. If it belonged to this other man I could only conclude that he had left it in a hurry. A little voice in my head told me he was a better photographer than he was a driver.

The ptarmigan called and I burned through ten shots in eight seconds, my motor drive whirring the sweet song of consumption and quiet desperation. My hands shook as I changed film, ready to burn again. Here I was in Denali, nervous, excited, alert, a hunter, an artist, an enterprising man, trying, like everyone else, *to be somebody*. To make my mark.

To *burn*. That's what I had heard photographers say. They talked about "burning through film." It seemed appropriate, as my impression of many nature photographers was of men mostly, and a few women, on fire with ambition to be published in Sierra Club calendars, or *Audubon* magazine, or in that tallest tower of all, *National Geographic* magazine.

Angst climbed in my throat. I suspected the other guy was getting a better shot. Why couldn't I just sit cross-legged on the tundra and meditate on the damn bird like I'd done in Reid Glacier, in Glacier Bay, five years before? It seemed odd to think that this ptarmigan could have a longer (and more meaningful?) life preserved on my thin piece of film than it would in real life, its image rendered in books, calendars, magazines, and postcards long after it was dead. A dozen editors affixing to it whatever captions they wanted.

In that regard the power bothered me. I remembered when Roderick Nash, author of *Wilderness and the American Mind*, said that Sierra Club calendars were to the American wilderness what *Playboy* magazine was to the American woman.

Though some nature photographers disagreed, essayist Susan Sontag picked up on the "burn" metaphor and wrote, "the need to photograph everything lies in the very logic of consumption itself. To consume means to burn, to use up. . . . As we make images and consume them, we need still more images; and still more. . . . The possession of a camera can inspire something akin to lust."

I had thrown away my first camera in Glacier Bay; pitched it into the sea on Richard's dare. I honestly thought it would make a bigger splash than it did. Now here I was, five years later, image-making with a new Nikon, being what Albert Einstein would have called a *Lichtaffe*, a "light monkey." Like Sontag, he had had little fondness for photographers.

Journalism, art, self-expression. What about Paleolithic hunters thirty thousand years ago who painted wild animals by torchlight on cave walls? They distilled the sensation and made a confession. Speaking through pigments on their fingertips they said, "These are the animals that feed us, clothe us, and sustain us."

"There's a minute of life passing," Paul Cézanne would say as he painted canvas after canvas. "Paint it in its reality and forget *everything* to do that."

When I first stood before the Tlingit totem poles of Alaska and the great cathedrals of Europe, I felt the crafts of many generations reaching through centuries, the stories of medieval stonemasons who worked their entire adult lives for the glory of God and a job well done, never inscribing a name on their work. It was perhaps a grand and humbling thing to find a purpose larger than themselves, yet one integral to their being. An act of gratitude.

I thought of Melanie on the cruise ships in Glacier Bay as she worked to connect every passenger with the natural world, asking them if the wild places they knew as children were still there. The backyard creeks? The neighborhood meadows? No, came the chorus of replies. Most were gone. All were gone. Wild places were falling off maps and memories like leaves off trees.

"We must work to save them," Melanie would say in her artful way. By saving or losing wild places we will ultimately save or lose the best part of ourselves.

She was somewhere in California, working her way toward Glacier Bay, northbound with the thrushes, warblers, and terns, to spend another summer with Richard and me and other good friends. She had sent me a note in Spain saying, "I can't wait to see you."

Me? The last time I'd passed by a mirror I wasn't much to look at. A spore on the wind, a seed unsown, footloose and free, that was me. But where was I going? Where did I belong? I loved to travel but had no idea how to be home, to contribute to a community. Whenever I thought of settling down I thought of Melanie, who had a way of believing in others even when they didn't believe in themselves. I'd heard about humpback whales, how they sing in their winter waters and resume each song from where they left it the previous winter. That was Melanie and me: together, apart, together again, singing our songs of friendship growing into love.

I'd confided in her that I didn't want to work for the federal government. I didn't want to work for state government either, all that security and surrender. I wanted to work for myself as a freelance writer and photographer.

"You can do it," she'd say.

I wasn't so sure. It sounded dangerous: deadlines, kill fees, contracts . . . such severe language. If you missed a deadline, did you die? "It's easy, after all, not to be a writer," Julian Barnes wrote in *Flaubert's Parrot*. "Most people aren't writers and very little harm comes to them."

WITHOUT WARNING the ptarmigan flew away, beating its wings into the gray gauzy sky . . . *poDAYoh, poDAYoh, poDAYoh* . . .

I shouldered my tripod and headed upslope toward the other photographer. As I approached I could see he was Asian. His position had indeed given him an image superior to mine. I recognized him from somewhere.

"Nice background," I said as I observed how he'd laid out his shot, how the distant snow-streaked mountains rendered a painting-like effect.

"Yes," he replied with a gentle nod, "background is important."

His inflection was Japanese. Then I remembered his broad, open face, his genuine smile, his tangle of black hair and the Inuit wool cap.

"You're Michio," I said.

"Yes." He extended his hand with a slight bow. "I am Michio Hoshino."

I could see a mild discomfort come over him, embarrassed that I knew who he was and he didn't know me. It was a balance I would learn meant a lot to him: to always offer what's received, in this case recognition. I gave him my name and reminded him of our time together in Glacier Bay.

"*So desu*," he said brightly. "I remember; that was you? Oh yes, I was very hungry."

Five years earlier Richard and I had seen Michio paddling north in Glacier Bay as we paddled south, our trip ending as his began. Like us, he would be the only kayak in the bay before summer arrived. Many days later, when he paddled back into Bartlett Cove, half-starved, wet, and cold, he was in the campground making a rationed meal over a tiny stove when Richard found him. He brought him to our trailer and sat him down for a full dinner.

That's when I first met Michio.

His English had improved greatly, though he behaved as if it had a long way to go. I reminded him that his English was much better than my Japanese.

"Oh no," he said after I fumbled through a few sentences, "you speak Japanese very good."

"I don't think so," I said. In my travels overseas I had learned just enough Japanese, mostly from books and fellow travelers, to get me into trouble.

Richard had heaped a full meal on Michio's plate that night: potatoes, vegetables, fresh-baked bread, and half a Dungeness crab. Ravenous, Michio ate it all. Seeing this, Richard reloaded his plate with more potatoes and the other half of the crab. Michio ate again, this time more slowly. Richard filled the plate again and Michio ate. This went on a couple more times with each man wishing to honor the other—Michio cleaning his plate, Richard refilling it—until poor Michio nearly burst from overeating. We had to carry him back to the campground.

"Thank you," he said weakly as we left him in his tent like a distended whale.

That was the last time I'd seen him until now, on this wind-raked slope in Denali National Park. Ice still embroidered the braided channels of the Savage River. Patches of snow lingered on the north-facing slopes of the foothills. The distant peaks wore glacial shawls of deep blue defiance above a landscape not yet green with summer.

Michio and I sat and shared our snacks. The wind rubbed dry branches of dwarf birch against our pants. Now and then a passing vehicle seemed small and insect-like on the road far below as it skittered around Michio's poorly parked van.

"Is that your van?" I asked him.

"Yes."

"Nice parking job."

"Yes, I think the ranger will write me a ticket when he comes by."

"You want to go down there and move it?"

"No, I'm waiting for the bird to come back."

"The ptarmigan? Back to the same tree? That could be a long time, Michio."

"That's okay." He pulled out a knife and carved me half an apple.

We hardly knew each other yet rarely ran out of things to say. If silence did interject itself it came with no discomfort. I think Michio was listening to stones. How simple it was then, before he became famous and had television crews following him everywhere. He didn't want to discuss photography. Instead, he had a fathomless thirst for natural history.

"Kim," he asked, "do golden eagles kill Dall sheep?"

I had to think about this. I told Michio that I'd heard biologists talk about how an eagle might dive-bomb a lamb on a cliff to frighten it into losing its balance. If the lamb fell and died, the eagle would feast on its carcass.

Michio nodded and said, "Keeping balance is important."

"In many things."

"Yes, many things."

For the last five years he had lived part of the year in Tokyo and the other part in Fairbanks where he studied wildlife management at the University of Alaska. Back in the early 1970s, when he was little more than twenty (and had never been out of Japan), he saw an aerial photograph of the Eskimo village of Shishmaref on the northwest coast of Alaska. How impossibly small it seemed in a big, sweeping land. He knew he had to go there to see how those people lived. He wrote to the mayor and asked if he could visit for one month. The mayor agreed and Michio came and stayed for three.

He returned to Japan, earned a university degree in economics, and for a while fit into the calculus of conformity. But the whisper in his head turned to thunder. By 1978 he was back across the big ocean with a camera, spending months alone in the mountains and fiords of Alaska, waiting for the perfect light. When I said something about how nice his camera was, Michio told me about a Japanese master photographer who used only one camera and one lens of a standard focal length. No wide-angle. No telephoto. With this simple arrangement he took the best pictures Michio had ever seen. It was his way of saying a camera is only a tool, and the simplest tool is the best. In the end, all good art comes down to the head and heart.

We talked about caribou and glaciers and moose and lynx. Michio had many questions.

"Why do caribou numbers go up and down?"

"I don't know. I don't think anybody really knows."

The Western Arctic Herd that had numbered about 30,000 animals in the late 1960s had grown close to 400,000 animals by the mid-1980s. The Denali Herd that had numbered 20,000 in the 1940s was down to about 2,000.

"Some biologists say it's not even a herd anymore."

"Will the numbers come back?" Michio asked.

"Probably. I don't think anybody knows for sure."

He thought about this as he peeled another apple. Despite the cold air, his fingers worked with supple dexterity. I would soon discover that no kitchen or galley—or lack thereof—intimidated him. Fred Dean, a professor in Fairbanks, said Michio was "a magician with a wood cookstove." Jay Hammond, Alaska's former governor who lived on a remote lake 150 miles from the nearest traffic light or hamburger stand, noted that when Michio came to visit, he charmed the first lady by "taking over the cooking chores and conjuring up delicious meals from exotic ingredients he had brought with him."

I watched Michio sprinkle something on a slice of apple. He handed it to me and asked, "You said the Muldrow Glacier galloped. What does that mean?"

Gallop, I explained, was a metaphor for . . .

"Ah, metaphor." Michio knew the word.

"Sometimes glaciers move forward very fast," I said. "They surge. Scientists call them 'galloping glaciers.' It happened to the Muldrow, the largest glacier on the north side of Mount McKinley, back around 1956 or '57."

"I was just a boy then," Michio said, "five years old."

"Me too. One theory why this happens is that meltwater collects under the glacier and creates a slippery surface that suddenly allows it to slide forward very fast. The Muldrow advanced up to hundreds of feet a day when it was galloping. It came within a mile or so of running over the park road."

"Really?" He seemed to like that. "Will it gallop again?"

"Yes, probably."

"When?"

"Nobody knows, Michio."

He looked across the valley at the high peaks of the Alaska Range where glaciers looked back at us from beneath dour, sculling clouds. "I like mystery," he said.

"That's good, because there's a lot of it in Alaska." I ate the apple and tasted the spicy juices. "This is wonderful, Michio. What'd you put on it?"

He laughed. "It's a mystery."

UNEXPLORED, read the U.S. Geological Survey maps of interior Alaska in the late 1890s. It was a label Congress couldn't abide. Thousands of gold seekers were flooding into the nearby Yukon Territory and would soon spill into surrounding areas. Among the scientific expeditions launched was one under the leadership of two Survey scientists, George Eldridge and Robert Muldrow. In 1898 they traveled into the upper Susitna and Nenana river basins where Muldrow used a sextant and theodolite to make the first professional determinations of the height of Mount McKinley. His guess was a good one: just over 20,000 feet above sea level. (The accurate height is 20,320 feet.) Four years later, another USGS geologist, Alfred Hulse Brooks, led an expedition of seven men and twenty packhorses on the first recorded traverse of the Alaska Range. He began at the head of Cook Inlet in early June 1902, and finished 105 days and 800 miles later at Rampart, on the Yukon River. Despite boot-sucking bogs, swift glacial rivers, thick brush, and maddening clouds of mosquitoes, Brooks and his men—skilled wranglers, hunters, and campmen—fared well. At one point Brooks climbed alone to seventy-five hundred feet on an icy flank of Mount McKinley (he hoped to reach ten thousand feet) and nearly fell to his death on the descent. Another time he scrambled above camp and counted more than one hundred Dall sheep on distant mountains. He believed that these animals, together with the bears, moose, and caribou, made the area "one of the finest hunting grounds in North America."

His observation didn't go unnoticed.

A few years later Charles Sheldon arrived. Raised in Vermont and educated at Yale Law School, he was, according to one observer, "a seasoned man of affairs who was astute in the ways of politics and could spot a rascal at a distance." By talent and force of character he became the general manager of a railroad, then made a fortune mining in Mexico. He retired at thirty-five and set his ambition on his true loves of hunting and natural history. He made two trips to Denali, one in the summer of 1906, the second for ten months, from August 1907 until June 1908. Every wild animal intrigued him, but none more so than the pure white Dall sheep of the high country.

For most of the summer of 1906 Sheldon found only bands of Dall sheep ewes and lambs. This frustrated him, until one day he spotted several rams on the north side of a peak he called Cathedral Mountain. He approached at a crawl over wind-raked rocks, coming to within two hundred yards. He lay on his back in a slight depression to steady his nerves, then rotated into a sitting position, elbows on his knees.

"Not a ram had seen or suspected me," he wrote later. "I carefully aimed at a ram standing broadside at the edge of a canyon, realizing that the success of my long arduous trip would be determined in the next moment. I pulled the trigger, and as the shot echoed from the rocky walls, the ram fell. . . ."

In less than a minute he gunned down seven rams with eight shots.

That night he made soup and tea and butchered the animals. He hauled the meat down the mountain and treated the skins and skulls for preservation and shipment to the American Museum of Natural History. He noted the stomach contents, physical condition, and measurements of each, and convinced himself that he must return to the region for a full year (1907–08) to understand the passage of the seasons and how the wildlife lived and died according to the larger laws of nature.

It was during this second visit, while camped near the Peters Glacier in January 1908, that Sheldon first articulated the idea of a Denali National Park, the essence of which would be, wrote historian William E. (Bill) Brown, "its heraldic display of wildlife posed against stupendous mountain scenery."

This first decade of the twentieth century was a time of keen interest in natural history in America. Botany walks were common among citizens of all ages. Bird watching began to soar. Women would bring butterfly nets to church so they could quickly head to the meadows to spend their afternoons as amateur lepidopterists. Junior Naturalists Clubs flourished from New York to Seattle. Naturalists sat as presidents of universities; one even occupied the White House. An avid outdoorsman and hunter (and a close friend of Charles Sheldon), Teddy Roosevelt extolled the virtues of what he called the "strenuous life." People were getting overcivilized, he said (in his straightforward way); it was time to get out and roll in the dirt before America went soft sitting in sofas and padded chairs.

John Muir agreed but harbored no illusions or false sentiments about Roosevelt's trophy hunting. After one of the president's shooting escapades, Muir said to him, "When are you going to get over the boyishness of killing things?"

"HE SAID THAT to the President of the United States?" Michio shook his head. "That is . . . *unbelievable.*"

I explained to Michio that Muir was the preeminent conservationist of his day, a man of great stature, and ten years older than the president, who in turn took the criticism in stride.

In America we honor the young; in Japan they honor the old.

The seniority of years brings with it a level of respect in Japan that we in America can barely fathom.

Michio said nothing.

We lay on our backs atop Primrose Ridge, low out of the wind as we waited for Dall sheep. Always waiting.

"They were friends," I added. "Teddy Roosevelt and John Muir went camping and horseback riding together. They corresponded by letter. The president liked and respected Muir, and often asked his opinion."

Michio shook his head, imagining, perhaps, someone in Japan saying such a thing to the prime minister, or worse, to the emperor. He might have been embarrassed by my culture, or *for* it. I didn't know. I could have jabbered on and on about the gray margins between civil liberties and common respect in America, but it was better to say nothing. It was better to watch the clouds.

Michio finally asked, "Do you think you know an animal better after you kill it?"

"Maybe. Do you think you know an animal better after you photograph it?"

A grin spread over his broad face. "I think I know an animal better—the best, I mean—just *before* I photograph it."

A cold wind sailed over us as sunlight leaked across the northeast sky. The hour was early. Neither of us wore a watch. We had met in the Savage River parking lot and climbed up the ridge in the dull light of the unborn day, not saying a word, hoping to find Dall sheep rams.

"There," Michio said.

Moving slowly toward us were half a dozen magnificent animals, each painted a soft pastel by the cloud-screened sunrise. They spotted us—heads up, eyes alert—but must have regarded us as no serious threat, as they resumed grazing. I noticed how at any given time at least one ram (sometimes two or three) had his head up looking about while the others had theirs down, feeding. Such watchfulness was the price of living with bears and wolves. It occurred to me that they would have been safer in a zoo, and less of what they were, like some people who devoted themselves to the pursuit of security, locked in cages of their own making.

"The wind is not so badly," Michio said. "Today we will get good pictures."

The rams began to move away. I wanted to follow but Michio suggested we stay.

"I think they will come back," he whispered.

That's how he worked: find the convergence of animal, landscape, and light—the harmony of the spheres—and wait for them to align like some cosmic event. Don't chase the animal. Let it come to you as it would to a good hunter; a hunter *who knows the spirit of all things*. Be ready. Chance favors the prepared mind.

I could hardly protest.

The day before, as we had looked across the valley at the foothills of the Alaska Range, the ptarmigan flew back and landed atop the same tree, as Michio hoped it would. I remembered how he fired off several shots while I stood there dumbfounded, downslope a few steps, already en route back to my van. It seemed best that I continue. The spot belonged to Michio, after all. It was his vision that had put us there, not mine.

"Stay," he called to me quietly.

"You don't mind?"

"No."

He had looked at me then—a look I will never forget—with the kind of peace that fills a man who is comfortable with himself, unthreatened by others, a man who dares to be different, uncaged. While most wildlife photographers jealously guard their best spots and seldom share them with others, Michio kept no secrets. For him, the territorial imperative simply didn't exist.

"No," he said, "I don't mind."

Side by side we took pictures and laughed quietly as the ptarmigan clucked and called, and Michio said, "I think this bird is in love."

Now it happened again. The Dall sheep rams of Primrose Ridge came nearer and nearer until they stood on pillared legs and stared down at us from only ten feet away, shoulder to shoulder, eyes fixed like golden jewels in the sky, the stars of a deeper existence. For a long time we didn't move. I could hear myself breathing. Then slowly Michio rolled to his left to get a better background, whirring off shots with his wide-angle lens. The cold rocks crunched beneath him. The rams cocked their heads but otherwise didn't move. I watched warm sunlight fill their nautilus-shaped horns and thought, *I'm dreaming; this can't be happening to me.*

Then they walked away, and I snapped out of my trance.

I looked over at Michio.

He grinned and whispered, "Kim, are you still alive?"

"Yes, I think so. Are you?"

"Yes, very alive, and very happy."

RICHARD ANSWERED the phone on the second ring. He was back from East Africa and staying in Juneau until summer would soon find him in Glacier Bay.

"Richard, I'm in Denali. Guess who I ran into?" I told him about Michio, and he laughed when I mimicked the call of a ptarmigan . . . *poDAYoh, poDAYoh, poDAYoh.* . . .

I asked if he had heard anything from Melanie. They were friends too, as most rangers tend to be when they work together in a national park.

No, he said. He'd heard nothing from her.

We said we'd see each other in a week. Standing in the phone booth near the sled dog kennels at Denali headquarters, cowering from the wind, I could hear the park huskies howl and was surprised at how deeply Richard's words warmed me, his voice like the tide.

"Did you see the Kenyan girl, your Christian Children Fund's daughter?" I asked him.

"Yes. She's beautiful, and bright. I also got to meet her mother, and the whole village. They gave me a cow."

"A cow? What'd you do with a cow?"

"It didn't fit in my luggage, so I left it there, on loan."

Michio had invited me for dinner that night at his campsite at Riley Creek. I found him bent over a little stove, working his magic. I can't remember exactly what he fed me, only that it involved rice and spices, and was excellent. Gray jays flitted about the nearby spruce trees, hoping for a handout. The sky threatened rain, but it was an empty threat. The wind cut through us and we huddled in his van. It was a simple time for us, a time when everything we owned—our books, music, and camera gear—fit into our rusty Volkswagens. No homes, no mortgages, no furniture.

Michio talked about a book he was photographing on bears. He wanted to call it *Grizzly*. He asked if I liked that name. I said it sounded good to me. He asked several questions about Charles Sheldon and Dall sheep, then said, "Why did he shoot so many?"

I could offer no good reply. The excuse of collecting museum specimens seemed a feeble one at the moment.

"Charles Sheldon was like Teddy Roosevelt," I said. "He was a hunter and a conservationist."

"But seven sheep," Michio said, ". . . that seems like many."

It came with an irony. The chief reason Charles Sheldon later wanted the area to be a national park was not to protect the mountains. They could take care of themselves. It was the fates of the Dall sheep that worried him. Prospectors and railroad workers had arrived and Sheldon feared that the sheep, so easily slaughtered by an "indifferent marksman," as he called himself, would fall victim (in devastating numbers) to sharp-eyed market hunters who sought to sell the meat to the workers. Having proved the vulnerability of the animals, Sheldon now felt obliged to save them. He fought long and hard for this protection. His efforts paid off in February 1917 when Congress established Mount McKinley National Park. (Its name was changed to Denali National Park and Preserve in 1980.)

Sometimes a man, like a glacier, must destroy before he can create. Perhaps it's another element of war, this conflict we have with nature. We must pass through the prism of our own destruction to see a new and better light, as Charles Sheldon did.

"As long as there will be man," Albert Einstein said, "there will be war."

The burdened physicist lived through one of the darkest periods of human history, a time that sent my father to fight in the Pacific with the U.S. Navy, and Michio's father to fight in China. We were the sons of soldiers, born in the shadow of a terrible war, sitting together in an old VW van in a national park in Alaska, sharing coffee.

That night in the Riley Creek Campground, Michio reluctantly showed me some of his photos after I saw them sticking out of a notebook. To this day I remember how they arrested me with their clarity and simple power, the balance of foreground and background, the perfect dew on tundra leaves, the glint in a caribou eye, the geometry of form and space, the ineluctable *something* that few (if any) of my pictures possessed.

"These are very good, Michio," I said.

He demurred that they were okay, adding, "I have much to learn."

I was reminded that the greatest artists have the greatest doubts; that supreme confidence (which I had seen in many other photographers) is granted to the less talented as a consolation prize.

I found myself wishing that Susan Sontag and Albert Einstein could have met Michio Hoshino; that maybe with one photograph I could change a life and persuade one human being—as Michio had been persuaded at a young age—to approach the bountiful, bleeding Earth with a new and deeper regard.

Michio asked if I had a girlfriend and I told him about Melanie, how we met in Glacier Bay and would soon see each other again. Did I tell him I was falling in love? I can't remember. Looking back on it now, it felt more like a soaring than a falling, as if whales in the sea were as free as eagles in the sky, flying in and out of each other's lives.

Michio listened keenly and asked if I thought I'd marry Melanie someday.

"Maybe," I said. My life was defined by maybes.

"What about you, Michio? Do you have a girlfriend in Fairbanks?"

"No."

"Why not?"

He flapped his arms like a bird. "I am always flying away. I will marry a Japanese girl someday."

"Really? Why?"

He smiled. "Background, Kim. Background is important."

FEATHERED FEET

Chapter Six

———————

ROAD CLOSED, announced the large sign atop the barricade. NO VEHICLES BEYOND THIS POINT.

It was the morning after my dinner with Michio. Still in Denali, I parked my Volkswagen and pulled a rusty mountain bike off the rack. I loaded food and water into a daypack and pedaled past the sign without looking back. Is a bicycle a vehicle? The sky offered no gesture of spring. Winter lingered like a guest who stays too long. The rising sun—I could only assume it was up there somewhere— was about as dispassionate as a medium-sized star could be in May. I suspected the only warmth I would feel that day was what I generated myself.

I crossed a bridge over the Teklanika River and pedaled hard through a forest of spruce, moving deeper into Denali National Park, uncertain where I was headed or why. Soon I passed over Igloo Creek and began to climb a gentle canyon incline with Igloo Mountain on my right and Cathedral Mountain on my left, their rocky flanks pressing in on me. Breathing hard, I kept my head down and arched my back to ease the cut of the pack straps in my shoulders. I passed Tattler Creek and began to side-hill Sable Mountain, my ears filled with the throbbing of my own heart.

At Sable Pass the topography opened up and a sign announced another closure, this one not of the road but of *everything else*. The Sable Pass Critical Wildlife Closure is a large upland tundra basin—prime grizzly bear habitat—that's been off limits to the public since 1959. Only the occasional researcher or winter sled dog patrol is allowed in for short periods of time. I coasted back down the road a quarter mile and stashed my bike in a ditch. From there I hiked down to a creek and began to climb Cathedral Mountain, where Charles Sheldon shot seven Dall sheep rams one summer evening in 1906.

My legs ached. My lungs began to sear from my fast pace. I skirted some snow patches and was forced to cross others, in a few places plunging down to my thighs. I gained a windswept ridge where the exposed rock gave me better footing. The sky should have brightened with each passing hour but didn't. I should have been more watchful as I gained elevation and exposure, but I wasn't.

Driven by impulse or obsession or both, I continued to climb. The clouds furrowed their brows. The wind died and the sky began to snow. I let out a wild laugh and pushed on.

Two hours earlier I had awoken in Riley Creek with no idea what to do. Go deeper and higher into Denali Park was all I knew. Michio had already gone, off chasing the morning light somewhere. My memory of him made me smile. He seemed to be part wondrous child and part wise elder, a disciple of different angels with their own definition of guardianship. I worried about the coffee stains on his pants and the peanut butter under his fingernails. I worried about his quaint absentmindedness among bears that lived by their noses and claws and teeth.

Perhaps I worried too much.

The snow fell harder as I scrambled upslope. Balanced on the angle of repose, I could reach to one side and touch hard rock; to the other, only air. The world fell away in whiteness. Catching my breath, I slowed my heart until I heard nothing. The snow made no sound. I stood surrounded by peace and fear, white and black, the acute present and the distant past.

I pushed on. Fifteen minutes later I reached a false summit, descended the other side, and climbed again, higher than before. One summit after another I climbed until no more ascending slopes greeted me and all directions fell away into whiteness. I felt equally part of earth and sky, too proud and breathless for my own good. There on the true summit to greet me, cradled in a small depression uncovered by snow, was fresh bear scat. Not warm but not cold, it seemed to say, *This mountain belongs to me*, Ursus arctos, *grizzly bear, survivor of the Pleistocene that claimed many large mammals but not you and not me. Watch yourself.*

I laughed and screamed and lost my bearings and had no idea which way to head down. The swirling snow had erased my tracks. The whiteout was completely disorienting. I had no compass. I huddled against a rock and ate my meager lunch. *Patience*, I told myself. As a young boy I had read stories about great explorers in high latitudes. One was about Fridtjof Nansen, the tough Norwegian who skied across the Greenland Ice Cap in 1888 and spent several months living with Inuit Eskimos before he sailed home. One day the Inuit journeyed out to gather grass along the coast. When they got to where they were going and found the grass stunted by a late spring, they sat down and in Nansen's words, "waited for the grass to grow."

The lesson was simple. Be patient, stay put. Let the elements of nature swing to your favor. Nansen mentored Ernest Shackleton, Roald Amundsen, and Robert Falcon Scott before each man plunged into the frozen ends of the Earth. As Shackleton later said on his *Endurance* Expedition, "Put footstep of courage into stirrup of patience." After crossing eight hundred miles of stormy seas in an open twenty-foot boat to reach the Island of South Georgia, Shackleton held offshore to let a storm blow itself out before landing. He knew that making landfall could be more dangerous than the crossing itself. One bad wave, and every overeager man would be dashed on the rocks and killed. So he waited. The next day, after the storm had passed, he and his bedraggled men landed safely.

I rocked back and forth to rebuff the cold. My toes ached. My fingers stiffened. I sang Beatles tunes to pass the time. After a couple of hours the storm abated. The snow stopped, the clouds lifted, and a patch of blue sky appeared. Below me was a land of pure white beauty, the Earth at once ancient and new. To the south, the Alaska Range showed its teeth and snow-fed glaciers. To the west, I could see the park road and beyond it the untrodden plain of Sable Pass where no people could go. I opened my journal and wrote:

> Glaciers, mountains, rivers, forests, tundra; a landscape rich with places that have never felt the tread of human feet. It thrills me not because I can break first ground, but because first ground remains unbroken.

I made it down Cathedral Mountain and back to my bicycle in less than an hour. Riding the wet road back through the spruce forest (it had rained at the lower elevations), I emerged at the Teklanika River to find a dozen people on the bridge, several of them photographers with tripods and large lenses, Michio among them, in his baggy sweater and tasseled hat.

He waved me over.

"What's going on?" I asked.

"Caribou and wolf," he said, "very exciting."

I looked downstream to see a young bull caribou standing still as stone on the edge of the river, the waters swollen with rain and snowmelt.

"Its back leg is hurt," Michio told me. "A wolf was here and . . . there it is!"

He pointed at the willows where a furtive gray shadow moved parallel to the river, perhaps to circle the caribou for a new attack. Wolves often hunt in packs in winter to bring down large prey, such as moose in deep snow, but will hunt alone in summer for smaller and easier prey—the injured, sick, and unwary.

Suddenly the wolf raced in. Already weak and without large antlers to parlay the attack, the caribou plunged into the river. It struggled for footing and was quickly consumed by huge waves. The wolf moved along the bank, watching it. Soon both wolf and caribou disappeared from view. People ran for their cars. The road paralleled the river for a short distance to the north, and everybody figured it might afford a chance to watch the action.

Michio's van was parked behind a ranger patrol car. I quickly loaded my bike inside and got into the passenger seat as Michio started the engine and looked over his shoulder to back up. He popped the clutch in first gear. The van lunged forward and slammed into the ranger car.

A minute later we stood on the road with the ranger, who said, "That's okay, Michio. It's only a small dent. That's what bumpers are for."

I couldn't believe it. I knew this ranger. He loved to write tickets. He wrote tickets like Stephen King wrote books. He even looked Stephen Kingish, bullet-headed, square-shouldered, humorless, his flat hat pulled low over his eyes, a big gun on his hip. And here *he* was making excuses for Michio. His bumper was crunched. His license plate looked like a taco. Yet Michio's sincere remorse for doing such a thing seemed to touch him with uncommon amnesty. Michio's van had its wounds as well, but I could see that all he wanted was to get down the road and find out what happened to the caribou and the wolf.

"Go," the ranger said with a wave. "Go get your pictures, and drive carefully."

Michio made a final apology and drove away like Mario Andretti. A few miles down the road we found the others at a viewpoint above the Teklanika River. The wolf was gone but the caribou was still in the river, floating on its side, apparently drowned.

Michio watched it disappear from view and said quietly, "That's too bad."

THAT EVENING, my final in Denali, Michio again invited me to his Riley Creek campsite for dinner. I played guitar while he juggled noodles and vegetables and stirred up an exotic sauce. I couldn't sing very well—still can't—but was able to pick out melodies by Paul Simon, Stephen Stills, and others from the 1960s.

Michio asked me to play several Beatles songs: "Here Comes the Sun," "Something," "While My Guitar Gently Weeps."

"Those are all George Harrison songs, Michio."

"Yes, George Harrison."

Of course, George was the quiet one, the spiritual one who went East to find a deeper vision. His music must have transcended time and place in a way that appealed to Michio but that I couldn't hear.

All that night we talked about caribou and wolves. Michio was making plans to camp alone for a month in the Arctic National Wildlife Refuge, in the far northeast corner of Alaska. He had many questions and I told him what I knew about caribou. Some years they did well, when eighty percent of the calves survived their first summer. Some years were hard, with calf mortality at nearly one hundred percent. Weather, predation, and available forage seemed to be the biggest factors. Born in early June, the calves could stand within an hour, walk in three hours, run in three days, and outrun a wolf or a bear in two weeks. They moved like gazelles over ankle-turning tussocks that bedeviled the strongest hikers. The herd of about 130,000 that occupied the refuge migrated there each spring from winter feeding grounds in Canada. It seldom moved as one large group, or by the same route. Instead it broke into aggregations—10,000 caribou here, 5,000 there—that flowed like separate channels of the same river, spilling over mountain passes and open tundra. The Inupiat Eskimo had a saying: "No one knows the ways of the wind or the caribou."

Michio nodded. He knew the saying.

"One month up there is a long time, Michio."

"Yes, long enough, I hope." He planned to get dropped off by small plane in the middle of the calving grounds. He would take a VHF radio, but no emergency location transmitter, global positioning system, or bear repellent pepper spray. I couldn't believe it. I knew of no other photographer in Alaska who approached a subject this way, going alone into places so remote for so long.

Michio thought for a moment and said, "We don't have much time."

I stared at him.

He grabbed *The Timetables of History*, a thick reference book I carried (and still do) that covers five thousand years of human history in seven hundred pages. I had shown it to him earlier to explore the parallels between Japanese history and European history. For example, in 1603 the Tokugawa family attained the shogunate in Japan while the Tudor monarchy ended in England (with the death of Queen Elizabeth) and Shakespeare finished *All's Well That Ends Well*. Stuff like that fascinated me.

Michio nodded through one of his preoccupations.

He held a thin wafer of the pages between his thumb and forefinger and said, "We are only alive for this long. All the rest of the time"—he hefted the tome in his hands—"we are gone . . . forever. Like the caribou today. We float away."

I told Michio about my climb up Cathedral Mountain, the snowstorm, and the bear scat on the summit. He became animated, his eyes flashing. I mentioned something about Sable Pass being closed for decades, how that gave me hope.

"Hope?" Michio said. "What do you mean?"

"Maybe there can be a place, maybe many places, where nobody goes. Sacred places that we all agree are best left untouched by human beings. They would be the apple in the garden, the symbol of our restraint. They would prove that we don't have to go everywhere and do everything and study everything and describe everything."

"Mystery," Michio said with a smile.

"Mythology," I added.

"I wonder," Michio said after some careful thought, "if one person could visit this place each year. A writer one year, a scientist another year."

"A poet. A photographer."

"I would like that. . . ."

"Michio, when you were kayaking in Glacier Bay, did you see anybody else?"

"No."

"You were the only kayak?"

"Yes, for awhile, I think."

"How'd that make you feel?"

"Oh, Kim . . . I was scared. I made many mistakes. I almost lost my kayak, and my tent too. I think I could have died. But I felt very *alive*. So much ice. So many bears. I don't think Alaska would be Alaska without ice and bears."

He said this as he made coffee, which I now understood for Michio was a ritual.

We talked for hours and arrived at this conclusion: Wilderness areas are places to explore deeply yet lightly; to exercise freedom but also restraint, to manage but also leave alone, to bring us face-to-face with a dilemma in our democracy. How do we convince people to save something they may never see, touch, or hear? A starving man can't eat his illusions, let alone his principles.

I explained the concept of a paradox and Michio shared with me its Japanese equivalent, *gyakusetsu*, which means "opposite theory."

Maybe Bronowski was right in *The Ascent of Man*, when he wrote that civilization has been our longest childhood; that until we accept limits and find new symbols of stability and success we will not live in harmony with the land and the sea, or with each other.

At one point I said something—I can't remember what—and Michio laughed and said, "Kim, you are pulling my foot."

"It's leg, Michio. I'm pulling your leg."

"Yes, that too."

I thanked him for another wonderful dinner and wished him a safe journey to the Arctic Refuge. As rare and vulnerable as I knew him to be, I took Michio for granted. I didn't realize that most people spend a lifetime searching for a friendship like ours, and die searching.

As I began to pack up my guitar, he requested a song. I put the capo on the eighth fret, pulled out a flat pick, set my fingers to D major, and strummed the opening measures of "Here Comes the Sun." Michio closed his eyes and hummed along, his coffee cup cradled in his lap.

THAT SUMMER in Glacier Bay I proposed marriage to Melanie. I didn't get down on one knee and present her with a diamond ring. She visited me where I lived in a small ten-by-twelve-foot cabin on a raft anchored in Goose Cove, a quiet nook in Muir Inlet fifty miles north of Bartlett Cove, and I baked her a loaf of bread. One afternoon as we lay together in the little cabin and her head felt right on my shoulder, and mergansers paddled past the door, and tidewater glaciers murmured of their return, I asked her if she'd marry me.

Without lifting her head she said, "I'd love to."

I felt no threat to my freedom as some men do when facing marriage. Yes, I'd heard the warnings—"Wedlock, a padlock"— and other witticisms from famous men who sat in European smoking parlors and dispensed wisdom like water. I found it ironic that these same men, having tamed every acre of their own land and colonized half the world, now complained that their wives wanted to tame *them*. Alaska gave us permission to be different. We would each be the guardian of the other's freedom. We would take flight in the fall, perhaps to Antarctica with the arctic tern, Argentina with the upland sandpiper, Hawaii with the golden plover, New Zealand with the bar-tailed godwit. We had already been offered jobs in Antarctica and the Galápagos Islands. The idea of hunkering down in Alaska for the winter and growing feathers on our feet held little appeal then. If the ptarmigan was talking to us, we didn't hear it. We failed to listen.

That changed in the fall.

While Melanie spent her summer as a naturalist on tour boats and cruise ships, I was a backcountry ranger who patrolled the upper reaches of Glacier Bay in a twenty-five-foot boat named *Arête*. It was my job to photograph glaciers from established field stations (to determine if the glacial termini had advanced or retreated), to run plant transects for succession studies, to fall asleep in the sunshine with my toes pointed skyward, to monitor wildlife and kayakers, and of course, to save lives when necessary, which—well, it never was. Not that summer. Everybody apparently saved themselves. As the days shortened with September and the night seas reflected northern lights and danced with phosphorescent algae, and storms rolled in from Icy Strait and stacked themselves onto remote, rocky beaches, Melanie and I planned a kayak trip to Dundas Bay, some twenty miles west-southwest of Bartlett Cove.

"Don't kill yourselves," Richard said with a laugh as we packed our gear.

We loaded our double kayak on top of the *Neve*, a sister boat to the *Arête*, and Bruce Paige, the chief naturalist at Glacier Bay National Park, ran us from Bartlett Cove out to an abandoned cannery that stood wet and rotting on old brine-soaked pilings above a barnacle shore. He would return to get us in seven days, give or take a couple for bad weather. We had food and fuel for ten. When he left, he took the rest of the world with him. Alone and in love, Melanie and I danced on the old cannery floor as the timbers groaned and wet splinters fell to the ground. Low tide made a heron of the cannery on its tall creosote-coated legs; high tide made it a duck, near to the water and the smell of autumn things, living and dying, coming and going.

Lewis Sharman, the park's biological technician, had given us a book of scary stories to read aloud each night. How pleased he and Richard would have been at its effectiveness.

"Stop," Melanie said as I reached the part where an unwitting woman was about to slip into a hangman's knot and walk off a plank. "Isn't there something else we can read?"

After two days at the cannery we paddled across flat water to Buck Harbeson's abandoned cabin on the east side of Dundas Bay. Rumor had it that Old Buck had fallen onto a bad end, and his cabin was haunted. He hung out there. We didn't believe it. We didn't *want* to believe it. The meadow surrounding his place was rich with nagoonberries, and Melanie had in mind a good harvest for making pies.

Two things you're not supposed to tell about in Southeast Alaska are the best halibut holes and the best nagoonberry patches. But for the purposes of this story and how we became blind to our peril, I must. That first afternoon we explored the meadow without picking a thing. Variegated golds and greens ran through the leaves of angelica and wild strawberry. Bear tracks wrote ancient scripts in the intertidal mud. Skeins of swans flew south with winter on their tails.

That night Melanie heard the cabin door open and close, once, then twice. The latch lifted and settled into its wooden brace. Was it Old Buck?

As we picked nagoonberries that next day, I watched high winds squirrel through hemlocks and spruce at the meadow's edge. I glassed the bay with binoculars and saw nothing ominous. Melanie was in no mood to spend another night with Old Buck's ghost. I estimated we could paddle back to the cannery in two hours. The weather didn't look great; it didn't look bad either. How much trouble could we get into in two hours?

"We'll be fine," I said as we loaded up and pushed off.

An hour out, with screaming winds and big waves slamming us hard and flooding our spray skirts and driving us off our mark, I admitted that we—I—had made a big mistake. It's a funny thing, trouble. It arrives with a smile and leaves with a sneer. You keep thinking you can *will* yourself out of it. But panic is a wild card that erases common sense.

With Melanie in the front of the kayak and me in the back, paddling for our lives, I heard her yell over the wind, "Kim, I'm scared."

"It's okay," I yelled back.

We stroked hard. I had to match my rhythm to hers so our paddles wouldn't hit one another. The wind threw spume off the waves that slapped me in the face. I couldn't see where we were going or where we'd been.

"Kim, I think . . . I think we're in trouble. . . ."

"It's okay."

"No, it's not. Don't tell me that. We have to do something."

The wind was hitting us from the southeast, pushing us up the long northwest arm of Dundas Bay. We could paddle as hard as possible and never get closer to our intended shore. We had to change tactics. Put footstep of courage into stirrup of patience? Too late for that. We should have never left Old Buck's. Better to live with someone else's ghost than make your own.

Melanie stabbed the sea with each stroke, bless her heart, paddling as hard as she could. She was weakening, though, slowing down. I began to high-brace with my paddle against the bigger waves, fighting to keep us upright and alive.

Melanie yelled, "Kim . . . WHAT SHOULD WE DO?"

"We're going to turn."

"What?"

"ON MY COMMAND, TURN RIGHT, OKAY? STROKE WITH YOUR LEFT PADDLE UNTIL I SAY STOP—OKAY?"

"Okay."

I watched the waves roll into us, lift us, twist us, how they came in sets, bigger ones followed by smaller ones, then bigger . . . smaller.

"TURN NOW."

We crested a moderate wave that freed our bow and stern and gave us, for a second, a stable pivot point. Melanie stroked left, I backstroked right. We spun ninety degrees and were suddenly surfing the waves, moving fast.

"Paddle, Melanie. Paddle hard!"

One instant she was above me, the next below. The crazy waves rolled into us, under us, through us. They slammed me in the back as I used my paddle for a rudder, desperately fighting to keep our kayak from turning broadside and flipping over. If we capsized we'd be dead.

The tide had turned against the wind, making the waves higher, steeper. I could see a low-aspect beach to the north, near the Dundas River. Then I remembered that the river had a large tideflat at its mouth that would make the waves crest far from shore. It was going to be a wild ride. Melanie's shoulders appeared to shake—from fatigue? Fear? Her strokes were much weaker now. I realized for the first time that it was raining hard.

"Melanie, are you okay?"

No answer. She kept paddling. The kayak began to corkscrew on a wildcat wave. I backstroked and ruddered with all my might. Nearly vertical now, the waves slammed us from behind. The water was no longer blue-green; it was brown, the color of river silt.

"Melanie, hang on, we're going to hit hard. Be ready to jump out of the kayak and haul it up the shore, okay?"

No answer.

We hit hard all right, as if a big hand lifted us five feet off the tideflat and dropped us. The rudder snapped. I thought I heard the kayak break.

I pulled off my spray skirt and saw that I was *sitting in water*. The central cockpit was one-third flooded. A wave slapped me from behind as I got out. The full force of the wind blasted my face as I helped Melanie. She was unable to free her frozen fingers from her paddle. I released them one by one, pulled off her spray skirt, and got her out. She fell to her knees. I lifted her and steadied her. She staggered up the beach.

The kayak weighed a ton. I bailed it, then dragged it up the wet tideflat as far as I could and began to unload it. Everything in the main compartment was wet, but the holds forward and aft were dry. Running on adrenaline, I carried one load after another up the beach and dropped them in the ryegrass. Melanie sat on a large rock with her sou'wester rain hat off and her useless fingers fumbling with coat buttons.

It didn't register with me what was happening until it was almost too late.

Half an hour later, maybe an hour, with all the gear stored and covered and the kayak dragged into a thicket of alder and tied there, I walked over to Melanie. She was sitting on the same rock, in the same rag-doll position, barely upright, her head down and face hidden.

"Hey, Sweetie," I said, "it's time to make camp."

I knelt before her and took her hand, thinking she was asleep from exhaustion.

"Melanie?"

I lifted her head and looked into her eyes and heard myself say, "Oh, God."

She wasn't there. She looked at me as if I were a total stranger. Her skin was a papery blue-white, almost colorless, transparent like an ice-fish, cold to the touch of my already cold hands. She had hypothermia. Her core body temperature had fallen sharply. If I didn't get her warm fast, she would die.

I can't remember what I did exactly. Everything was strangely silent then—the wind, rain, and sea—as if each element belonged to a dispassionate jury that watched me run around like a crazy man. I got hot water on the stove, erected the tarp and tent, spread out the sleeping bags.

I got Melanie out of the wind and into the bags. Once the water was hot (but not scalding) I began to nurse it into her, working her lips around the rim of the cup, forcing her to drink. She was limp in my arms. With her sleeping bag under us and mine on top, I dried her hair and wrapped my naked body around hers and forced her to drink more. I filled three plastic bottles with hot water, sealed them tight, and put them in the bags with us. I told her stories. She was cold beyond shivering, almost cadaver-like. I didn't want her to fall asleep. She might not wake up. Ernest Shackleton knew this. Men suffering from hypothermia and extreme exhaustion get to a point where they are no longer cold. A seductive warmth creeps over them and they welcome it. They lie down, almost smiling, and close their eyes to dream of home. That's how they freeze to death. Not in pain, but in peace. They fall asleep and never wake up.

"When men cease to explore," said Fridtjof Nansen, Shackleton's mentor, "they cease to be men."

How trite it sounded to me then, as I held Melanie's coldness close to me. Face-to-face with the consequences of my own poor judgment, I wanted to explore the most daring place of all—my own heart. My own capacity to love. I wrote in my journal:

> Let men plant a Union Jack inside their souls and explain the peaks and valleys of their own evolution. Ask them to stay put, to make a home, and build a community. Would Shackleton, Amundsen, and Scott have gone to Antarctica if they had to stay there?

No.

In America, we love "the road" and write about it all the time. Some of our best literature and music comes from the empty highway. But they're not empty anymore. Roads run both ways, and the greater challenge, I believe, is learning to stay rather than to leave, to stand still and listen to one elegant piece of land where the trees whisper and the light is just right after the rain, and you say, "Okay, this is it. This is where I will live, love, and die."

Every winter I had been off to Spain, Turkey, Mexico, and Russia to satisfy my wanderlust, as if Alaska weren't enough. Richard too. But lately he had begun wintering in Juneau. He talked about teaching and settling down.

"A thousand branches and no roots," he told me, "you fall over in the first big storm."

With Melanie in my arms and slowly warming, I realized that all I knew of Alaska was its summers. October storms were foreign to me. Winter, a stranger. I had little understanding of—or respect for—the suite of seasons that made Alaska what it was, that gave full measure to the trust we put in each other. For that I nearly paid a terrible price. The storm that hit me in May on Cathedral Mountain was brief and largely benevolent. My risk then involved only myself. The storm that hit Melanie and me in Dundas Bay was different. It lasted three days. The only kayak was suddenly very small in the hands of a summer naturalist and a sunshine ranger.

By midnight Melanie was talking and eating. The next morning she was the same little furnace I knew her to be. I held her tight and apologized and she said it was okay. All that day and night we stayed in camp. I closed my eyes and saw the caribou in the river, floating away. I saw Michio, his head back, listening to my guitar gently weep. I wrote a final entry in my Dundas Bay journal:

What soft-bodied, vulnerable creatures we are.

By evening of the following day the water was flat calm. The storm had exhausted itself. We patched the kayak with duct tape and prepared to paddle to the old cannery. Melanie gripped her paddle and set her jaw.

"It's your call," I said. "If you don't want to go, we don't go."

"No," she said, "I want to go."

The shore was littered with uprooted kelp, broken shells, the shredded remains of lives lost in the storm. As I walked back and forth to load our kayak, I must have brushed through rain-soaked grass and the downy remains of a mew gull.

"Kim, look at your boots," Melanie said as I approached the kayak.

I looked down, and knew. I had been too much the tern, too little the ptarmigan. Stuck to each wet boot was a single feather, ancient and elegant as the oldest glacier. It was time to stay put. I had feathered feet.

PART THREE

MAKING TROUBLE

GARFORTH BEAR

Chapter Seven

———

THE PACKAGE arrived postmarked from Japan, with a return address in Fairbanks. I walked down to the shore in Bartlett Cove and sat against a rock to open it. Never had I seen such a book before. *Grizzly*, announced the cover. The letters stood above a sun-splashed bear with half its face in golden light, half in deep shadow.

"For Kim," read the small inscription inside, "from Michio, your friend."

I turned the pages slowly. There were eighty or so, yet they seemed to go on without beginning or end. It was not so much a book as it was a wheel. The final page came and went and I simply rolled back in again, feasting on images that broke a dozen rules and made new ones. No standard portraits. No sunny-day postcard pictures. No cute shots. No snarling beast on its hind legs. Michio understood metaphor all right. Using just two dimensions he conveyed the power and grace of every wild bear: the claws and paw of a pillared leg over a dying salmon, a splash of whitewater from a ghost-like charging burst of fur, a pensive sow framed by an immense palette of autumn tundra, a fat boar in pursuit of an arctic ground squirrel, two cubs boxing in September snow.

He understood cliché too. Not a single one blemished the book.

I felt many things: pride to be called a friend, gratitude that such wild places still existed with wild animals in them, and—I have to say this—jealousy. I could never take photographs like that. I was in the company of a genius. The book would win the prestigious Anima Award, and contribute to Michio being named Japan's Photographer of the Year.

Richard found me down by the water sitting on a rock. I shared the book with him.

He looked through it carefully and after a minute said, "How'd he get pictures like these?"

"I don't know."

"He must have been close, to get some of these shots."

"Yes. . . ."

Clouds rolled over the shoulders of the Fairweather Range. A bald eagle called from the forest's edge. The tide rose around us and licked our boots. We looked across the water and without a word acknowledged that we were no longer young men. The innocence and bravado we had known in the only kayak some seven years earlier seemed distant and strangely abstract. We had recently graduated from a 240-hour law enforcement course in North Carolina and qualified as National Park Service backcountry rangers. Now, on the day Michio's book arrived, I was told by the chief ranger that as a federal law enforcement officer trained in the use and safety of firearms, I had to shoot a bear in Glacier Bay.

"You okay?" Richard asked me.

"I'm fine," I said unconvincingly.

That night I phoned Michio in Fairbanks and got no answer. I called a Japanese woman, Mrs. Nishiyama, who told me he was somewhere in the Alaska Range taking pictures. I thought, *Michio doesn't take pictures, he* makes *them.* I left a message asking that he call me when he returned.

"It may be awhile," Mrs. Nishiyama said.

"I know."

SO THIS BEAR, the one I was supposed to shoot, it was a pioneer. It had stepped into the cold, deep waters of Glacier Bay and swum to an island where bears had rarely been seen before. From the moment we first heard about it—Richard, Melanie, and I (and everyone else in Bartlett Cove)—we wondered if it acted on impulse or by calculation. Could it have seen the island from the mainland? Smelled it? Tasted it as a salmon does its spawning stream after years at sea? Or did the bear just step into the sea and begin swimming with no idea where it was going?

New land, old ice. Life is a gamble in Glacier Bay. Every salmon is descended from a salmon that probably lost its way and by dumb luck or sheer boldness started a new run of fish. Pilots have reported seeing mountain goats crossing vast mazes of crevasses to reach islands of green alpine slopes surrounded by ocean-like icefields. Mountaineers have seen furtive wolverines plodding through snow at ten thousand feet. Every July cottonwood trees send their lacy white seeds into the sky to play the odds of a one-in-a-million landing where they can take root and grow. A beaver will suddenly appear in a pond where beavers have never been seen before, as if one day it decided, *That's it. I've had it. I'm going for a long walk.* And so it did. It walked until it found a new home. In such a young, vibrant geography, every piece of open ground spells opportunity. Every ridge, valley, island, pond, and stream. It was time then, apparently, for a bear to claim Garforth Island.

We broke out the maps.

We traced the island with our fingers, measured it, and talked about it late into the night. Richard commented on how small it appeared. To me, it seemed to punctuate Glacier Bay as a comma would a word-filled page, with modesty and grace, giving cadence to the larger story of ice and rock and the thin margins of life between one glacial advance and another. Ignored by summer's daily cruise ships and tour boats that throttled upbay to see tidewater glaciers, the little island lay demurely along the east shore off Muir Point. Roughly three-fourths of a mile long and not very wide, it probably emerged from beneath the great retreating glacier—the one that buried and then unveiled Glacier Bay—shortly after the American Civil War. It would have been nothing more than naked rock and sediment then. A dozen decades later, by the 1980s, it supported a young spruce-hemlock forest fringed by alder, ryegrass, and beach greens.

Long ago the Tlingits picked berries and hunted seals there. Later, the National Park Service closed the bay to subsistence harvests. Then vacationing sea kayakers found Garforth Island an inviting respite in their journeys through the bay. Weary from paddling and hungry for landfall, they made camp, cooked dinner, and probably missed the obvious signs of occupancy in the island's forested interior: the scat and tracks on rain-soaked trails, the claw marks on spruce.

The bear stayed hidden at first. It watched. It waited. It learned.

It had no doubt found some food on the small island, but not enough to spend the summer. Bears follow their noses and for the most part make an honest living. It certainly was not the first bear to reach the island, nor would it be the last. But when these noisy, two-legged creatures arrived in their long, narrow boats and pulled exotic foods from canisters and heated them over little stoves, it was too much. Turkey stroganoff, chicken Alfredo, shrimp fettuccini. Add to that some fresh fruit, the ubiquitous squeeze tubes of peanut butter and jelly, a box of crackers, Swiss and cheddar cheeses, and sundry inventions (and invitations) of chocolate, all imbued with that human scent. The bear stepped out of the forest and sniffed the possibilities.

Some reports said it was reddish-brown with a pointed nose, indicative of a black bear. Others said it had a large shoulder hump and a dish-shaped face, suggestive of a brown bear. Everyone agreed it was bold. It approached the kayakers with the same authority that had brought it to the island, the same sense of opportunity that had enabled its ancestors to outlive mammoths and mastodons. For this it would be punished. By me.

The kayakers did precisely what they were not supposed to do. They backed off—some even ran—and left their food.

Everybody talked about it in Bartlett Cove. For awhile we called it The Garforth Island Bear. But as its reputation grew it became The Garforth Bear. And when no others in the bay seemed worth talking about, it simply became The Bear.

"Have you seen The Bear?" people would ask.

"Any word about The Bear?"

In developing a myth about The Bear we of course developed one about ourselves. The Bear became a talisman. The bay was his now, not ours. We didn't talk about other bears, black or brown, big or small, the ones out there eating berries and sleeping in the forest and nursing their young. Run-of-the-mill bears. Middle-of-the-bell-curve bears. Minding-their-own-business bears. Glacier Bay was rich with them, but we insisted on being poor and allowing one bear to fill our thoughts as if it filled the entire bay.

The chief ranger called it a "problem bear."

Problem bear? That night I looked through the pages of Michio's book for such an animal and didn't find one.

Richard suggested that we excavate a few words. He pulled out his dictionary and I pulled out mine. We made popcorn, opened a couple beers, and fell back through the centuries.

Think of it. We speak of that which is *bearable* and *unbearable*. In acts of restraint and abstinence we speak of *forbearance*. We engage in *horseplay* and *monkey* around, but from bears we borrow our most precious acts. We *bear* witness, *bear* our young, and *bear* glad tidings. We see in bears a little too much of ourselves and take that familiarity as a threat on one hand, a consolation on the other. In moments of grace we regard bears not as followers but as shamans of the animal world, creatures from a spiritual dimension far richer and more ancient than our own. Every native culture in North America has myths and legends about the bear, many of them tributes to wisdom and strength. "The bear is good to talk with," say the Yupik Eskimos. "If the bear wanted to speak with you, all it needed to do was remove its mask and there beneath was a human." The mirror sees both ways.

So this bear, this being within and without me, I wanted it to live forever. It had pioneered Garforth Island and I wanted to let it be.

The decision wasn't mine. I was a GS-5 seasonal ranger with a gun on my belt and a badge over my heart. Something had gone wrong. To achieve more time in the wilderness, I had become a cop. My stomach made noises it never made before. I began to speak in acronyms and staccato sentences from the Code of Federal Regulations. Everybody talked about the *resource* and I wondered: If Glacier Bay was the *resource*, what's the *source*? If we came here to *recreate*, where did we go to *create*? For that matter, why have refried beans? Wasn't frying them once enough? Reflex, recoil, rebound . . . rebel.

Where was our language of reverence? Of sacredness?

Every year in America we add hundreds of words to our dictionaries that describe our infatuation with pop culture and technology, but none that describe a deepening regard for the natural world.

"The middling, politically correct language of the professions is incapable either of reverence or familiarity," wrote Wendell Berry; "it is headless and footless, loveless, a language of nowhere."

Couldn't we do better?

I was asking too many questions. When the Notice for the Paperwork Reduction Act arrived and was ten pages long, I knew I was in trouble. Career rangers told me I had the training and jurisdiction to save people's lives in the wild, and to save the wild too. But a little voice in my head said it was all bullshit.

I had my strengths as a ranger, though offhand I couldn't remember any. I saved nobody's life. I rescued not a single stranded kayaker or mountaineer. I patrolled the waters of Glacier Bay and contacted backcountry users, but for the most part I stayed out of their way.

"The woods are full of wardens," Kerouac wrote in the last line of *Lonesome Traveler*. Law enforcement was everywhere in the United States. The last thing visitors to wild Alaska needed to see was a uniform. Besides, my low-key approach would free up more time to write poetry and study tidewater glaciers, the important things to do in Glacier Bay.

"Why not just let the bear have the island?" I said (naïvely). "Tell the kayakers to go somewhere else."

No. The chief ranger shook his head. The kayakers had gone to great expense and effort to get to Garforth Island. Moreover, the problem bear might swim back to the mainland and teach bad manners to other bears. It needed to be conditioned.

"Conditioned?"

The chief ranger explained that another ranger and I would go to Garforth Island and pretend to be unsuspecting kayakers. We would make landfall and begin cooking. When the bear appeared we would back away as if frightened (our faces filled with terror) while keeping our guns concealed. Just as the bear was about to eat our towering brick of Tillamook cheese (extra-sharp cheddar with artificial orange food coloring), we would shoot it in the butt with birdshot. The bear would then associate people with pain, a lesson learned by a vast compendium of North American wildlife over the past five hundred years. It would be a stimulus-response experiment with Garforth Island as the Skinner Box, the bear as the pigeon, and we rangers as B. F. Skinner, the famous behavioral psychologist who so loved his little box he put his daughter in it.

We would contribute to the myth as I contribute to it now, responding to one bear as if it were a Belial, a man-eating Grendel, a dragon in need of slaying. We rangers would make the wilderness safe for the very kinds of people who had made it more dangerous than it needed to be.

"WHAT IS THE BEAR?" anthropologist Richard Nelson would ask at a bear symposium in Gustavus, the little town next to Glacier Bay. After some silence he answered his own question. "More and more I believe we have no idea. At best, science can tell us only half of what there is to know. What about the other side of the mirror, the one that doesn't reflect back on us? Are there bears up the bay right now having a conference about us? Can we open ourselves to the idea of being studied by that which we study?" Having lived with Inupiat Eskimos and Koyukon Athabascans in Arctic Alaska for many years, Nelson said it was an enormous responsibility and privilege to share our world with bears. When asked questions, he would preface his answers as the Koyukon elders had with him, "Well, what little we know about that . . ."

Richard Carstensen, another symposium speaker and a self-taught naturalist who lives in Juneau, said, "There's no human botanist in Southeast Alaska who knows the plants the ways the bear does."

Intrigued by people's acute fear of bears, Carstensen asked the Juneau Police for some statistics. Here's what he found: In twenty years one woman in Juneau was "run over" by a bear (that appeared to be running away from something else), while in a single year 79 people were injured by dogs, and 577 were assaulted by other people.

Greg Streveler, a former National Park Service biologist who lives in Gustavus in a home he built himself using hand tools, would mentor any ranger who came asking. Upon leaving Wisconsin for Alaska as an eager young biologist in the 1960s, Streveler was told by one of his fellow graduate students, "Go ahead, Greg. You go up to Alaska and preside over the destruction of the wilderness. I'm going to stay in Wisconsin and help put it back together."

The caveat seemed especially keen years later when Alaska's Governor Walter Hickel, a champion of development, builder of shopping malls, and proponent of wolf control, told NBC News, "You just can't let nature run wild."

When Streveler talked about bears, you became the bear. He put you in its skin. He put you behind the mask. With one hand he could mimic a near-perfect bear track in intertidal mud—forepaw, hind paw, black bear or brown bear. Once after reading aloud a Mary Oliver poem, Carstensen said it was remarkable how she could write so powerfully about bears, since she lives in Cape Cod and there aren't any bears left at Cape Cod.

After a moment Streveler said quietly, "There aren't even any cod left at Cape Cod."

The long shadow had marched from one end of the continent to the other.

"There are no more pre-contact cultures of bears," Streveler said. "The bears are still out there, but something is missing now. Something is gone."

I recalled John Muir's last trip to Glacier Bay in 1899 when he came as a guest of Edward H. Harriman, president of the Union Pacific Railroad. Harriman wanted to shoot a bear, so Muir sent him and some colleagues into Howling Valley. You'll bag one there, he told them. The men returned empty-handed and exhausted. They could see from Muir's expression that he'd misled them. No bears lived in Howling Valley.

Harriman got his specimen later that summer on Kodiak Island.

"Toiling in the treadmills of life we hide from the lessons of nature," wrote Muir. "We gaze upon our world clad with seamless beauty and see ferocious beasts . . . but bears are made of the same dust as we."

In the Juneau airport, prior to the symposium, I had watched a young girl study a brown bear stuffed and encased in a huge glass box. She craned her neck to absorb the full height and ferocity, the beast so very tall, the teeth polished and pointed, the eyes bright but unblinking. A *Tyrannosaurus rex* with fur. She finally backed away to find her mother's hand, unaware that the man who killed the last grizzly loved the mountains. A copy of *Outdoor Life* on the gift shop magazine rack announced GIANT BEAR ISSUE. The author, Chris Batin, warned everybody that "Before you stand toe-to-toe with a brown bear, you must first confront and pass through an equally formidable adversary: the Alaska wilderness. . . . Alaska storms and typhoons sink boats, flip airplanes, demolish cabins. They blow tents away as if they were puffs of smoke. To survive, you either dig a hole and pitch your tent in it or you die of hypothermia."

I checked my hands to see if I was shaking.

Batin wasn't finished. "With such potential for pain and suffering," he asked, "is there more to wilderness brown bear hunting than the obvious trophy? There is, of course, the clear realization of either you killing the bear or the bear killing you."

That night, after the symposium, Richard said it best: "More people die each year from potato salad than from grizzly bears."

THE CHIEF RANGER knew better than to pair Richard and me for the Garforth Island assignment. Earlier that summer, the deputy director of the Alaska Region of the National Park Service, had arrived in Bartlett Cove (from Anchorage) to give the seasonal rangers some serious medicine. Too many of us were making careers out of jobs that were supposed to last only a summer or two, or three. We were expected to grow up and either get permanent positions with the NPS, or move on to other occupations. The Deputy announced that only ten percent of us would receive a "highly recommended for rehire" for the same seasonal jobs next summer.

Grim silence. Nobody said a word until Richard stood up (disheveled hair across his brow) and asked The Deputy how long he'd been working for the Park Service.

"Twenty years," he said proudly.

"You mean you were better than ninety percent of your coworkers each year for twenty years?"

"We didn't have that same standard for us."

We seasonals had to understand that he, The Deputy, and others like him had passed through some magical door that bequeathed upon them "permanent" status with very little chance of ever being fired. They were exemplary, the Guardians of the Gate.

I guess I knew then, and have known ever since, that Richard and I wouldn't make it in the NPS. Richard was a crazy Jack Kerouac to my Aldo Leopold, the trigger-happy young man who shot the wolf in New Mexico and became forever haunted by the fierce green fire in its dying eyes. And Miss Rachel Carson who pounded out *Silent Spring* because nobody else would, even while dying of cancer. And Cactus Ed Abbey who monkeywrenched his way across the Colorado Plateau and pitched beer cans out his truck window, saying it wasn't the cans that were ugly, it was the highway. Beer cans are beautiful. All three had worked for the federal government and taken what Richard called "a sharp left turn at Truth Serum Gulch."

No truck. No wrench. All I had was the Garforth Bear roaming in my gut, telling me that recruitment, security, and advancement in any bureaucracy would eclipse boldness and risk, and turn upside down and reward in reverse the very traits nurtured by wild places. That alone scared me more than any bear.

"I am glad I shall never be young," wrote Aldo Leopold, "without wild country to be young in." He was the professor Dr. Folsom had told me about, the one in Wisconsin who found the last stand of tall grass prairie in the corner of the little triangular cemetery.

That night after The Deputy's edict, Richard paced about, agitated, singing an Eric Clapton song about shooting the sheriff but not the deputy. The chief ranger had sent him to Graves Harbor the previous summer, where he and his partner swamped their skiff and had to swim to shore. Now he was about to be shipped off to Dry Bay, farther up the coast, where people fished and hunted and ran all-terrain vehicles across beaches and estuaries as if God himself had invented the four-stroke Honda and left it for Adam in the Garden.

The Deputy was probably right. Richard and I needed to move on. Grow up. Join the team or get out. We were ptarmigan who wintered in Alaska, but that wasn't enough. To gain a career foothold in the NPS we would likely have to work at Grant's Tomb in New York City, or the Liberty Bell in Philadelphia, or take GS-3 secretarial jobs in Denver, Seattle, or Anchorage. We would be caged birds with plucked feathers hoping someday to soar with eagles.

It would never happen.

Many of the best people I knew—the people I respected most—worked for the National Park Service. They read Aldo Leopold and dedicated their lives to something larger than themselves. They formed a family and worked hard and dreamed of leaving a piece of the Earth as they found it, wet with dew, newness, rhythm, and promise. It wasn't the Park Service that disappointed me, or even the cold corners of bureaucracy. It was myself.

Our frustration with others is always greatest when we're frustrated with ourselves. The answer to my troubles wasn't over the mountains; it was in the still waters of high tide, where I saw nothing more clearly than my own reflection.

A BEAR TASK FORCE was assembled and the chief ranger enlisted Leigh Selig and me to go to Garforth Island to condition the bear. Leigh was the *beau ideal* ranger: cool, calm, courageous, always on the job but not seduced by position or power. We anchored our patrol vessel, *Arête*, off the east side of the island and paddled our kayaks ashore to reconnoiter. I carried a twelve-gauge shotgun, Leigh a bolt-action Remington .30–06. We found evidence of the bear but not the bear itself. It was either hiding or gone.

Studies by the U.S. Forest Service and the Alaska Department of Fish & Game on Admiralty Island (a national monument southeast of Glacier Bay) have shown that brown bears cover vast areas in search of food. Several times through spring and summer, as different foods become available, they move from the subalpine to the shore and back, zigzagging up and down and contouring mountainsides to work berry patches, salmon streams, sedge flats, clam beaches, and fen meadows. Skunk cabbage in May. Blueberries in June. Pink salmon in July. Strawberries in August. Silver salmon in September. Devil's club berries in October.

Tillamook cheese, anytime? We'd find out.

Garforth Island was probably just one of many places covered by the Garforth Bear. With no more kayakers coming ashore to make fettuccini, the temptations of the mainland might have called it back. Leigh and I visited the island several more times. No bear. On our days off we returned to Goose Cove, twenty miles north in Muir Inlet, where we lived in our cabins on rafts (the same cabin where I asked Melanie to marry me). I would pound away on an old Smith-Corona typewriter, while Leigh cleaned the *Arête* and built spice racks and bookshelves from clear-grained Sitka spruce. Melanie came to visit and joined our next patrol to Garforth Island.

While Leigh and I were hiking the west shore in search of the bear, we heard Melanie yell.

I ran through the forest with my heart in my throat, lugging the shotgun. Limbs and branches thrashed at the safety latch. Leigh followed, gaining on me, breathing hard. We emerged on the east shore and saw Melanie a hundred yards away in her kayak, near the anchored *Arête*.

"Melanie, are you all right?"

Her voice trembled. "It came after me. The bear. It swam right for me."

"Where is it? Where'd it go?"

"Over there," she pointed. "It swam over to that point and went ashore and ran into the woods."

It was on the island. So were we. Melanie stayed on the *Arête* while Leigh and I searched all afternoon and evening. The bear had disappeared into the mossy forest where the light was low and apple green. The island felt bigger than before. Smaller too. We didn't have this bear. It had us.

How foolish I felt. At law enforcement school I had learned to drive fast backwards through orange cones on a parking lot, to disarm a terrorist and search a Winnebago for drugs, to wrestle a felon to the ground and read Miranda rights. Using a .38-caliber revolver from fifty meters on a firing range, I had perforated the chest of a silhouetted square-shouldered man and tasted the sweet, acrid smell of gunpowder.

Now here I was, sweat-faced on a wilderness island in Alaska, outwitted by a bear.

Our range master at law enforcement school had been a humorless military man we called "Gunnery Sergeant." One day Richard asked him if the square-shouldered FBI silhouettes we shot at could be changed to something more appropriate for national parks. A small woman holding binoculars? An old man with a walking cane? The Gunnery Sergeant flushed red and told Richard to get back to his position, get his earphones on, and start shooting.

Thus we became lawmen ready to defend Glacier Bay from all manner of mayhem and the criminal element. At one point Leigh found a perfect set of bear tracks on a muddy forest trail. I remembered William Clark in the Bitterroot Mountains writing about *bearfooted* Indians. Maybe it really was a shaman, this Garforth Bear, here to make us see only ourselves. We searched until nightfall and didn't find him.

"We're doing this all wrong," Leigh said. "We have to let the bear come to us."

I wiped the sweat from my eyes and remembered the good hunter who knows the spirit of the animal. He listens. He waits. The animal comes to him. I thought of Michio, patient Michio, waiting for one month in one place for one photograph. A thousand mosquitoes might feast on him and still he would wait.

"I felt an intense awareness of existence itself," he wrote in *Grizzly*, about his moments alone with a bear. His fear was not for himself, but for Alaska. "Nature here may be the most vulnerable to change, and easily scarred, of all places in the world. Even the grizzly, standing at the peak of the food chain, cannot escape this destiny."

ANOTHER MONTH WENT BY. Visitors came calling at Goose Cove. Two Australians arrived in their double kayak. Having paddled a thousand miles from Seattle, they intended to go up Lynn Canal to Skagway, sell their kayak, hike over the Chilkoot Pass, build a pole raft, and float the Yukon River to the Bering Sea. They broke out a bottle of Scotch, played guitar, drank past midnight, and passed out drunk on my floor. A week later, three women pulled into the cove in single kayaks and told me they were breast cancer survivors. Each carried the wing of a bird on her kayak. They had met in chemotherapy, attended Outboard Bound, and left corporate jobs to find something more meaningful in their lives. The Aussies had left some Scotch and red wine, and these gals dusted it off.

Next came Lewis Sharman and his seventeen-year-old research assistant, Hank Lentfer, a long-legged, gangly-armed kid with a shock of wavy brown hair. A photographer named Tom Bean was visiting then. I invited Leigh over for dinner (his cabin-on-a-raft was anchored fifty yards from mine). That night the five of us told stories and ate a lasagna the size of Montana. I liked Hank immediately but had no idea he would one day become the third in a trio of friends who would help me find hope and laughter in a world of long shadows. He was fifteen years younger than the rest of us, with a quick wit and a wheezing laugh that made his eyes disappear. His ribald sense of fun reminded me of Richard. He was a rule breaker, a rebel; the only one among us who had been raised in Alaska. His father, Jack, a renowned polar bear biologist, had taken his family from Juneau to Barrow to Anchorage to Spitsbergen (Arctic Norway), and back to Juneau.

We talked about bears, how our lives were filled just knowing they were out there crossing glaciers, swimming inlets, owning islands, breaking boundaries. We talked about the ABC islands—Admiralty, Baranof, and Chichagof (immediately south of Glacier Bay)—that have lots of bears but no wolves, and Prince of Wales Island (farther to the south, due west of Ketchikan) that has wolves but no bears. Lewis had worked on the Greater Yellowstone Ecosystem Grizzly Bear Project and said any one of the ABC islands had more brown bears on it than existed in all the Lower Forty-eight States (where once an estimated 50,000 to 100,000 grizzlies lived). We talked about bears and humans, how each is capable of ferocious acts and delicate gestures. Sharing stories that night was as nourishing as sharing good food and water.

Hank challenged Tom to a popcorn-eating contest and Tom, born and raised in Des Moines, beat him with the "Iowa Roll," curling handfuls into his mouth without dropping a single kernel. When his mouth was empty and Hank's stuffed, Tom said something funny and Hank spit out his entire cache, making a wet popcorn patina on my cabin wall.

A couple days later came a radio call from Bartlett Cove. The bear was back on Garforth Island. It had raided another kayaker's camp.

This time Leigh and I went undercover as Special Forces SWAT SEAL Rangers. We anchored the *Arête* five miles away, covered our uniforms with drab shirts and rain parkas, and paddled to the island in two single kayaks with no NPS insignias on the bow. We meant business and we got it.

Ten minutes after we began cooking on the beach, the bear emerged. It walked our way from the forest fringe and turned sideways to intimidate us with its large profile. We stood as if alarmed (faces filled with terror). The bear huffed, then advanced.

We scrambled into a retreat, keeping our guns concealed at our sides (like real gunslingers). The clever animal approached our pasta primavera and Tillamook Tower. As I shouldered my shotgun I saw this bear as every bear, the ones that once owned the foothills of Denver and the oak forests of San Francisco, the ones that chased bison and antelope and napped atop Arizona's rhyolite peaks and Idaho's basalt colonnade. I remembered Aldo Leopold's story about the mountain called Escudilla, where there lived one bear, the last bear, a great huge almost mythological beast that every spring would come down to the valley and bash in the head of one cow. The ranchers tried to find it to kill it, but could not. Determined to make the valley safe for cattle and sheep, they hired a bounty hunter who went up the mountain and set a tripwire. The bear walked into the wire and shot itself. The great hide covered an entire barn wall. Everybody came to see it. Not until many years later, when fifty times more people filled the valley with their tract homes, strip malls, golf courses, and gang wars, did anybody question the rules of progress.

"Escudilla still hangs on the horizon," Leopold wrote, "but when you see it you no longer think of bear. It's only a mountain now."

Saliva poured off its lower lip as it closed in on the Tillamook Tower. The insubordination of not shooting The Bear had disappeared. I was all adrenaline, flushed with the moral certainty of a Greek god.

Five feet from the Tower, approaching fast, The Bear was a living allegory of *self*.

Leigh fired two shots into the sky. The Bear turned to run and I blasted it in the rear with number-nine birdshot—strong enough to sting (from our pre-measured distance) but not enough to break the skin. It scampered into the forest. Leigh and I looked at each other with grins. I wondered what Michio would say.

Nobody saw it after that. The NPS discouraged kayakers from camping on the island for the rest of the summer, which by then was nearly over. The chief ranger complimented us on our noble deed. Other rangers nodded as if to say, *Good job*. Richard dropped me a line from Dry Bay telling me not to "gestalt" the whole thing. I got out my dictionary and looked up gestalt. These were the words that followed it: "Gestapo," "gestate," "gesture," and "get away." That's what I wanted to do: get away.

I went for long walks with Melanie. I told her that what struck me most was this: Once upon a time before spears, arrows, guns, and bombs, men battled their adversaries face-to-face. They looked each other in the eye. Now a coward could kill a king from a distance.

MICHIO CALLED. It was mid-September. He had had a great summer with brown bears at McNeil River in July (watching a mother nurse her cubs only twenty feet away) and with Toklat grizzlies in Denali in early September. Now he was packing to go to Katmai National Park in Southwest Alaska, a place famous for its volcanoes and bears. Would I like to come along?

"No," I said, I had to finish my ranger duties. He asked about my summer. I told him it was fine but said nothing about the Garforth Bear. I thanked him for the book and wished him a good trip to Katmai. It never occurred to me to tell him to be careful.

It's a strange thing, making friends and losing them. Family is made of blood; friends are made of water. Friends come together like the braids of a glacial river, then separate and come together again without obligations, laws, or bonds. In the years ahead, Richard,

Michio, and Hank would be my river, flowing through the rapids and calm water of their love for wild Alaska and their fear, like my own, that it could slip away.

On my last night with Melanie and friends in Bartlett Cove, we spread maps over the table and talked about the summer. Richard had survived Dry Bay. People up there would talk about him for years. We traced the boundaries of our experiences and sang Beatles songs and ate beer-batter halibut.

When everybody went into the kitchen to get slices of nagoon-berry pie, I was alone for a moment with the map. My finger found Garforth Island and hovered there.

"Hey, Kim," I heard somebody call from the kitchen, "you want a slice of pie?"

"Please."

I drifted back to the bear, how beautiful it was, the fur-dappled legs and blond-tipped ears, the paws flicking onto the ground with each step, the broad face, elegant shoulders, and enormous gait so fluid, frightful, and strong, so capable of crushing a skull and picking a berry. It was every bear, and I was every man.

My fingers brushed lightly on the map. I looked back at Garforth Island and let it go.

It was just an island now.

DEEP TIME

Chapter Eight

———

IT STARTED as a pillow fight and escalated into a wrestling match. Michio and I against Hannah and Ben. I had just turned forty; Michio was about to. Hannah was eight, Ben a toddler. Yes, Michio and I had size and strength. But Hannah had grit. Ben had a pacifier. They knew the terrain.

They were the children of Roy and Kim Corral, who lived in a small apartment in downtown Anchorage near Roy's office, where he worked as photography editor at *Alaska* magazine. Martial arts expert that I was, or imagined myself to be, I pinned Ben to the floor. Michio struggled against Hannah, a natural athlete, and lost. She was quick and soon had *him* pinned. He begged for mercy as she sat on his chest and demanded that I release her little brother. We called it a draw and launched into a gallon of ice cream.

That night Michio and I slept on the living room floor while Roy, Kim, Hannah, and Ben retired to their bedrooms. "Do you think I'm old?" Michio asked me.

We'd been over this before, but I decided not to remind him. Michio was worried that life was passing him by. To be honest, so was I.

If fifty is the youth of old age, then forty is the old age of youth. We were there. The round Earth rolls, John Muir said, and takes us with it, like it or not. It's not always easy to know where your worry comes from, unless you sit on a sofa and listen to your prostate grow. Part of my ailment arose from the four years in the late 1980s when Melanie and I had lived in Anchorage. After a handful of memorable summers in Glacier Bay, Melanie had landed a permanent position with the National Park Service as an assistant manager of a public lands information center, located downtown on Fourth Avenue. It wasn't her long-sought-after goal of being a full-time naturalist in a national park, but it gave her the "permanent status" she needed to apply for those places. With its congestion and crime, Anchorage was as far as you could get from Alaska without leaving it. Every spring when the thrushes sang and early-June light sliced through pale green leaves, my heart ached to be in Glacier Bay.

Then one dark winter day in December 1990 the phone rang. It was Denali National Park asking Melanie if she would like to be the west district naturalist on the Toklat River. We would live not far from where Adolf Murie, the famous wildlife biologist, lived with his family while doing research on wolves for three summers from 1939 to 1941. She said yes in a West Anchorage minute. The next day Kenai Fjords National Park called from Seward and offered Melanie the position of chief naturalist. We couldn't believe it. She said no, thank you, and explained to me that night, "I'm more park than Park Service." She would rather take a cut in pay and live in a park (Denali) than get a raise and live in a bustling town outside a park (Seward). The position of chief naturalist sounded tempting, but in truth she wouldn't be a naturalist, or a chief. She'd be an administrator. So we went north to live on a river where wolves lived too. It was January and minus forty. George Bush the Elder was preparing to attack Saddam Hussein in Operation Desert Storm. American blood would soon run black with oil. We loaded up our possessions and drove to the land of tundra and little trees, where we would live for five years.

Michio's work had by now made him famous, but he seemed disenchanted with it all. He wanted children. He wanted a wrestling match every night.

"You know, Kim," he told me after we had turned out the lights, "I would give up all my books and awards if I could have kids like Hannah and Ben."

"You need a wife."

"Yes. . . ."

"Is that a problem?"

"A little. . . ."

I suspected so. I had heard that he was engaged to a woman in Japan but had broken it off at the last minute—no doubt an embarrassment for his family and a bigger one for hers. We never talked about it much, though he had many questions about my marriage to Melanie. Were we happy? Did we laugh together? Did we plan to have kids?

Yes. All the time. Maybe.

Five years had passed since my encounter with the Garforth Bear. No longer a ranger with the National Park Service, I was gainfully unemployed as a freelance writer and photographer. Michio had nursed me along as a photographer. While his pictures taught me a lot—how, for example, to frame a wild animal in a large landscape—it was his grace and poise in a crowded field of wildlife paparazzi that touched me most.

While living in the Talkeetna Mountains a short distance north of Anchorage, Melanie and I had returned to Glacier Bay for one week in August 1986 to be married.

"Just come back for your wedding," said Dave Nemeth, the supervisory backcountry ranger, my former boss. "We'll take care of everything here in Bartlett Cove."

And they did. They opened their homes for our relatives. They caught halibut, salmon, and Dungeness crab for the evening feast. Musicians arrived from Gustavus to play past midnight, busting down the walls with their banjos, fiddles, mandolins, and guitars. People made many toasts, the most memorable from Melanie's eighty-year-old Aunt Ella, who lived in Chicago. She had attended a women's dinner the previous night in Gustavus and marveled at how our friend Lynne Jensen had cleared her own wooded land, peeled the logs, built an elegant little six-sided house filled with books and love, and then called the square dance that night.

"To the women," Ella said as she thrust a can of beer into the air.

"To the women," we all shouted in response.

Richard couldn't be there. He was a backcountry ranger that summer in Gates of the Arctic National Park in the central Brooks Range, high above the Arctic Circle. It would be his last season in green and gray.

Hank was in Bolivia living with a family of poor people who slept on a dirt floor and considered themselves rich because they had one cow and forty potatoes.

All this time the glaciers of Alaska were misbehaving, and I loved them for it. A short distance north of Glacier Bay, near the town of Yakutat, Hubbard Glacier had surged from the St. Elias Mountains and occluded the dogleg turn from Disenchantment Bay into Russell Fiord, which effectively dammed the fiord and made it into a thirty-mile-long lake. As snowmelt from the surrounding mountains filled the lake, the shoreline climbed, the salinity dropped, and the ice dam groaned under increased pressure. Still, it held. Several dozen harbor seals, trapped in the lake, attracted international attention when a team of so-called "eco-rescuers" arrived to save them. The seals avoided capture, so the rescuers caught a salmon—the prized food the seals needed to survive—grilled it, and ate it. Critics howled with indignation.

The *Anchorage Daily News* called it "The Great Fiord Fiasco."

Later that fall, during heavy October rains, the ice dam broke after six months (the lake level had climbed eighty feet) and released a torrent of water estimated at thirty-five times greater than Niagara Falls.

Richard and I talked by phone (he was back in Juneau) about other brother glaciers that might surge. Mendenhall and Lemon Creek glaciers would reclaim their valleys in Juneau, smother the big store Fred Meyer, bulldoze Kmart. "Today's blue light special . . .

glacial ice." Mount Rainier would send an icy battalion into Seattle to topple the Space Needle and the King Dome. Completing a pincer movement from the Olympic Mountains, glaciers would retake Puget Sound, which they owned twenty thousand years ago. Continental glaciers would advance again over the Canadian Shield and the Great Lakes, reaching down to obliterate Chicago, Cleveland, Cincinnati, and Detroit, birthplace of Ford Motors, the modern assembly line, and the sport utility vehicle. Another glacier would settle into its old terminal moraine at Cape Cod and sit there for a thousand years or so.

Sometimes in the darkest part of the night I dreamed of ice walls marching down from distant mountains and snapping tall conifers like matchsticks.

SEVEN HUNDRED years ago, climates cooled around the world and glaciers advanced throughout much of Europe, Asia, and North America. This Little Ice Age (also known as the Neoglacial Period) lasted roughly five hundred years, from A.D. 1350 to 1850. Some years had no summers then. European villages were abandoned. Churches and taverns were consumed by ice. Crops failed. Entire ways of life ended. In Glacier Bay, Tlingit oral history said the ice advanced "as fast as a limping dog could run." The Tlingit who lived there paddled their canoes south and in time founded the village of Hoonah, across Icy Strait on Chichagof Island.

Devastating as this must have been, it was a mere postscript in the two-million-year-long Pleistocene Period, or Ice Age, that sent massive pulses of glaciers back and forth across the Earth's higher latitudes at least four times, with some advances lasting hundreds of thousands of years.

In my geotheomorphology class, Dr. Folsom had spoken enthusi- astically (he could speak no other way) about an eighteenth-century Scottish physician-turned-farmer named James Hutton who never did farm very well. He didn't have to. He was independently wealthy. Hutton's real love, Folsom said, was geology. Trudging about in the cold Scottish rain in his frock coat and three-cornered hat, Hutton would watch water carry topsoil into ditches and streams, and down rivers to the sea. Along coastal cliffs he found rock strata turned ninety degrees on end, hundreds of feet high, and atop that more strata, perfectly level, as if new frosting had been applied on to an upended layer cake. How much time must have been needed, he wondered, to create such features?

"The destruction of the land is an idea not easily grasped," he wrote in 1785, "though we are the daily witness of its process." Anything can happen, will happen, given enough time.

Hutton offered no ideas catastrophic or Wagnerian, nothing apocalyptic or apologetic. He knew the religious dogma of his day that said all sedimentary rock had been deposited during Noah's Flood, just six thousand years ago. He also knew that in some parts of Europe a man could still be put to death for uttering the phrase "millions of years." Yet his eyes and powers of reasoning told him otherwise. He was a critical thinker, not a faithful believer. Rain, wind, waves, ice, earthquakes, volcanoes, given enough time—vast amounts of time—will shape entire continents. They will level a mountain or build a whole new range of them. They will lift ancient sea floors into high summits. Give them enough time and they will turn the entire world upside down, literally and figuratively. Hutton was not the first to debunk the Flood theory. According to John McPhee in *Annals of the Former World*, Leonardo da Vinci found marine fossils in the Apennines, a good distance from the Adriatic Sea, and said, in effect, "that it must have been a talented clam that could travel a hundred miles in forty days."

As for the application of Hutton's ideas to the life sciences and the study of evolution, McPhee wrote, "In six thousand years, you could never grow wings on a reptile. With sixty million, however, you could have feathers, too."

The Earth was much older than anybody had ever imagined, James Hutton said, all of it shaped by "little causes, long continued."

With his writings came the idea of *deep time* and the concept of uniformitarianism that said the present is the key to the past. The same processes that shaped the Earth all that time continue to shape it today, at the same pace, in the same way.

Hutton influenced Charles Lyell, the father of modern geology, whose mission, he said, was "freeing the science from Moses." Lyell in turn influenced Charles Darwin, one of the biggest troublemakers of the nineteenth century. "The result, therefore, of this physical inquiry," concluded Hutton, "is that we find no vestige of a beginning, no prospect of an end." What has been will be.

Nearly two centuries later, in the early 1970s, another geologist—a glaciologist, to be exact—sat before a committee of distinguished men who represented their own *dogma du jour*. Bearded, white-haired, and wearing dark horn-rimmed glasses, this glaciologist worked for the U.S. Geological Survey in Tacoma, Washington, and had vast experience in Alaska.

His name was Austin Post.

The committee he sat before was charged with finding a proper route for transporting crude oil from Prudhoe Bay, in Arctic Alaska, to refineries down south. Two options looked feasible. One: carry the oil from Prudhoe Bay east into Canada, then to Edmonton, Alberta, where it could be refined and transported south by truck and train. Or two: construct an all-Alaska pipeline eight hundred miles south to Valdez, in Prince William Sound. Then transport the oil by supertankers to refineries in Washington and California.

Austin Post told the committee that Alaska had fifty-two major tidewater glaciers, and all but one, Columbia Glacier, immediately west of Valdez, had surrendered its fiord to the sea. That is, Columbia Glacier could recede twenty miles into the Chugach Mountains and still be tidewater. Only one thing prevented this: an underwater moraine that anchored the glacial terminus. When (not *if*) the terminus backed off that moraine, the glacier would enter a phase of "catastrophic retreat" and discharge a tremendous number of icebergs into Prince William Sound. Some of those icebergs would find their way into the proposed supertanker shipping lanes, Austin Post said. *Just thought you gentlemen should know that.*

The Senate voted. The Trans-Alaska Oil Pipeline was approved by a single vote, a tiebreaker by Vice President Spiro Agnew.

Seventeen years later, on the night of March 23, 1989, while Melanie and I and a quarter million other naïve souls slept in Anchorage, the single-hulled supertanker *Exxon Valdez* radioed the Valdez Coast Guard and asked permission to leave the southbound shipping lane due to "icebergs ahead." The Coast Guard approved. The *Exxon Valdez* diverted but failed to return to its course in time. It struck Bligh Reef at four minutes after midnight on Good Friday—twenty-five years to the day after the massive Good Friday earthquake of 1964—and spilled 10.8 million gallons of Prudhoe Bay crude oil into the cold, rich waters of Prince William Sound.

The following day an EXXON spokesman stood before the cameras of the world and said his company would clean up "all the oil."

Was it a law of didactics? Tell people what they want to believe and they'll believe it? Curled into a fetal position in front of the television, I felt my trust shatter. I felt my fingernails dig into my palms. I felt darkly aware that Alaska wasn't Alaska anymore; it was Saudi Alaska, an oligarchy, an *oiligarchy*. The sons of men who had pumped dry and paved over so many other places would do the same here. A man driving a gas-guzzling pickup was once asked by a television reporter, "What kind of vehicle do you think Jesus would drive?"

The man answered with a smirk, "A stretch limo, for him and those twelve apostles he always had to have with him."

Later on television, as the American public continued to pump gas at EXXON stations everywhere into their single-occupant vehicles that got poorer gas mileage than Henry Ford's Model T of seventy-five years earlier, I saw a long-haired protestor carrying a sign: AMERICA: A NATION OF SHEEP, OWNED BY PIGS, RULED BY WOLVES.

It broke my heart.

Richard called, then Michio. All morning we shared the medicine of each other's voices. Richard was solemnly philosophical. He tried his best to tell me that we'd get through this. Michio was different. If I read his voice correctly, he wanted me to tell him it would be okay, that the oil would be contained and cleaned up and wild Alaska, like the Earth itself, would abide forever.

"I don't know, Michio," I said. "I just don't know."

For three days the black tide spread slowly west in clear, cold, windless weather as EXXON, the U.S. Government, and the State of Alaska assigned blame and debated the "right course of action." The fisherfolk of Cordova took to their boats with buckets and makeshift containment booms in a futile attempt to save their ways of life. On the fourth day the winds came, and over the next two months the oil smeared more than 1,500 miles of coastline from Prince William Sound to Kenai Fjords to Kodiak Island and across Shelikof Strait to the Katmai Coast, and beyond.

Richard called it "the crude awakening."

Enlisted as part of a National Park Service task force, Melanie and I were sent from Anchorage to the Katmai Coast to inventory wildlife—birds and bears, primarily—before the oil got there. That way, when the casualty list was later assembled, the NPS would know the relative losses caused by the spill. We arrived on April 20 and left on April 30, three days before the oil arrived. Ten miles off Hallo Bay, en route back to Homer, we hit the killer tide. Thick and brown, it appeared more like chocolate mousse than oil. Then came the smell and the carcasses of thousands of seabirds (mostly murres) in a line of death as far as we could see. We vomited over the side.

This terrible tragedy, said Alaska's Senator Frank Murkowski, should in no way discourage us from drilling for oil in the Arctic National Wildlife Refuge. He didn't actually say, "Arctic National Wildlife Refuge." He said, "An-wahr." In fact, he said "Annnwhhaaarr."

Not everybody can give an acronym four syllables, but he did.

My father died that spring, leaving me parentless. Edward Abbey died then too. He was sixty-two. Friends put him a pine box, took him out into the desert and stuck him in the dry earth covered by a pile of rocks. It was important to live right, he had said, and die right. He had visited Alaska a couple times in the 1980s and found the topography more impressive than the people.

He wrote: "Alaska is not, as the license plates assert, the 'Last Frontier.' Alaska is the final big bite on the American table, where there is never enough to go around. . . . For Americans, Alaska is the last pork chop."

AFTER OUR wrestling match with the Corral kids in Anchorage, Michio and I flew to Cordova, in the southeast corner of Prince William Sound. It was early May 1992, three years after the spill, and the little town still carried the burden of its loss, weighted down further by its David-versus-Goliath litigation against EXXON. The herring fishery had collapsed. Salmon runs were depressed. Dozens of boats sat idle in their slips. Nearly three thousand sea otters had died, plus three hundred harbor seals, a quarter million seabirds, and thirteen killer whales. Those were the verifiable statistics. The actual numbers were probably much higher. From Cordova, we headed down the Lost Coast toward the St. Elias Mountains and the Fairweather Range, and beyond to Glacier Bay. Along the way we found a little lodge and a large tideflat, and settled down to wait for the birds.

They came with the promise of the millennia, northbound by the hundreds of thousands, headed for nesting grounds on the Arctic tundra. They were western sandpipers and dunlins mostly, flying with the same magical choreography Richard and I had seen in Bartlett Cove thirteen years before, always winging off into the horizon but never into each other. Michio and I would lie on the sand— sometimes in the mud—and watch them pass, cameras in our hands. Now and then they would alight all around us and chirp their soft conversations as they probed the mud for small invertebrates. Then suddenly—*whoosh*—they were up again, flying, spiraling, changing direction as quickly as a sheet snapping in the wind.

"I'm getting too old for this," Michio would say with a laugh as we cleaned the mud off our elbows, bellies, and legs.

"You're not old," I told him. "Age is a state of mind."

He looked at me. "State of mind?"

"Yes, Michio. A state of mind is . . ." *How to explain . . .?* "It's . . . an attitude."

"An attitude?"

"You know how some people are young but think they're old? And some people are old but think they're young, all because of their attitude? It's how they feel about themselves, about the world around them. That's state of mind. Understand? *Wakari-mas-ka?*"

He nodded slowly. "Yes, I understand. *Wakari-mas.*"

I doubted that he did. My explanation wasn't clear enough.

My doubts were confirmed the next evening when Michio, bent over his dinner soup and slurping loudly with his hands cupped around the bowl, made an announcement. He had been out all day in the rain, wind, and sun, working his artistry beneath brilliant shafts of light that cut through heavy clouds.

He looked up and said, "Oh Kim, by the way, I now have a state of mind."

"That's good, Michio. What is it?"

"Alaska," he said. "Alaska is my state of mind."

He didn't get it. But as the days went by I began to think that I was the one who didn't get it. So carefree Michio seemed, so unburdened by all the things that weighted me down. I'd heard it said that by the time a man reaches middle age, he's half-dead; he's met so many people, every new person he meets reminds him of someone he's already met. Not so with Michio, or with Richard or Hank. They were original, unlike any friends I'd known before, shaped by wild Alaska as a glacier shapes a mountain. In turn they shaped me. Michio, with his Alaska state of mind, had more than just light inside him, he had illumination, his own aurora. Richard had married one of the most likable girls in Juneau, Luann McVey. At their outdoor wedding north of town, Luann stood in a vast circle of family and friends and shared the reasons she loved him: He was kind, compassionate, funny, a bit unpredictable (like a glacier), intelligent, responsible. She ended with, "I love you, Richard, for being so caring and creative." She looked at him when she said this, straight-backed, poised, and clear-eyed, her voice breaking, and I knew that Richard was going to be fine. With Luann he could be what he'd always been: Kerouac's hobo, Muir's mirror, out there on the curve of binding energy, a particle as vibrant as Michio's wave, forever shining and in motion. He would take Luann to Africa, Australia, and Asia. They would become teachers and make remarkable children. He would grow old with love in his life. I was happy for him.

Back from Bolivia and grown into a man, Hank had apprenticed himself to Richard Carstensen and Greg Streveler, two of the best naturalists in Southeast Alaska, and found work as a summer field biologist in Glacier Bay. I saw him on a short visit to Bartlett Cove before Michio and I jumped on a charter boat in Juneau to photograph whales.

I hadn't been to Glacier Bay in the six years since my wedding. The changes alarmed me. More cruise ships, more tour boats, more kayaks, more airplanes, more commercial fishing boats, more research, more buildings, more administrators, more money, and more reasons to have more of the moreness. First the Moors invaded Spain, then the Mores invaded Glacier Bay. The important thing, it appeared, was to pretend that the moreness was necessary, insignificant, or unavoidable, and to keep pretending until the pretense became real.

I asked the superintendent about it, and the chief ranger. I asked the chief of this division and the chief of that division. So many chiefs. So many divisions.

Did it have to be this way? Can't something change?

Their blank faces reminded me of a line from Nelson DeMille's chilling novel, *The Charm School*: "[They] were now thinking about things, but a good number of them had that neutral, vacuous expression that people wear when they hear a call to arms and pretend the speaker is addressing someone else."

Was the Ibach cabin still standing? Nobody knew. Had anybody seen the Garforth Bear? The *Sphere Princess*? Did rangers still range?

"Nope, rangers don't range anymore," Hank told me. "They attend meetings, balance budgets, and write safety briefings."

It wasn't the people Hank distrusted. They were honest, hard-working, and in most cases, big-hearted and well-intended. It was the nature of the organization—any organization—that grew and grew and in so growing rewarded people with the good life. So comfortable and secure did they become in the good life that they seldom attempted the great life, living on the edge, crossing the crevasse.

Potatoes in exhaust pipes. Vaseline on door handles. Telephones disconnected. Mischief was Hank's only means of maintaining sanity in a Bartlett Cove office culture that he said had more in common with Washington, D.C., than with the bay out the window.

"All right now," he'd mutter as he walked the warren-like maze of desks and partitions, "everybody in your little cubicles, it's time to think outside the box."

It was the brave new world of "risk management, quantifiable outcomes, and information-based decision making," as if every deci-sion made prior to then had been made in ignorance. Maybe one day the scientists—all those -ologists running their powerboats and lin-ear regressions—would discover something so illuminating that the managers could base an unassailable decision on it. Maybe, too, Humpty Dumpty would put himself back together again.

And risk management? A little voice in my head told me that Emerson had it right (he knew John Muir, after all) when he said that it was wiser in a storm to pray for safety from peril than for deliverance from fear.

I reminded Hank that the NPS itself was handcuffed by an impossible mandate, as written by Frederick Law Olmsted, Jr., the son of the co-designer of New York City's Central Park. This "Organic Act" of 1916 stated that the fundamental purpose of the national parks (and thus the role of the National Park Service) was to "conserve the scenery and the natural and historical objects and the wild life therein and to provide for the enjoyment of the same in such manner and by such means as will leave them unimpaired for the enjoyment of future generations." The first time I read it I got cross-eyed. The second time, a headache. The third time, depressed, as I could see it depressed Hank, who found the language ponderous and unlike any of the rhythms he knew from the wilderness. Mr. Olmsted no doubt intended for the act to be effective. It might have been possible in 1916, when national parks were remote and America had few miles of paved roads, no interstate, no jet travel, and no grasp of the common man with discretionary money, time, and the ability to travel. Today, that remoteness has been obliterated. National parks have become playgrounds. The Organic Act, constantly interpreted by opposing ideologies to fit their agendas, has been boiled down to little more than a recipe for dichotomy. Who then defines "unimpaired"? Or "enjoyment"? The guy on his snowmobile sharing his fumes? Or the guy on cross-country skis looking for silence? The Organic Act does little to keep national parks off the slippery slope of ecological erosion, a slope well-oiled by unctuous lobbyists and don't-tread-on-me libertarians.

I suggested to Hank that the NPS needed a reauthorization act. Remove it from the Department of the Interior. Give it unprecedented fiscal autonomy. Create a twenty-one-person board of directors chosen in equal one-third parts from members of Congress, the American Academy of Sciences, and the American Academy of Arts and Letters, who, in turn, choose the director. No more appropriations blackmail. No more pork barrel. No more "national parks." As novelist Mary Roberts Rinehart wrote in *Ladies Home Journal* in 1921, "The word 'park' is too small a name, too associated with signs and asphalt and tameness." Call them "American Origins." Sanctuaries of open space. Only one big problem: It would take a national referendum. It would require the will of the American public to wake up and say "We cannot lose these places."

In a nation where less than 5 percent of the voting public ranked the environment as their number one priority, it seemed unlikely to happen anytime soon, if ever.

A sadness—almost a fear—rimmed Hank's eyes as we spoke. At six-foot-four with a mossy beard that covered his chin but not his grin, he was a tree in an office, a bear in a barn. I wondered how long he would last, how much of his spirit would die before he quit.

I had hoped for a trip into the backcountry with Richard or Michio. We could be the only kayak again, one last time before we grew up. But Michio had things to do in Juneau. Richard too. Besides, the bay had many kayakers in it, everybody wanting to be John Muir. Everybody wanting to be different from everybody else.

The Buddhists were right. Impermanence wasn't just something to ponder, you had to embrace it. You had to pass it on and grow old gracefully, damn it.

There were other changes in the bay, exciting ones. Steller's sea lions had arrived at South Marble Island. Sea otters had arrived as well, their numbers increasing each year, mostly in the lower east bay around Beardslee Entrance, Boulder Island, and Leland Island. More humpback whales too, swimming invisible spirals below thick schools of forage fish. Moose had shown up in nearby Gustavus, first a few dozen, then a few hundred. The long-legged, big-nosed calves would stand on the side of the road and watch traffic (there was more of that too) before they slipped away to join their mothers who disappeared into thick willow. Sandhill cranes stopped by Gustavus every September and occasionally stayed deep into autumn as if their compasses had failed and they were unable to continue south.

Half the people in town wanted to feed them, the other half wanted to eat them.

Winters were milder, summers wetter. Most of the glaciers in the bay continued to retreat. One or two advanced. One of those advances, while short-lived, involved Lamplugh Glacier, a sibling of Reid Glacier that also flowed north out of the Brady Icefield. The summer before, a tour company had announced it would bow-land about a hundred boat passengers onto a rocky outcrop near the tidewater face of Lamplugh Glacier. Not possible, said the National Park Service. Too many people. It's unsafe, and would damage small pioneering flowers. Too late, the tour company said. We've already announced it in next year's brochure. Too bad, said the NPS, you should have checked with us first. Not so, the tour company said, as it appealed to the gilded men it financed in Congress. Much debate ensued as the tour company and the NPS explained their imperatives to anyone who would listen. That winter, Lamplugh Glacier advanced over the rocky outcrop and the pioneering flowers, and over the imperatives of the tour company and the National Park Service.

It was conflict resolution by ice, and I could hear Dr. Folsom quoting John Muir: "The last days of this glacial winter are not yet past . . . and the world, not yet half made, becomes more beautiful every day."

IN JUNEAU, I held in my arms little Lydia Steele, Richard's new daughter. How vulnerable she seemed, and tough too, easy to win your heart and change your life.

Muir was right. The world had become more beautiful in one day.

Richard and I stayed up late eating popcorn while mama Luann and baby Lydia slept, at least for a short while. We spread our old maps over the kitchen table, the ones of Glacier Bay, and talked of future adventures, the risks we would never be too old for. Men being boys. Out the window the last cruise ship of the season, ten decks high and lit up like a Christmas tree, sailed down Gastineau Channel in heavy October rain. Passengers on board must have wondered what happened to the blue-sky Alaska they paid for in the glossy travel brochures.

I had been on board one of those ships recently and met, of all people, a man who worked for EXXON. When I mentioned to him James Hutton and deep time, he rolled his eyes and asked me for my address. A few weeks later a Bible arrived in a box (two actually, one for me and one for Melanie, our names gold-embossed on the covers).

On the outside of the Bible box was written: "Every once in a while you experience something that changes you forever." And below that, in smaller type: "What would happen if you received a letter from God?"

I have. Every time it snows I receive a letter from God. Was it okay to believe that? Was it okay to regard the Sistine Chapel as no more beautiful than new-fallen snow on a western hemlock, how the crown of the tree bowed as if . . . well, in prayer? Was it okay to believe in deep time and a heaven on Earth and a rebirth in Glacier Bay? Or should I have gone to church on Sunday as Senator Frank Murkowski did, filled with faith and embraced with the belief that we can—we must—grow ourselves out of every problem? Without growth we have decay. That's what he said. Whatever economic woes we suffered in Alaska, we suffered largely at the hands of environmentalists who took nature off the auction block. He called their ideology "BANANAs." Like ANWR, it was an acronym: Build Absolutely Nothing Anywhere Near Anyone.

Addressing the Anchorage Chamber of Commerce, Senator Murkowski talked covetously about Texas, where nearly all the land was privately owned and open for development. Alaska was sixty percent federally owned, much of it "locked up" in officially designated Wilderness, with a capital W (which stands for Wrong). Now that he was a committee chairman in the U.S. Senate, he intended to do something about it. I thought he might move to Texas.

Honestly, he scared me. From my anger came disillusion and fear. I was beginning to question the fundamentals of my own country, believing that as precious and hard-won as freedom is, we in America were drunk on it. Our loss of open space, our apocalyptic urbanism, our corporate raiders and sold-to-the-highest-bidder politicians were all part of the hangover.

I had met commercial fishermen in Glacier Bay who after fishing there for one year behaved as if they were fifth-generation hand-trollers in the Sea of Galilee. Where did such possessiveness come from? If you owned the fish, did you own the waters they swam in? Did we all? John Muir was right. Nothing dollarable was safe.

I heard Governor Hickel say that population wasn't the problem, crowding was the problem, as if one had nothing to do with the other.

Never mind Gertrude Stein who wrote, "In America, there is more space where nobody is than space where anybody is. That's what makes America what it is."

It was apparently time for America to be something else. Houses on every horizon.

"What's wrong with that?" a developer once asked me.

In 1968, the year the Beatles released the White Album, Garrett Hardin (a pesky academic like Aldo Leopold and Michael Folsom) wrote a little paper called "The Tragedy of the Commons" that became very big, very fast. It described "the commons" as a field open to all, where each man could keep one sheep or cow to supply his family with wool or milk. But of course the time comes when a man introduces one animal too many onto the commons and they all produce less. Not as much milk per cow, or wool per sheep. A developer builds too many houses atop a failing aquifer. Same thing. "Therein is the tragedy," wrote Hardin. "Each man is locked into a system that compels him to increase his herd (his profit) without limit—in a world that is limited . . . natural selection favors the forces of psychological denial. The individual benefits as an individual from his ability to deny the truth even though society as a whole, of which he is a part, suffers."

Then as now, on land and in the sea, the man who steals a cow (or fish) off the commons is arrested (maybe), while the man who steals the commons from under the cow isn't even fined.

AS RICHARD AND I traced our fingers over Glacier Bay, we remarked on how tattered and worn the maps were, as if they had memories, a skin. They took us back to the only kayak, and our time as backcountry rangers. Penciled notes filled the margins:

June '79, wolf hunting in meadow.
September '80, eagle's nest in cottonwood.

September '83, forty crab pots in wilderness waters.

August '84, black bears & salmon, strong flooding tides.

June '90, two cruise ships and three tour boats at Margerie Glacier. Somebody call the harbormaster.

Luann came into the kitchen with Lydia and asked Richard to hold her. How impossibly small she seemed in his arms, making those cooing sounds babies do, talking to themselves. I could practically see his heart beating in that big chest of his. It dawned on me then that Richard had embarked on a new risk, one with deeper crevasses and higher summits than anything he'd faced before—fatherhood.

Sitting there and holding Lydia myself, I felt my own deep time, measured not in millions of years but in the intensity of the single moment, the millions of feelings you feel when another life—the future of Alaska—is in your hands. No wonder Michio wanted children.

"How long," I asked Richard, "until this little girl will be ready for a wrestling match?"

As it turned out, Lydia would prefer pillow fights. Together with her little sister Laura, born two years later, they would thrash me. Though in all fairness I believe I got in a few good shots before they pummeled me to the floor and pinned my arms.

A few years later, in 1996, Melanie and I moved from Denali back to Gustavus, next to Glacier Bay. We loved the sense of community there, the creativity and compassion that comes from smallness and quietness, the rusty old trucks and funky rubber boots, the acts of gratitude versus pride, the potlucks and music and unlocked doors, the smoked salmon left in the car that meant someone was saying thanks for something. We knew of other couples there like ourselves, happily married, in love with each other and the land. We wanted to grow a garden and pick berries and heat our home with wood. Melanie and I had met in Glacier Bay, fallen in love, and been married there. We wanted to grow old there too, holding hands in our kayaks for as long as our knees would allow.

ON ANOTHER VISIT with Richard, I asked, "Remember how it was? How the table in the Ibach cabin at Reid Inlet was set?"

He nodded. "It makes you wonder how many of us leave a place intending to return, and never do."

I knew then, and suppose he did too, that the only kayak was a paradox, yes, but also a kind of fantasy. For many people who want to change the world, the idealism they chant for free in their twenties is too expensive in their forties.

"Did you hear?" I said. "I'm the new president of Friends of Glacier Bay. We're going to take on Murkowski and commercial fishing."

Richard got that wild look on his face, the one I'd seen years before in the grocery store when he threw twenty pounds of popcorn into the shopping cart and convinced me to go kayaking with him.

"You may not know karate," he said, "but you know craaaa-zy."

I didn't laugh. I didn't even smile.

"Hey, it's okay," he said. "Frank the Bank is only a senator. You're a president. You're John Muir. You'll kick his ass."

"Yeah, right."

Inside I didn't feel like John Muir. I felt like little Stickeen.

UNELECTED, UNIMPEACHED

Chapter Nine

I HAD NEVER BEEN a president, or wanted to be.

The September sky was blue and black, the cottonwoods a monarch yellow with their crowns open and charitable. Overhead, sandhill cranes spiraled into heaven and flew south in perfect formations, skein after skein with necks boldly outstretched and spirits undaunted by dark clouds. The flight happened during our annual Friends of Glacier Bay meeting at the Gustavus School. We went outside to watch and listen. It occurred to me then, showered by those ancient voices, that if loons invented the music of being alone, cranes invented the music of being together.

Back inside, we settled down to our self-appointed task of protecting "ecological intactness and opportunities for solitude" in Glacier Bay National Park. No easy thing. Thirty of us had arrived that morning. By the end of the day, after hours of sitting and talking, only ten remained. We discussed the park's general management plan, vessel management plan, Bartlett Cove concept and development plan, backcountry management plan, and the hottest issue of all, commercial fishing. Now came the financial report and elections. The position of president was open, and somebody suggested me. Nobody opposed, and—*whoosh*—like birds taking flight, I was president of Friends of Glacier Bay. Everybody else was out of the room. Gone.

Wait a minute. What does it mean to be president?

A "splendid misery" is what Thomas Jefferson called it. The people pick you, then pick *on* you. But I wasn't even picked. I was nominated and unopposed. No speeches. No election. It took two minutes. I had no vice-president, no salary, no Secret Service, and no Secret Agenda, though as the commercial fishing issue heated up I would be accused otherwise, at least on the agenda part. I never flew in Air Force One either.

Did I really have to be a president? What about a director, a dictator, a prime minister, or a czar? What about El Presidente? On the marble steps of my capital I would stand with sword in hand, my chest heavy with medals as I challenged infidels and spoke of war and watered the land with the blood of my own faithful. Couldn't I just be an independent, no-name writer living at the end of a dirt road, quietly crafting my never-to-be-published sedition?

When I stepped outside the school, the cranes were gone. The sky seemed empty. In a strange way so did my heart. I was flattered to be entrusted at the helm of a small, grass-roots conservation organization with a fifteen-year history of good community relations in Gustavus. But I was worried. Big issues loomed ahead. I wasn't sure I could carry the banner with as much integrity as it had been in the past.

Melanie and Hank were waiting in the parking lot.

"How does it feel to be president?" Hank asked.

"Weird."

"You'll be fine."

"I guess."

"Just don't say anything."

That night, back in the house Melanie and I rented near the center of town, she told me she was confident I'd do the right thing. I was reassured, yet a little haunted. For all but a few men, power brings abuse, and abuse more power. After Melanie had gone to bed, I pulled out my old nylon string guitar and played a few bars of Lennon and McCartney's "Nowhere Man."

I PHONED MICHIO the next day. He invited me to join him in Katmai to photograph bears. As before, I said no. I was too busy. I must have thought he'd live forever; that the invitations would never end.

"Okay, Kim. Then we photograph whales next summer?"

"Sounds great. Hey . . . how's Naoko?" His sweetheart.

"Oh, she's good. She's very happy, thank you."

One day in Denali, during Melanie's and my last summer on the Toklat River (a year or so after the wrestling match with Hannah and Ben Corral), Michio had dropped by our little A-frame cabin and introduced us to her. He didn't say it then, but Melanie and I could see it in his eyes. This was the woman he would marry. She was much younger than he, petite, attractive, and delicate without being fragile. She reminded me of a leaf suspended over a stream, inches above the rushing water yet absolutely still. Later, while driving the Denali park road, I saw them together at Stony Dome. Michio was lying on the tundra, photographing wildflowers while patient Naoko stood beside him holding a windscreen. Driving back two hours later, I saw them still there, sitting side by side, eating their lunch and reading a book.

On the phone, Michio told me that he was happy to know that Melanie and I had moved back to Glacier Bay and were looking to buy land in Gustavus. He wanted to buy land there too, he said, so he and Naoko could "enjoy the rain."

"I like the rain," he added. "It makes Alaska seem . . . new."

A mutual friend, Karen Colligan-Taylor, a professor of Japanese in Fairbanks and a longtime landowner in Gustavus, was looking for possibilities for him.

"That would be great, Michio," I said. "We could be neighbors."

"Yes, I have thought about that. Kim, do you still play the guitar?"

"A little. I was playing the Beatles last night."

"George Harrison? 'Here Comes the Sun'?"

"No, Lennon and McCartney. 'Nowhere Man.'"

"'Nowhere Man'?"

He didn't know the Beatles as I did, how those songs were therapy for me. I could have explained, but I didn't want to burden him with the weight of my new presidency. I understood now the differences between his relationship to Alaska, and my own. We both loved the wild, open, roadless spaces, but when it came to addressing the threats to them, Michio had a way of skipping stones over those dark waters while mine sank straight to the bottom, heavy with worry.

Senator Murkowski wanted a second road in Denali National Park, and oil drilling in the Arctic National Wildlife Refuge, and more cruise ships and tour boats in Glacier Bay. Landscapes I saw as full (with rivers, ridges, birds, and bears) he saw as empty (in need of development and more people). He wanted commercial fishing forever in Glacier Bay, snowmobiles in Denali, and more high-volume clearcut logging in the Tongass National Forest. All those trees going to waste, standing there with nothing to do, overmature, falling and rotting. Best to harvest them, he said. Near as I could tell, no place was more sacred to him than the act of harvesting that place.

For Michio, gentle soul that he was, the specter of a thumping, grinding industry in his sacred temple was too unpalatable to think about. So he didn't. He needed to do what he did best. Be out there. Sleep on the ground. Create photographs unlike any others and share them with the world. Show everybody what we have to lose.

One night in Denali, years before, as we drank coffee in his Volkswagen van, I mentioned more threats to Alaska—a bad habit—and Michio grew quiet.

He rotated his warm cup in his hand and said, "Kim, do you have hope?"

"Hope?"

"Yes, I am wondering . . . where does your hope come from?"

"I don't know, Michio. I don't know if I have any hope."

MY FIRST ORDER OF BUSINESS as president of Friends of Glacier Bay was to write a state-of-the-park address, a sort of State of the Union Address without Congress or television. I didn't deliver it as a speech in a venerated chamber of redwood and marble. I wrote it in a small, drafty house while watching a horse that belonged to our neighbor, Kate Boesser-Koschmann, stare over a fence at a moose, and the moose stare back, each trying to understand the other. "There is still magic here," I began. "Melanie and I awake every morning and look out the window to see the world always different, always the same, always Alaska. . . ." I quoted Aldo Leopold and Alvin Toffler, and listed the important points of the annual meeting. "Accelerated industrial tourism has arrived in Glacier Bay. What will this place look and sound like in the year 3100? Fifty general management plans from now? Fifty Bartlett Cove concept and development plans from now? Fifty holy writs from now? Already there is more money, staff, research, and visitation, and less solitude, than ever before. This troubles me, and brings me to a confession. I like poetry and stillness. I like pulling up survey stakes. I rejoice in living in Alaska not for what it can become but for what it is and has been for a very long time, a place where only glaciers do the excavating. I like the notions of sacredness and restraint, and feel at times that compromise is the act of taking the object of our desire and cutting it in half again and again until it is no longer desirable. Think of it. Charles Sheldon in Denali. William Cooper in Glacier Bay. They stopped the Juggernaut of the Mores and gave us two national parks. It goes to show what ten years of conviction will get you versus one hundred years of compromise. Today, that same conviction is needed just to keep these places quiet and unsullied by what Aldo Leopold called 'a tyranny of small decisions.' "

I opened a beer and continued. "I'm forty-three and probably have fewer tomorrows than yesterdays. My high school reunions are beginning to look more like archaeological digs than social events. I can't take my money with me; it's not true wealth anyway. My last fortune cookie told me so. True wealth is family, friends, and place. True wealth, if you've ever paddled a kayak for six days in the rain, is watersong, bear tracks, and dry socks. Can we find solutions? Can we stop the Juggernaut of the Mores? Or are we fooling ourselves? As an independent writer I've been told by other writers (Ed Abbey, mostly) that it is my right—*and duty*—to attack, when necessary, the powerful, rich, well-connected, mythic, sentimental, and traditional. Abbey was dying when he wrote that, and probably afraid. Afraid not of his own life ending, but of a *quality* of life ending, a way of being that may never be again, unless we close some doors in front of us and leave a few places exempt from our buying and selling."

Abbey's call to arms had a certain appeal. He probably read Kerouac. I ended my letter with this: "For now I'm happy to be back home, enfolded in a community of creative, kind, independent-minded people. I intend to listen. Contact me."

I mailed it out in 120 newsletters, and the phone began to ring. People liked it. I received nice letters, including one from Bob Howe, the former superintendent of Glacier Bay, retired and living in Gustavus. His wife, Doris, had served as the volunteer park librarian for the past thirty-five years. Their two sons were respected commercial fishermen in Icy Strait. Bill Brown, a retired National Park Service historian, called and thanked me. Greg Streveler asked how I was doing. These men were my elders. They looked out for me. Hank dropped by. He came through the door with wood chips on his pants and a grin on his face. As he did, the phone rang.

How to describe the woman on the other end? She had a lot to say, which meant I had a lot to listen to. It was more of a lecture than a conversation. First my one ear got tired, then the other. Then one arm, and the other. I cleaned the toilet bowl and did my taxes, saying now and then, "Uh-huh . . . yes . . . of course, commercial fishing is an honorable way of life." Peter was a fisherman, we all know how much Jesus loved him. I considered putting the phone down and eating dinner, picking it up in time to say, "Uh-huh . . . yes . . . of course."

If this woman was anybody's Miss Right, her first name must have been Always. After a couple hours she hung up. Maybe she got hungry, or had to go check her crab pots in Glacier Bay wilderness waters.

"You okay?" Hank asked. He had read an entire book while I listened.

"Uhhhh . . ." My head was ringing. I wanted to be in Katmai with Michio, sipping coffee (I didn't even like coffee) and waiting for bears. I wanted to be in Juneau, pillow-fighting with Richard's girls (*that* I liked).

Hank pulled out a baseball and two gloves and took me outside to play catch in the dark. It began to rain but we kept throwing until Melanie came home from work at the park. We sat down to eat, but my appetite was gone. I kept hearing the Phone Woman blather on about how things are in Alaska, fishing and freedom being one in the same and all that. I could hardly wait for her to call again; I knew she would. The storm was coming.

That winter the membership of Friends of Glacier Bay voted by a sixty to forty margin to align with the National Park Service (and several national environmental organizations) to phase out commercial fishing in Glacier Bay itself. The other marine waters of the park—from Excursion Inlet to Icy Strait to the outer coast of the Gulf of Alaska, where eighty percent of the commercial fishing occurred—would stay open.

Didn't matter. The storm hit. The nasty federal government was stealing people's liberties and ways of life. The *Juneau Empire*, the same farsighted newspaper that opposed the creation of Glacier Bay National Monument in 1924, said it was an injustice to take honest, hardworking fisherfolk—men, women, and their rosy-cheeked children—and kick them out of Glacier Bay.

I flew in to attend a "fish summit" at the Alaska Department of Fish & Game, and stayed that night with Richard and Luann in their home in Douglas, across Gastineau Channel from Juneau. The instant I came through the door, the girls ambushed me in the pillow fight of the century. After hugs and brushed teeth, they went to bed. Richard and I stayed up late talking.

"Fishermen are the cowboys of Alaska," he said. "You want to end commercial fishing in Glacier Bay, you might as well outlaw John Wayne."

"He's dead."

"He is and he ain't."

"He's mostly dead."

"In Alaska he's mostly alive. This is the last frontier."

"Filled with the last frontiersmen."

"Freedom versus restraint."

"John Wayne versus John Muir."

"Paradox, dirty socks, glacier rocks, Goldilocks."

I laughed. I hadn't heard him say that in fifteen years.

He thunked around the kitchen making popcorn, and said, "History is one thing when it talks about heroes. It's another thing when it talks about victims."

"Somebody should write a book on the history of history."

"And the evolution of evolution."

"You know," he said, a serious expression coming over his face, "we tell our children to take risks and use their imagination, to reach for their dreams. We tell them to be what they want to be and the money will follow. But what do we do? We spend our adult lives in a neurotic pursuit of money, status, security, and comfort. We get lost."

I looked at him.

Was he speaking about himself? I didn't know. I didn't want him to be. I wanted that crackling wit of his, the occasional bad boy behavior and husky laugh, the tilting at windmills and flying French phrases you'd never find in Berlitz. I wanted him back in a kayak, paddling hard, pushing the ocean behind with each powerful stroke. It could be any kayak, metaphorical or real, duct-taped or new, so long as the water was deep and cold, and a glacier stared back at us with icy indifference. For several years since leaving the Park Service, he had worked as an education grant writer in Juneau and done well. Recently he had applied for a teaching position in the local school district. Once, long ago, I believed he wanted to be a career ranger with the National Park Service. But as the years went by I could see—and I think he could too—that he was too much a mustang for the federal stockyard and corral. He would make a great teacher, and I told him so. It was the second most important job in the world, after parenting, was it not? It seemed a perfect fit for a man who loved history, literature, and kids, and could find in those young faces a depth and light worth his journey.

After a minute he asked, "Is the Ibach cabin still standing?"

"I don't know," I said. "I think so."

A COUPLE MONTHS LATER, I rode my bicycle to the end of the Gustavus pier. A cold fog had settled over it and onto the floating dock below. The tide was low, the ramp steep. No wind. Flat water. Glaucous-winged gulls stood atop the pilings as if waiting to be painted, white on gray. A single commercial fishing boat was tied to the dock, a crabber name *Audacious*, the letters large so nobody would miss them. A truck was parked on the pier, a rusty flatbed with a cracked windshield. Stacked atop it were half a dozen Dungeness crab pots. A bumper sticker read: GOVERNMENT WORK ETHIC: IF IT AIN'T BROKE, FIX IT 'TIL IT IS.

The owner of the boat and truck was a funny guy who no longer shared his humor with me. He came up the ramp wearing a rain-soaked cotton T-shirt and torn, oil-stained pants. He carried a Dungy pot on his shoulder and dropped it onto the truck. He'd lost all the hair on his head, or shaved it off. A rebel of sorts, impervious to the cold, he huffed back down the ramp, refusing the handrail, lifted another pot, and carried it up. He didn't ask for help and I didn't offer. We'd been there before.

With the pots loaded, he pulled off his gloves and threw them into the cab of the truck. We spoke tersely about the weather, the basketball season, that kid in Anchorage who was bound for Duke University and probably the NBA. Joe Millionaire, the American Dream. Then we hit on fishing, the great divide.

"What does it hurt?" he asked as he faced the water, thinking perhaps the sea would have a better answer than me.

Nothing I could say would change his mind.

"I don't know," I said. "How do you define 'hurt'?"

He looked right at me. "Taking away a man's livelihood. That hurts."

I nodded. "I suppose it does."

That's when he got in his rusty truck and drove away, the tires clattering down the tar-smeared planks of the pier.

We had been friends once, back when I was a naturalist for the Park Service and he a deckhand on a tour boat. We laughed hard then, free in our youth, unburdened by ideologies. One day a few years later he decided to be defiant. He dropped a crab pot in the bay, and another, and another. The National Park Service told him it was illegal, but wrote no citation. He began to sell his catch to local tour boats.

"Fresh Dungeness crabs," the galley chefs would say, "straight from the bay today." Finest seafood in America.

Sacred cows make the best hamburger.

Let's all be fishermen in Glacier Bay, icons of the rough, tough, right-stuff men who roll up their sleeves, defy authority, make their own way, and prove that hard work is its own virtue. If this funny rebel could do it, couldn't we all? Some of us? Any of us?

Half of the seafood caught in the United States comes from Alaska, where there are more miles of coastline—34,000 total—than in all the contiguous United States.

"And not one mile of it," a scientist told me, "is closed to commercial fishing. Imagine running a huge experiment with no control or baseline. Add to that a shifting climate and sea surface temperatures. Would any forest ecologist approve of selective-harvesting an entire national forest and leave no part of it unlogged? I don't think so. But that's exactly what fishermen want to do in the marine waters of Southeast Alaska. They want to fish everywhere. It's ridiculous."

A graduate student standing next to him said, "Every farmer knows it's important to let a field go fallow now and then."

I was attending a marine biology conference, where one scientist said, "There are many ways marine ecosystems differ from terrestrial systems—life histories, energy vectors, trophic levels, reproduction rates, lots of ways. But none are as important as the fact that humans are terrestrial, not marine." And another said, "Our own ecosystem is more visible and understandable to us. It's more of a home. The sea is a mystery. Most of what goes on out there we can't see, including the damage we do. Out of sight, out of mind. The myths of super-abundance and inexhaustibility. The tragedy of the commons. Buy a bigger boat to go after fewer fish. Blame the other guy, the govern-ment, anybody but yourself. No wonder fisheries have collapsed around the world." And yet a third said, "I'll tell you what. Go down to Halibut Point [near the dock in Bartlett Cove] and for every crab, salmon, and halibut hauled out of Glacier Bay, take a rock of the same size and pile it on shore. In just a few days you'd have a hill. In months you'd have a mountain. Let the press photograph it. Explain the double standard to every visitor. Tell them why commercial fish-ing and sportfishing are allowed in a national park, and commercial hunting and sport hunting are not. Then see how quickly it takes for fishermen to be kicked out of Glacier Bay."

"They should never have been allowed in there in the first place," a feisty woman told me. "They're opportunists."

Opportunists? Like the Garforth Bear? And Joe Ibach? I sus-pected that Joe would have agreed with General Douglas MacArthur, the scrappy old soldier of his same generation who faded away and said, "There is no security on this Earth; there is only opportunity."

According to most scientists, the reasons for closing Glacier Bay to commercial fishing were many and convincing, but you never read them in any scientific journal, or on the op-ed page of the *Juneau Empire* or the *Anchorage Daily News*. You never heard them in a Senate hearing where Chairman Murkowski decided who would speak and who would not. People called those hearings "dog and pony shows." These fisher-men, he said, were decent, salt-of-the-earth people.

I agreed. The Funny Rebel was the boys' basketball coach. He arrived at Halloween parties with the best costumes and jokes. He imitated characters from *The Wizard of Oz* and *Monty Python and the Holy Grail* and had people crying with laughter. Other Glacier

Bay fishermen volunteered for the fire department and saved homes. They got up in the middle of the night to fix the town generator. They walked school kids around Point Gustavus and taught them natural history. They built their own homes, fixed their own cars—other people's cars, too. Some built their own boats. If they didn't know how to weld, they learned. If an elderly woman living alone needed help, they were at her doorstep in an instant. None had what Joseph Conrad called, "the soft spot, the place of decay, the determination to lounge safely through life." With hard work and good humor they built a little town, and now they wanted to know what they had done wrong. Why did they have to leave a place they loved as deeply as any kayaker?

Through National Park Service hearings and testimony from Seattle to Anchorage, and many places in between, I kept thinking about Aldo Leopold and the little cemetery in Wisconsin that held the last remnants of American tall grass prairie, the former ocean now an island, destroyed by good people who loved the land. I kept thinking about Ed Abbey and the last pork chop, all those pioneers eating off the same plate, crammed into the last frontier, banging their elbows together.

I never heard Senator Murkowski say our own runaway appetites were the problem. No, it was the National Park Service, together with "extreme environmentalists." In a hearing he held up a photograph and said it was a picture of a Tlingit village the NPS had burned to the ground. Not true. It was an old cannery that had fallen down. To justify his agenda and maintain his myths, the senator apparently needed to demonize others. Somebody said that he should apologize. Hank and I shook our heads.

In order to arrive at where they are, the powerful have already done what you're afraid they're going to do. That which should expel them is what put them there.

A week before I was scheduled to testify for Friends of Glacier Bay, the phone rang. It was Phone Woman, wound up tight. She had a thousand points to make about the virtues of commercial fishing

in Glacier Bay, and didn't bother to ask if it was a good time to talk.
I listened for half an hour before I started throwing her tone back at
her, tossing out a rejoinder or two, playing the echo chamber so she
could hear herself. A mistake. The cheese fell off her cracker.

"You're ruining my life," she screamed over the phone.

I was about to tell her that only one person could do that, and it
wasn't me, but she hung up. Slammed that sucker down hard.

For an hour I played my guitar and tried to wipe it from my
mind. Not even Lennon and McCartney could help. Her words were
serious, dire. I began to worry. Would she do something crazy? To
herself? To me?

I phoned Bill Brown, the snowy-haired retired historian. He had
just spoken to her and calmed her down.

"She'll be okay," he said.

For most people who move to Alaska, history begins the day they
step off the plane. Not with Bill. A deep time guy, he had come north in
the 1970s with an NPS task force that presaged the 1980 Alaska
National Interest Lands Conservation Act, which created more than
forty-three million acres of new and expanded national parklands.
Having spent months with Eskimos and Athabascans in the Brooks
Range and beyond, he understood the depth and importance of indige-
nous hunter-gatherer cultures, and the shallowness of our own.

"Seventy percent of Americans say they believe in conservation,"
he told me, "but only seven percent belong to a conservation organization, and few of them are true activists. Now you know why. It's
damn hard in today's hyper-consumptive, shop-till-you-drop ethos
with its crass commercialism and everything for sale. You stand
before the tanks of growth and greed, and sure as hell they'll run you
down."

"I'm beginning to see that, Bill. Thanks."

That night I wrote in my journal,

Conservation is the brake on the wheel. Preservation is the sud-
den stop.

OUT THE WINDOW, the moose was back. Kate's horse stood at the fence, nervously staring at it. Four legs, two eyes, a long nose, and sizable ears, but beyond that, very different. That's how I felt— different, confused, a little scared as I peered at a future I couldn't comprehend. What frightened me most was this: One hundred years from now, maybe a thousand, after global warming has run its course and the glaciers of Alaska are all gone, the last remnants of a once-upon-a-time wild bay will exist only in the corner of a cemetery somewhere. The epitaph will read, GOBBLE GOBBLE ECONOMICS— SEEMED LIKE A GOOD IDEA AT THE TIME.

Melanie and I had recently visited England to research a book I was writing for National Geographic on the Antarctic explorer, Sir Ernest Shackleton. We spent ten days at the Scott Polar Research Institute in Cambridge, northeast of London. One morning we visited the public market and found every selling stall packed into a small area, while across the street a huge, empty courtyard fronted a church and college. Standing on those ancient cobblestones, I felt another kind of deep time, the weight of centuries saying this was how it has been and will be: commerce on one side of the street, religion and education on the other. Matters of fact, matters of faith.

I said to one of the merchants, a woman selling scarves, "Does anybody ever go across the street over there and set up a selling stall in that courtyard?"

"Oh, no," she said. "Nobody."

"You'd be arrested?"

"Yes, but that's not the reason. That's sacred ground over there. You'd be shunned. This is Cambridge, you know. We have an important history here."

To have something sacred requires sacrifice. It takes a long and deep history, which we in America are just beginning to attain. We build our churches and schools with sweat, money, and time, and they become venerable in ways that wild fish and primal forests are not. We love our national parks and open vistas, but they're not sacred. They're not silent. We build roads into them, and ride our cherished machines. We bring our selling stalls across the street and say with audacity that it's our right. And we ask, "What does it hurt?"

I read the Friends of Glacier Bay testimony at the National Park Service hearing in Gustavus, and the sky didn't fall. The fishermen regarded me as a moose would a horse. Had I told them how much I respected them, would they have believed me? I doubt it. Bill Brown and Greg Streveler, my mentors, agreed that a commercial no-take marine preserve in Glacier Bay could serve as an important fish nursery. It could help to sustain good catches in Icy Strait, maybe even improve them, as I said in my testimony. But what a sad impoverishment if this closure were to cost us something irreplaceable: these colorful, authentic, hand-me-a-wrench-and-I'll-fix-it-myself fisherfolk, ptarmigan-footed, raven-wise men and women whose knowledge cannot be written down or found in computers and books. Without them, Alaska would sink deeper into the come-and-go, been-there-done-that superficiality of tourism, a thousand façade-fronted shops and ships run by ten thousand façade-fronted people, an industry dedicated at all costs to growth.

Things improved in the spring when Lynne Jensen asked me to be the Easter Bunny, and Michio called. Lynne had the kids assembled in the library, reading to them, when I appeared at the window jumping up and down with my floppy ears and big tail. They squealed with glee and dashed outside after me. We hunted for eggs and shared our lunch in the April sunshine. I stayed in costume and enjoyed being anonymous among little people who passed no judgment on fishing or any other issue. Only this: Did I make a good rabbit? I thought I did. I had a blast. Though the next day my legs were sore from too much hopping. Hazardous duty, being a bunny.

I phoned Michio and we set up the whale photography trip for July. We would meet in Juneau. I told him I was looking forward to it. We needed to get together and catch up.

"Yes Kim, get together." He began to sing, "Get together, right now . . . over me."

I laughed and almost cried over the beauty of his soft, cajoling accent. The song was "Come Together," but I wasn't about to correct him. He and Naoko were married, and expecting a baby in November. He was doing more and more photography in distant places, Haida villages in the Queen Charlotte Islands, Chukchi reindeer herders in Siberia, polar bears in Manitoba, brown bears in Kamchatka, and always caribou in the Arctic National Wildlife Refuge. I felt lucky to see him once a year.

One June evening I was on the dock in Bartlett Cove when the *Audacious* came in with the Funny Rebel at the helm and his wife on the aft deck, stern line in hand. After docking, he went up the ramp to fetch his truck while she organized gear.

A young crewman from a tour boat asked her, "How's fishing?"

"Not good," she said.

"Oh," he was taken aback. "Why not?"

She motioned toward me. "Because it makes him mad."

No, it didn't make me mad. It made me sad, and sadder still to hear her words. I had never shown anger, while it seemed to me that her husband made a habit of it. We'd all seen the tiger of his wrath. Somebody said it would have done him good to live in Bulgaria or Bhutan for a year or two, or ten, teach him perspective. Instead, he calcified into something hard-edged, and used that edge to cut an image of the dispossessed, downtrodden populist hero—John Wayne with a hobbled horse and no gun. I lost respect for him, as I'm sure he had for me. That too, made me sad. No wonder his wife dealt in the currency of anger. She knew it well and applied it to others as if we all lived in a house of mirrors. Maybe we did. Reflections are everywhere in Alaska.

Sunset that night set the sky on fire. Spokes of cinnabar light shot over the Fairweather Range and turned the clouds crimson. Two blue herons lumbered through the last embers of dusk and roosted in shoreline spruce. Looking north, I saw above Lester Island a coil of deep blue clouds, and above them a salmon-colored sky, belly-warm with soft pastels. The clouds were that same vitriol blue John Muir described in glacial ice. The Tlingits had seen it too, right where I did. But where I saw clouds they saw ice from their summer fish camp hundreds of years ago. The women would watch their men return from over the great glacier, foot-weary on blue ice, hauling back the bounty of their hunt. They had only one word for starvation, but many for gratitude. The first salmon caught each spring was eaten ceremonially, the bones set beside the stream so it could return to the great spirit. Every fish was a gift. Not one salmon went to a cannery, tour boat, or restaurant. All this while the gentry of Boston and New York ate cod by the millions, fresh from the Grand Banks, and believed it would never end. Had you told them then the great fishery that fed them and their world would one day be dead, overfished, in economic collapse, they would have called you a fool.

I heard the Funny Rebel imitating Dorothy on the Yellow Brick Road, "Oh Toto, there's no place like home. . . ."

Somebody laughed, and I found myself wishing I could laugh too.

The waters of Bartlett Cove were flat calm, darkening like ink yet still harboring the warmth of sunset. Another reflection. How deceptive the sea can be, considering all the stories it knows and the ones it chooses to tell. I agreed with Conrad, that the sea has inspired great prose and song, but at most ". . . it has been the accomplice of human restlessness."

BASTILLE DAY. To honor the peasant rabble that stormed the infamous prison in Paris on July 15, 1789, Richard was flying the French Tricolor over his Douglas home.

Folded up in a closet he had more than forty flags representing forty nations. He flew one whenever an event warranted it—a holiday in Mexico, an earthquake in Turkey (sending prayers), a peace march in Zaire (more prayers), that sort of thing. Some flags had designs nobody recognized. Passersby would slow down or stop to study them. Word got around and people wondered, *Who is this guy?* The newspaper sent out a reporter and a photographer. Richard told them the flags were his way to celebrate diversity, to connect Alaska with the rest of the world.

He asked about my presidency, how it was going.

"Fine," I said.

"How's John Wayne?"

"Tougher than I thought."

"Well, you're not dead. I guess you haven't been assassinated."

"I haven't been impeached either."

"Not yet anyway."

I always felt inspired by the confidence my friends had in me.

I drove out to the airport to get Michio. Either I was late or Michio was early, I can't remember. I found him sprawled atop his bags like a grizzly on a carcass. Summer tourists bustled around him, but Michio slept, exhausted from late hours in the Arctic Refuge with the midnight sun, chasing a heavenly light. He was having caribou dreams. I shook him awake. He sat up and smiled that big smile.

"Kim, I've been waiting for you."

After shopping for food and other items, we found Lynn Schooler aboard the *Wilderness Swift* in the Juneau boat harbor. A writer, photographer, and outdoor guide, Lynn wore a beige beret and long graying hair tied into a ponytail. He spoke with an arroyo drawl, the kind you don't give up easily after spending your first fifteen years in the desert country of West Texas. Alaska had been his home ever since, first Anchorage, then Juneau. He moved about his boat like somebody who lived and worked on the water.

We headed south down Gastineau Channel, and I began to relax. Michio and Lynn had done many trips together and were hungry to catch up. They talked in the wheelhouse while I sat out in the wind, thinking it might cleanse me. The more I tried to purge my mind of the Glacier Bay fish fight, the more it cemented itself. Was there ever a president who didn't want a second term? Yes, me. I didn't even want the first one.

It took us three days to find the whales. Even then, *they found us.* We were anchored off Tyee, at the south end of Admiralty Island, and awoke the third morning to spouts and blows over a breathless sea.

"Let's go," Lynn said. "Breakfast can wait. Only cruise ships build their schedules around food."

We weighed anchor, and for the next several days in Frederick Sound our cameras seemed extensions of our hands. We seldom stopped shooting. Did we ever eat breakfast that morning? I can't remember.

We had humpback whales everywhere, big and small, mothers and calves, sometimes five or more feeding in groups that would lunge after fish or dive deep and ascend in a spiral, releasing bubbles as they did. These "bubble nets" concentrated the fish into a tight ball and enabled the whales to surge up through them with mouths agape, swallowing hundreds at time. Curtains of baleen hung from their jaws. Pleated throats swelled with each catch. Dark eyes looked directly into ours, neither asking permission nor giving it. We smelled their oily, fishy breath and heard their deep groans. At first I was too stunned to take a single picture. Rising all at once, they appeared as a volcano, a massive flower, their jaws like petals opening and closing as herring leapt through the air to avoid capture and death. Again and again the whales did this. The herring too.

Between eruptions we waited in tired, elated silence, whispering to one another until the ingenious net, its mesh made of air, reappeared. When it did, it encircled the boat and we realized . . . we're *inside* the bubble trap. Lynn throttled back just as the whales exploded off our bow, dousing us with their splash. Michio never stopped shooting.

"Hey, Lynn," he said as he changed film. "I think whales are like cruise ships. They schedule everything around food."

"They eat a ton a day, Michio, and need every bit of it. There's no such thing as an overweight whale."

After a summer of feasting, the humpbacks would swim two thousand miles south to Hawaii to mate and give birth before returning north in the spring, the mothers nursing their new calves the entire way. All that time in warmer waters they would eat little or nothing. Small wonder they were hungry in Alaska.

Michio wondered if any of the whales we were seeing might be from Glacier Bay. Could one of them be Garfunkel? Snow? Tic-Tac-Toe? Lynn didn't think so. Neither did I.

Humpbacks have what biologists call "strong feeding site fidelity." Those in Glacier Bay and Icy Strait almost always return there, as do those in Frederick Sound. Each whale has a unique pattern on the underside of its fluke, or tail, much as each human has a unique fingerprint. Biologists have identified, named, and catalogued hundreds of humpbacks, and tracked them through generations to learn behavior, life histories, and family lineages.

FARTHER NORTH in Chatham Strait, we found a single humpback that breached dozens of times, its sleek body rising in elegant arcs from the sea, water streaming off its pectoral flippers. Michio fired away. The photography was better, he said, not just for the whale but for the mountains behind. The sharp peaks of Baranof Island.

"Good background, eh Michio?" I said.

"Yes, background is important."

Earlier in Frederick Sound, we had had the clearcuts of Kuiu Island to contend with. Not a pretty sight. Michio was always asking Lynn to maneuver the boat to avoid having those scars in his frame. Lying due south of Admiralty Island, Kuiu appeared to have been carpet-bombed, with entire valleys stripped of every tree. Studying those cuts from afar, I wondered if someday chain saws would be seen as weapons of mass destruction, and modern men too, each of us in an industrial society fighting our long war with nature, some more than others.

"Nowadays, the worst cuts aren't on Forest Service land," Lynn said over one of Michio's magical dinners, "they're on Native corporation lands."

Logging on the seventeen-million-acre Tongass National Forest had run rampant in the 1970s and 1980s (heavily subsidized by the federal government at a huge loss to American taxpayers), but had slowed down and in some places stopped altogether with a shifting economy and passage of the 1990 Tongass Timber Reform Act. Cutting on Native corporation lands was different. It continued unabated until there was less to cut and the corporations moved into tourism, the selling of picturesque Alaska.

"If you think Kuiu is bad," Lynn said, "you should see Prince of Wales. It's been nuked."

Prince of Wales Island. Sooner or later I would need to go there. I was working on a large photographic coffee table book on Alaska, and I knew it would be incomplete without a shot or two from Prince of Wales. People called it POW, Prisoner of War, where ancient trees were cut like grass and every job was a good job. Never mind that the timber went to Japan to make throwaway cellophane, rayon, and diapers, and the world's largest roller coaster, the so-called "White Cyclone," built with enough wood to make one thousand homes.

"The first duty of the human race is to control the Earth it lives upon," said Gifford Pinchot, the Yale-educated forester who in 1905 became the first director of the U.S. Forest Service. He wanted the new agency in the Department of Agriculture. John Muir did not.

Trees are crops, said Pinchot.

Trees are sacred, said Muir. "Any fool can destroy a tree."

Pinchot won. He had more pull with Teddy Roosevelt who also believed in the doctrine of utilitarianism: that the land should be used to the greatest good for the greatest number of people. It fit nicely with Adam Smith's Invisible Hand Theory, a hand so invisible you couldn't see it when it picked your pocket or slapped you, as it did John Muir.

Picturesque Alaska. Is that what Michio and I were after? In a nation obsessed with beauty, celebrity, vitality, money, and youth, Alaska was a celebrity too—the last wild place, the last frontier, the last great land, the last of the past. As a passenger once said to me on a cruise ship, "I came to Alaska to see it before it was ruined."

On the final day of our trip, we pulled into Tenakee Inlet and went ashore. Lynn wanted to share a favorite place with us. We walked across a tideflat rich with bear tracks, then slipped through a fringe of alder and entered the ancient temperate rainforest of the Kadashan Valley, one of the most magnificent groves of old-growth trees still standing in the Tongass. Spruce and hemlock climbed so high I could only imagine where their crowns might be. Michio stared up as though he were a child in a chapel. Kadashan. It was the name of one of the Tlingit chiefs—the son of a Chilkat chief—who had paddled a canoe with John Muir into Glacier Bay in 1879. It had a powerful drumbeat quality to it—*Kad-a-shan.* I found myself saying it over and over, quietly, like a mantra.

After several deep breaths I set about making pictures, trying and failing to record the scope and majesty of it all. I framed the tall trees, but nothing worked. I discovered a bear trail and shot that, and a luscious fern with its fronds curled together like the arms of the Milky Way.

Michio did none of this.

I found him at the base of a tree, focused on a small deer skull, white bone on green moss. I sat down and watched him work. He must have composed that skull ten different ways, slowly, patiently, positioning his camera to let the curve of white mandible marry into the sweep of tree trunk where it spread out and embraced the earth. It wasn't picturesque Alaska. It wasn't brutal Alaska either, like the devastation on Kuiu Island. It was something in between, a story of growth and decay. A story of growth *from* decay, artful, hopeful.

"This is everything," he said. "This is the whole forest, right here."

WE SAID GOOD-BYE in Juneau, each convinced we'd see the others again. Richard was out of town, so I went alone to Costco to shop before flying by small, single-engine airplane back to Gustavus. It took a minute to adjust to the huge racks of goods and oversized carts, all designed for me to buy more than I needed. From there I headed to Fred Meyer for their shiny fruits and vegetables. Near the checkout stand I noticed a stack of Monopoly games. Not the Monopoly I knew as a kid. This was a special Alaska Monopoly. A trigger went off in my head. My photos were often sold through an agency that sent me monthly royalty checks and source-of-sale statements. I had recently received a statement that listed the source-of-sale as "board game." It made no sense to me until that moment, standing in Fred Meyer. A little worm of worry turned over in my gut. I grabbed the Alaska Monopoly and threw it in the cart.

Out in the parking lot I ripped it open. The names had changed but the game was the same: buy property, a house, two houses, three, four, until you get a hotel and take all the money and win. In this version Illinois Avenue was Portage Glacier. Atlantic Avenue was Kodiak Island (with a photo of a brown bear). A caribou was on the five-dollar bill. Water Works had become the Alyeska (Trans-Alaska Oil) Pipeline. Boardwalk was Denali National Park. Park Place was Glacier National Park, sandwiched between Chance and Luxury Tax. All of them had photos, and some of the photos were mine.

I stood there, dumbfounded. Traffic streamed by on Egan Highway. Helicopters sliced the sky, taking cruise ship passengers to and from Mendenhall Glacier. I wanted Richard with me then, to say something corny and make me laugh. Paradox, dirty socks . . .

It was just symbolism, the Monopoly game. But symbols mean a lot. People build their lives around them. Flags are symbols. Men have died holding them. A boat named *Audacious* is a symbol. A cabin in the wilderness. A lone kayak.

As I boarded the plane back to Gustavus, I sat next to a big fellow, a commercial fisherman who had nothing to say to me. He knew who I was, and what I stood for.

What did I stand for? The more I knew, the less I was certain. On the *Wilderness Swift*, Lynn had mentioned that fishermen all over Southeast Alaska had been instrumental in stopping irresponsible clearcut logging in the Tongass National Forest in the 1980s. I could have struck up a conversation with this big fellow sitting next to me in that little plane. I could have asked about his wife and kids. I could have been bigger than my pride, presidential, thankful. But it was hard.

It was easier being Nowhere Man.

It was easier being the Easter Bunny.

Part Four

FINDING HOPE

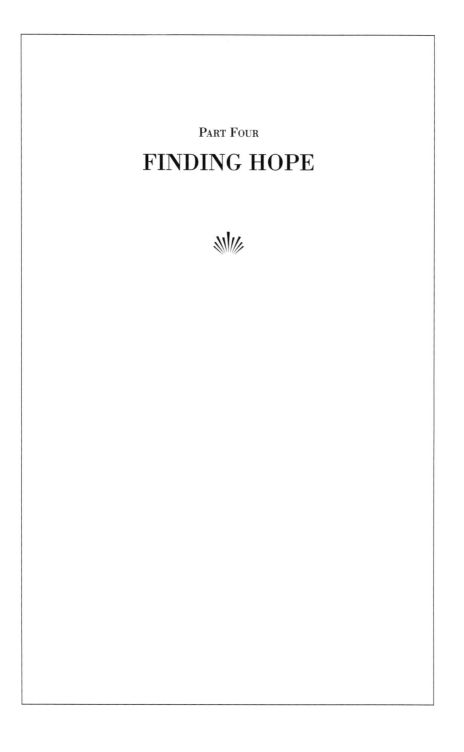

TERRANE WRECK

Chapter Ten

———

THE FIRST LIGHT of dawn hit Mount Fairweather at ten minutes after four. A pink glow, demure as a pearl, warmed a thick mantle of ice that spilled down the summit fifteen thousand feet above the sea, thirty miles west of our campsite in Queen Inlet, in the West Arm of Glacier Bay. I was already up and out of the tent, packing while Melanie slept. The sky was clear, the sea calm, patterned with reflections of mountains and glaciers. Every edge gleamed as if sharpened by a whetted knife. Near shore, green alder and spruce mirrored themselves in silent, profound testimony to a bay returning to life, healing, breathing, photosynthesizing even on the glaciers, where single-celled algae grew on ice and snow.

It was July 1996.

I had a routine for early morning paddling. First, I listened. So many voices out there, most familiar but a few not. Conversations of secret senses. Second, I hoisted the single-man kayak against my hip and hauled it from the alder fringe down to the shore. A handsome boat, it was an Eddyline Raven, white below and purple-red on its flattened dorsal side, with a bow that swept up like a Viking ship. I had given it to Melanie on our tenth wedding anniversary, and would use it now, as it was the faster of our two single sea kayaks. Perfect for a four-day solo trip. She called it the *Boysenberry Raven*.

Third, I set the kayak on wave-rounded rocks where I estimated the flooding tide would be by the time I had everything loaded, and I could push off. The tide in Glacier Bay can rise one foot every fifteen minutes and twenty feet in six hours. It does this twice a day, with the middle two hours (midway between slack high tide and slack low) the most extreme. Every summer the tide catches people off guard. It steals boats. It floods tents. A kayak off by itself, drifting upright and empty, usually belongs to someone stranded somewhere who underestimated the reach and speed of the flooding tide. The ebb is equally dramatic. Water drains from tidal basins with the exuberance of young rivers. At Sitakaday Narrows, in the lower bay, the tide rushes over an underwater recessional moraine (deposited in the early 1800s by a retreating glacier) and creates severe vortexes that can upend kayaks and other small boats. Once when camping in the Beardslee Islands, Melanie and I awoke during an extreme minus-five-foot tide and couldn't believe our eyes. Broad aprons of mudflats and mussel beds bridged islands where the sea used to be. The ocean had disappeared.

Melanie said, "Who pulled the plug?"

We told Hank about it. He grinned and said it was a glitch. The park was now so thoroughly computerized that tides, like rangers, were automated.

"Must have been a malfunction," he said with a laugh.

Fourth, I packed the kayak, balancing heavy items fore and aft, port and starboard.

Fifth, I ate breakfast and considered the journey before me, where I was going, where I had been; why I felt compelled to paddle alone to the Ibach cabin, seventeen miles away and seventeen years in my past, all across deep water. Melanie would be picked up in a few hours by a large boat, and returned to Bartlett Cove where she was a supervisor. Once a summer naturalist, she now worked year-round and mentored new rangers. I had asked Richard to join me, and Michio. They were too busy. Richard had gotten his teaching job in Juneau and taken summer work for the Department of Education. Michio was in the Arctic National Wildlife Refuge photographing Gwich'in Natives and the caribou that sustained them. More and more he aimed his camera at Native peoples, focusing on what the land and sea gave them that technology and money never could. Wild salmon versus Tyson frozen chicken. Caribou that can run forty miles an hour versus Thanksgiving turkeys that can't even walk let alone fly, reduced to meatballs pumped with growth hormones and taste additives. Memories of the wind and water and the river at your feet, the crisp taste of fall, versus McDonald's in the mall.

Hank was still employed with the National Park Service in Glacier Bay, though not for long. The clinical, loveless language of the bureaucracy was driving him nuts. Policy without any poetry was a dangerous thing, he told me. Be careful what you get good at—you may end up doing it for a long time. We joked that if Glacier Bay should have a public information officer, then why not a mystery officer? Hey, who erased all the names on these maps? Who took the GPS? Who burned the guidebooks? Must have been the mystery officer. And if a safety officer, then why not a risk officer? Hey, who scheduled the maintenance guys to go kayaking this afternoon? They never go kayaking. Must have been the risk officer, just doing his job.

One day as Hank sat in his cubicle pretending to write an environmental impact statement, his boss, the so-called "chief of resource management," dropped by with several Hoonah Tlingits and introduced Hank as "our wilderness expert."

One of the Tlingits smiled through a wind-etched face—like that of his people who hunted and fished in Glacier Bay centuries ago—and said softly, "Oh, an expert. I always wanted to know what an expert looked like."

"I knew then," Hank told me, "it was time to go."

He bought six acres in Gustavus and with help from his sweetheart, Anya Maier, built a small home on the edge of a meadow, its size and placement loyal to Frank Lloyd Wright's rule that a house should be *of* the hill, not *on* the hill. Anya's father Frank had been a respected Juneau architect who passed his talents on to his daughter, though medicine, not architecture, would be her profession.

Michio had bought land in Gustavus also. Eight acres. When I spoke to him he could hardly contain himself as he said, "Oh Kim, it's beautiful. Now all our dreams can come true."

He was finally a father. On a cold November day as he struggled to get back to Japan after photographing polar bears in Canada's Hudson Bay, Naoko gave birth to their son, Shoma. The name meant "flying horse" in Japanese. I suspected that the boy, like his father, would move differently through the sky.

I hadn't met Shoma yet, but Lynn Schooler had. In his lyrical book, *The Blue Bear*, Lynn would describe Michio when he came off a jet in Juneau with his new son over his head. "'My *aka-chan*! My baby!' he exclaimed as he danced in a circle, chattering in a mixture of English and Japanese. Naoko was drooping, drained from the long journey and ongoing surprise of being a mother, but somehow she managed to be radiant at the same time."

A friend and fellow photographer in Denali, Tom Walker, told me that Michio had stopped smoking his pipe. Tom said that Michio wanted to live a long time and have a full life with his wife and son.

In a conversation with Michio shortly before my solo paddle to the Ibach cabin, I asked him about Shoma.

"He's sleeping now," Michio said quietly over the phone from his home in Fairbanks, "but I talk to him even when he's sleeping, so he knows I am here."

It would be the last thing he ever said to me.

TWO YEARS had passed since I became president of Friends of Glacier Bay. When my term ended and nobody else wanted the job, I stayed. Again, no Secret Service or Air Force One. No impeachment either.

The fish fight continued. While Senator Murkowski rebuked the National Park Service for its terrible intentions, Ted Stevens, Alaska's senior senator and chairman of the Senate Committee on

Appropriations, cut a deal with Secretary of the Interior Bruce Babbitt to create a federal government buyout for the commercial fisherfolk of Glacier Bay. Lawyers circled, their briefcases like dorsal fins in the moneyed waters as the injured pleaded their case. The Funny Rebel who wasn't so funny anymore drove the stakes higher and higher. You could find him dropping crab pots in the Beardslee Islands from the *Audacious* right up until he and his wife got a handsome sum of compensation money and moved to Washington State. The town of Gustavus was scheduled to receive compensation as well, which angered the Not-So-Funny-Rebel. He said the town deserved nothing. The Associated Press arrived in Gustavus and photographed the Phone Woman standing outside her home looking forlornly at her unused crab pots. She and her husband also got a nice bundle of cash.

Still, she complained, saying Friends of Glacier Bay was "the nail in the coffin."

Another woman saw things differently and told me, "They traded one form of theft for another. They should have been kicked out of the bay years ago, and fined."

What a cat fight it would have been to set them loose in a small room to shred each other, each screaming her moral certainty, the luxury of the closed mind. It seemed crazy to me. How to combat fundamentalism without resorting to it? I didn't know. Part of me wanted to scream too, throw back my head and shout good-bye to all the places we seemed incapable of leaving alone.

I needed clarity.

I needed to be by myself, to paddle alone.

In his acclaimed book, *The Abstract Wild*, Jack Turner said it was essential for each of us to be alone at times in our busy lives. A corporate friend had told him about the importance of team sports in America, how they instilled social values and prepared young people for cooperative adult life and success.

Turner responded, "Yeah, a happy life in the hive, like an insect, with the drone as hero, or an interminable larval bliss with no metamorphosis to individuality. . . ."

While leading a group of school kids into the mountains, Turner asked them to stop talking if only for a minute; to be quiet and listen to the Earth. John Muir was good at listening, he told them. He talked to the trees.

"Muir was probably bipolar," a kid said.

It reminded me of a story about a young boy who had never been off the concrete of the inner city. His teacher (fourth grade?) took him into the mountains, and when the boy stepped off the bus he asked, "Who put all the dirt on the road?"

I HAD NO ILLUSIONS about being the only kayak. They had died years ago. Three or four dozen kayaks were in the bay the day of my solo journey, plus two cruise ships, three tour boats, twenty-five private vessels (yachts, sailboats, cabin cruisers, and skiffs) and at least eight National Park Service research and patrol vessels. An armada.

And me? I wanted to find the Ibach cabin, see if it was still standing.

Melanie walked down from the tent to say good-bye, sore-legged from the previous day when she had climbed to three thousand feet on Mount Merriam. A satisfied smile graced her face. She didn't tell me to be careful. She told me to come home when the tides and winds allowed. She squeezed my hand the way she did after we nearly drowned in Dundas Bay all those years ago. I pushed off and pointed my bow toward Reid Inlet, took a compass heading, and began to paddle.

It took awhile to settle into a rhythm. I stroked to the beat of the songs I sang, Beatles mostly, with Jackson Browne and James Taylor thrown in. The Fairweather Range glittered white from the bold ascent of the July sun. After an hour the shore I left behind had become distant, the campsite indistinguishable, yet Reid Inlet, my objective, appeared no closer. It wasn't fair. How could I get so far from one shore and no closer to the other?

Some three hundred years ago René Descartes put his arm in water and saw how it bent—or *appeared* to bend—and said it was proof that we cannot trust our senses. Maybe I was halfway to Reid

Inlet. Maybe the sun, four hundred times larger than the moon but four hundred times farther away, was in fact the same size as the moon. Each occupied the same portion of the sky. Maybe we humans are the paragon of species, the paradox too, and Tlingit elders are right when they say ravens know more than we ever will. Maybe Descartes had rocks in his head. The West Arm of Glacier Bay is nothing compared to the open ocean. But it's big water when you're out there in a kayak, sitting low and eating stale crackers and watching lenticular clouds form over ten-thousand-foot peaks. On clear days, afternoon winds can rise quickly and fill the bay with rows of white, foaming waves. It's best then to paddle early in the morning.

So there I was, impossibly small and alone, beginning to relax in my smallness and aloneness as I rode the laminar bare back of Glacier Bay and told myself I didn't have far to go. The risk officer would have laughed the way a joker laughs. The water was smooth as skin. I tingled with fear, excitement, gratitude, a deep sense of . . . what? I wasn't sure.

I had stopped paddling and singing. For a moment the kayak glided forward, leaving behind a thin, elegant wake. I cradled my paddle over the cowling and felt as if I too were made of water, like the sea, pulled by the sun and moon. Slowly, very slowly, a powerful force picked me up as if to break me, but instead embraced me. The sea became the sky, the sky the sea, and all I knew in some cosmic way was that my heart and soul would get me where I needed to go.

I closed my eyes and for a moment was at peace.

Then I heard the ship. A low hum, the future coming straight at me. I turned and saw *Planet Princess*. My God, it was big, approaching fast off my port quarter. I stared, mesmerized at how it sliced the sea, this marvel of industry and technology, if you can marvel at such things. I laughed, which came out as a nervous squeak. Then paddled like hell. Descartes would have too. Never mind one's own senses and what—or what not—to trust. I moved west and the ship moved with me. Targeting me? I had no radio to make a call. No cell phone.

Hey, anybody see me? You guys awake? How's the weather up there?

Cruise ships follow a mid-channel course in Glacier Bay. Near as I could tell that's where I was, mid-channel. I had no GPS, GPA, GIS, EIS, ELT, BLT. Nothing. Just my funky Cartesian senses, unreliable as they were. By paddling west toward Reid Inlet I might have put myself more in the ship's path. Then again I might not. The ship could have been changing course in its standard route to Tarr Inlet and Margerie Glacier, and not seen me. Or maybe a Republican pilot up there knew me for the Marxist-Lennonist (Groucho and John) that I was, and intended to run me down. What to do?

Imagine a Pleistocene hunter separated from his tribe. Alone, he comes face-to-face with the beast of his dreams, the great mammoth that feeds him, frightens him, defines his purpose in life. It's bearing down on him, hard. With only a spear (in this case, the kayak's Viking prow) for a weapon, he knows he's going to die, so he decides to die well. He charges. The mammoth is ten thousand times his size, making twenty knots, filled with the innocent consumers it has consumed. Still, the intrepid hunter charges. He does this because, well, he's intrepid. He might not know karate, but he knows craaaa-zy. He aims his Viking prow to slice the ship in two. Eye to eye, the ship blinks.

Planet Princess turned five degrees to starboard and passed me on its port side, some seventy yards away. It felt like a mountain going by. I saw nobody on deck. Two thousand passengers were inside battling for bacon at the breakfast buffet. But as the ship went by I saw an elderly couple on the aft stratosphere deck standing at the rail with a young boy. Their grandson? I waved but received no response. They must have been looking at the scenery beyond me, at Scidmore Glacier tucked into the mountains where it plotted its return. I waved again. The boy saw me and waved. He pointed. Too late. His grandparents had gone inside. He gestured to them. *Grandpa, Grandma, come look, there's somebody out here in a kayak. There's dirt on the road.*

But they were gone. The boy waved a final time and disappeared into the warmth and security of *Planet Princess*.

THE IBACH CABIN was still standing. I walked to it quickly, hoping it wouldn't fall down before I got there. A sense of relief came over me to see it on its feet, defiant of wind, rain, frost, rot, gravity, ice, and snow.

Seventeen years before it had been Richard who found this cabin charming, while I wished it wasn't there. Now with my youth and harder edges behind me, I reverently touched the rotting timbers, the patches of moss and a swallow's nest under the eaves, the rusty spoon lying on the ground. Red runners of wild strawberries coursed past an old leather boot. Broken glass lay about. Had it been there before? I couldn't remember. A thicket of alder and willow grew full-leafed around the cabin like teenagers tangled up in green.

Inside, the roof was about to cave in; the walls sagged under beams blackened with fungus. The floor was half rotted away. All the warmth was gone, and with it the feeling that Joe and Muz would return any minute. Condensation dripped from a rafter onto a tin plate on the damp table, ". . . *poink . . . poink . . . poink*."

The 1935 copy of *LIFE* magazine was gone, and the Henry Nash Smith book, *Virgin Land*. The cabin looked looted, defiled beyond what the wet and cold could do. Joe the prospector had been prospected himself, his articles taken away by people who wanted a piece of him just as he had wanted a piece of Glacier Bay.

I sat against the door frame and wrote a letter:

Dear Joe and Muz:

　　We never met, but I miss you. I'm here in Reid Inlet at the cabin you built more than fifty years ago, sitting in the sunshine, hoping you're together in a place that's good for gardening. I often look at the photo of you two, the one made on Lemesurier Island. There's something about your postures relative to each other that tells me big hearts don't require big homes.

　　Your little cabin is falling apart. I hope that's okay with you. It has given many of us something to think about over the years.

I stopped for a moment and reflected on how hard I was on them when I first came here, before I had feathered feet. I had judged them in the context of my time, not theirs, and now felt a little ashamed. They were capable of so much, I wanted them to be capable of forgiveness too.

I understand your attraction to gold, Joe. I've heard it said that even at sixty below it has a warm, seductive glow.

What would Joe have had to say about how the quartz veins he followed to find gold are in a strange way more valuable today than gold itself? Quartz is silica dioxide, SiO_2, which is used to make computer chips that store information. Would he shake his head to discover that computers are machines that run our lives in an information revolution and a growing global economy? Would he understand—or *want* to understand?—that information is knowledge, knowledge is power, and power is no different than it's always been? Those who have it often abuse it. Those who don't have it want it.

The gold lies where it always has, Joe, along faults and smaller breaks in bedrock where pieces of the Earth's crust have crashed into each other. You might have heard of continental drift, a theory that was just gaining acceptance when you left us. It's true, the continents move. As they do they create earthquakes and volcanoes along subduction zones where pieces of the Earth's crust dive below other pieces of crust. As North America has drifted northwest for many millions of years, smaller pieces of crust called terranes have slammed into it and accreted along its leading edge, one after another in a dramatic pileup from Puget Sound to Prince William Sound. I call it a terrane wreck.

I'm telling you this because I believe all our lives run together in the same way. We collide and accrete and become something of a whole, an amalgam of hearts and dreams and broken dreams, of friends, neighbors, and fellow travelers who influence each other across generations. It's the glaciers that tie us together. Atop the terrane wreck of our lives and the chaos below, these icy rivers sculpt and carve and bond us; they create, destroy, and create again. They give us new beginnings.

As I wrote I thought about "Études sur les Glaciers," a scientific paper written by the Swiss-born scientist and teacher, Louis Agassiz, in 1840, one hundred years before Joe and Muz built their little cabin. *Étude* is French for "study," but in a modern sense it's also a piece of music made famous by Frederick Chopin. Muz may have known this, as I heard once that she played pianoforte as a young girl before she headed north and met and married Joe. The double meaning no doubt pleased Agassiz, who was a contemporary of Chopin. He lived in a hut on a glacier to study its movements, and found such perfect music and rhythm in the ice that he titled his paper with his favorite composer in mind. Chopin was three years younger than Agassiz, and wrote two études, "Winter Wind" and "Raindrop," that sound as if influenced by Agassiz.

Agassiz concluded that the glaciers of the Alps in his day were the last gasp of a dying dynasty of ice; that Switzerland was once entirely covered by a single massive ice sheet, like Greenland. He was right, but wrong in that he said it happened only once. We know now that northern Europe and much of northern North America (including Glacier Bay) was covered by ice many times during the last two million years.

When somebody asked Chopin why his piano pieces were so appealing, he answered, "Because the length is in exact proportion to the content."

So it is with glaciers.

They come and go, like the tides. They pluck rocks from distant peaks and deposit them far away as evidence of their travels. We call these rocks erratics. I found some at the foot of the Ibach cabin. The German word for erratic is *findling*, which means orphan. It applies to each of us, does it not? We are orphans in this wild corner of the

Earth, deposited by forces we cannot explain, the ghosts of glaciers. I continued my letter.

> You may have heard that glaciers are in retreat these days. Around the world they are shrinking. We live in an age of global warming that some people say we've caused by burning so many fossil fuels. Others say it's hogwash, that the Earth has warmed up and cooled down before, and will warm up again, and there's no reason for Americans to stop driving their kids to violin lessons in gas-guzzling vehicles the size of small tanks. One theory says global warming and rising sea surface temperatures could produce more rain in temperate regions, and more snow in tall coastal mountains such as the Fairweather Range. If so, the glaciers of Glacier Bay could actually advance.
>
> Amid all this there's plenty of talk about saving the Earth. I'll tell you, the Earth has taken some hard hits in the past. It'll survive. What needs saving, I believe, is the human race and our ability to restrain ourselves, if we have such a thing. What needs saving is the rich tapestry of life around us that we take for granted. What needs saving—perhaps even found to begin with—is the intrinsic value of nature beyond any human utility.
>
> You may not agree, Joe. This probably sounds like gobbledygook to you. That's okay. People here still live fiercely independent lives. They create; they don't inherit. Alaska is a big state but a small town where friends have a way of becoming family. Even when we don't see eye to eye we look out for each other. We look into each other. I thought you should know that.

Joe and Muz were blessed with great friends, as was I. The four points of my compass were Richard in the East, a rising sun and teacher of young minds; Michio in the North, a patient follower of caribou and the oldest stories; Melanie from the South, a coyote refugee from California's freeways and smog; and Hank facing West toward the last wild shore, wondering where we go from here.

What had my friends taught me? That you can only be alone and comfortable in your aloneness when you know someone out there cares. Through the miles and mountains you feel it. Emerson thought young Thoreau spent too much time alone in his cabin at Walden Pond. By his very caring he gave him permission to be there. It's the love we receive from others that gives us wings.

Do you miss sleeping on the ground, Joe? Waking up to the drama of all the wondrous little things? Do you miss hunting and trapping, returning home from your adventures as John Muir did, "wet, weary, and glad"?

They say a moment of silence is the highest honor you can pay someone. It's not as quiet in Glacier Bay as it used to be, but I hope you two find the silence here you always did. I hope visitors pay you the respect you deserve. You should know, Muz, that there are wild strawberries all around here, and little blue forget-me-not flowers, and rufous hummingbirds feeding in a patch of fireweed next to those three spruce trees you planted. It's a beautiful, bountiful world. I hope we can keep it. Oh yes, one last thing; I wear a wedding ring now. It's made of gold.

Thank you for making me cross the deep crevasses.

Kim

BACK IN GUSTAVUS, a couple of weeks after my day at the Ibach cabin, I packed for my trip to Prince of Wales Island. En route I would need to visit a radio station in Juneau for a live debate about commercial fishing in Glacier Bay. I looked forward to it about as much as a root canal.

Melanie kissed me good-bye and told me to hurry home. We'd been married ten years, but I swear at times it felt like ten days. The honeymoon was still on.

Stuck in her office in Bartlett Cove, she'd get a telephone call. "Howdy, ma'am," came the voice from the other end. "My name's Vince Walznizchski and I'm callin' you from the Natchez Trace

Scenic Parking Lot here in Tennessee, not far from the Grand Ole Opry, and I'm thinkin' about workin' for you fine folks as one of them ranger naturalists who get on them cruise ships and eat chocolate éclairs and tell everybody everything about wild Alaska."

"Yes, Vince . . . what can I do for you?"

He'd keep her on the line for a couple minutes asking irritating questions until he'd say, "Hey, Melanie, it's me, Hank."

"Hank?" She'd slam down the phone with a laugh and tell me later, "I never had a mischievous brother. I'm beginning to understand what it's like."

I flew into Juneau, got my VW van out of storage, and drove to Richard's home in Douglas. He was at school, preparing his classroom and lesson plans. He wouldn't begin the school year for another week, but there was a lot to do. Nothing substituted for readiness.

Lydia was at the piano, working through the chords of Paul McCartney's "Yesterday." I sat next to her and watched her delicate hands explore the keys. I told her the melody came to McCartney in a dream. He woke up one morning and there it was, the entire song in his head. He didn't have words at first, so he called it "Scrambled Eggs."

Lydia looked at me the way a child appraises an adult who has a history of playing practical jokes. (Michio would say I was pulling her foot.)

"It's true," I said. "It came to him in a dream."

"Scrambled Eggs?"

"Yep."

"I don't believe you."

We settled it over a pillow fight. Lydia won. Secretly though, I didn't drop my claim about "Scrambled Eggs." I might not have known karate, but I knew the Beatles.

When Richard came home I was surprised at how tired he looked. He was working two jobs, raising two kids, and serving on several committees and boards.

"Richard, guess what? I got to the Ibach cabin."

"Oh?" He was making dinner. Luann was at a meeting. The girls were roughhousing in the living room. "Lydia, Laura, stop jumping on the sofa."

"The cabin," I said, "it's still standing."

"Really?"

A phone call distracted him, then the girls again. More gymnastics on the sofa. Another pillow fight (my fault). Richard and I discussed other topics and the Ibach cabin never came up again. For some reason he asked about Michio. I didn't think it odd at the moment, but later when I looked back on it I realized that Richard seldom asked about him. The only thing they had in common was their friendship with me. Yet Richard had great respect for Michio's work, which by now appeared in galleries, museums, magazines, and books around the world. I had recently traveled to Africa on a magazine writing assignment and seen one of his pictures in a store window in Harare, Zimbabwe.

"Michio's in Kamchatka," I said.

"Kamchatka?" Richard gave me a puzzled look. "What for?"

"To photograph bears."

"Russian bears," Richard said quietly. "I wonder what they're like."

I WASN'T FEELING WELL the next day when I reported to the radio station for the Great Fish Debate. Phone Woman was there with a smartly dressed attorney representing the injured fisherfolk of Southeast Alaska. The chief ranger and I would represent the anti-freedom Darth Vader dark side. The moderator, a guy named Joe, was yucking it up in the back with Lew Williams, the former publisher of the *Ketchikan Daily News* and a vocal advocate of the economic credo "If-we-don't-have-growth-then-we-have-decay." Whenever I heard it I wondered, if we don't have love, do we have hate? If not peace, then war? If not day, then night? What about twilight? If anybody understands shades of gray, it's the people of Southeast Alaska who live beneath clouds and rain.

To my fevered mind Mr. Williams had shaved his face the way he liked to see Alaska's Tongass National Forest: cut from one horizon to the other, close to the roots for maximum yield. The irony was this: in a temperate rainforest (one of the rarest biomes in the world), you cannot have growth without decay.

I imagined Joe Moderator and Lew Williams talking about America as men did three hundred years ago, as Fitzgerald described in *The Great Gatsby*—men flushed by the fertile green breast of a new continent lying at their feet, yielding, a young land not for the saving but for the taking, plundered by those who saw themselves not as guardians but as gardeners; men who moved across the mountains and plains and preached about sustained yield but never really practiced it, and so kept marching, road-building, tilling, filling, and spilling until they arrived here with the same mentality they began with, leaving us with only remnants of primal America; islands in a restless sea of greed, eaten away one grain at a time, one tree at a time, one memory and sacred place at a time.

Should I have been surprised? Most people in power see their world as they want it to be. They embrace whatever justifies their convictions, and ignore or condemn the rest. It's been that way for a long time.

At that moment, however, it seemed acutely American to me, given our infatuation with progress and convenience.

And who writes the definition of progress?

According to William Manchester in *A World Lit Only by Fire*, peasants in medieval Europe toiled so hard they collapsed in their fields. For a thousand years popes and kings "chose to believe what they wanted to believe. . . . No startling new ideas had appeared, no new territories outside Europe had been explored. Everything was as it had been for as long as the oldest European could remember. . . . The church was indivisible, the afterlife a certainty; all knowledge was already known. *And nothing would ever change*."

Yet it did change, didn't it? The Renaissance arrived and turned Europe upside down. Or right-side up.

Now we say that change is as constant as gravity, as unbreakable as the lack of change was back in feudal Europe. We say it's a good thing; that we've come a long way. If so, then let us be the better students of change, not the instruments of change, lest we ransack nature and suffer our own feudalism. Let us begin in Glacier Bay, itself a renaissance place, a time of new beginnings. Let us remember that hunter-gatherer cultures around the world have lived for thousands of years without changing their homes, certainly without plundering them. Let us remember that these people didn't merely survive, they *lived*. They struggled but also prospered. They excelled at being most human: strong, smart, and acutely aware of everything around them. They lived robust, sensual lives and knew every bright star in the sky, every birdsong, every flower and animal track in forest and glade, every pattern of rain and wind on land and sea.

We are all descended from a long line of people who slept on the ground and dreamed good dreams, who made love under the sky and filled their lungs with each new day. Given such a rich history, rich in things we've nearly forgotten, *The Great Gatsby* isn't just a tragic tale, it's a cautionary one about money, greed, and yes, the seduction of new beginnings.

What was I doing then, in the studio at the radio station that morning? Pining for an ancient world I couldn't occupy?

I didn't know.

I could feel my hands sweating, my anger rising. I wanted fresh air. I wanted the idea of freedom to apply to wild rivers and bears. I wanted a Bill of Rights for the earth and sky. I wanted an Emancipation Proclamation for the land and sea . . . I wanted . . .

Too late. The radio show producer asked that everybody please be seated. We hadn't even started our little debate and I was already agitated.

Joe Moderator said in a venal tone, "I'm going to take a brief moment to thank our sponsors. We're very proud of our sponsors."

Somebody get a glass of water for the Marxist-Lennonist.

I was trying to remember a line from Fitzgerald when Joe asked me a question. The debate had begun. I gave a feeble answer.

I had to concentrate, pull myself together.

Phone Woman said something about fishermen mentoring kids; how conscientious the fishing community was in Alaska to take such good care of the ocean. She equated subsistence fishing to commercial fishing; men feeding their families in the 1920s to men supplying restaurants in the 1990s.

Wait a minute. In commercial fishing there's no end to the hunger. . . . I needed to say that. I wanted to speak.

The slick lawyer rattled off a sound bite.

Phone Woman smiled.

Joe Moderator turned to me. "Kim, you once said that commercial fishing in Glacier Bay is nothing more than 'good gardening.' What's wrong with that?"

Uhhh . . . I hesitated. The chief ranger came to my rescue but was so long-winded that nobody understood what he said. Not even me, and I was on his side.

"Can I tell a story?" I asked.

Joe Moderator shook his head. Nope. No time for stories.

I fumbled through my final comments. The debate ended, and I headed for the door.

Outside, I held my face to the gray, misty sky and drank the rain.

TWO DAYS LATER, after taking an Alaska state ferry south to Ketchikan and another ferry west to Hollis, I rolled onto Prince of Wales Island and drove toward the town of Klawock. I must have been the only guy on the island driving a VW van with a Nature Conservancy sticker on the bumper. People flipped me off. Dogs barked. Even ratty old tomcats snarled at me. I pulled off the pavement and followed old logging roads up a mountainside, higher and higher until I was alone with the devastation, out of view from the main road and all those friendly islanders. I stopped and got out. No other people. No other vehicles. No living, breathing trees either. No deep-throated ravens or chattering winter wrens. No footfalls of deer or howls of wolves. The silence was too silent, like that of a neighborhood after a theft, with all the doors shut and curtains drawn. As far as I could see below me, a valley that had once cradled a lush temperate rainforest undisturbed for ten thousand years lay dead or dying, with every large tree gone.

It'll grow back, Lew Williams would say.

Only four percent of the Tongass timber is considered by foresters "high-volume old-growth." Half of that has been cut. To get it back (an old-growth temperate rainforest with its biological diversity and complexity) would take five hundred years or so. Never mind Descartes. My senses told me it was wrong. Nature is resilient, but that doesn't give us the right to test it. In his acclaimed book *The Island Within*, Sitka writer Richard Nelson said it was one thing to find a stump in a forest; it was another to find a forest of stumps.

How could men do this? A thousand years ago the Vikings had warriors called "berserkers" who swung their swords with such ferocity they couldn't stop; they didn't want to. Supercharged on killing, they went from village to village and valley to valley, destroying everything and everyone in their path. They were never arrested. In their culture, one thousand years ago, it wasn't a crime.

Standing above that violated valley, I felt people in the future looking back at us, measuring our humanity by what we regarded as atrocities, and what we did not.

I grabbed my camera and worked my way through the clearcut, navigating the destruction as I climbed over the broken limbs of smaller logs. I framed a splintered stump in the foreground with mountains in the distance.

"Background is important."

Farther along I found a lone scrawny tree still standing, its trunk battered where dozens of bigger cousins had been chained and dragged against it. Nailed to its skinny trunk was a piece of plywood with names and numbers written in black. Instructions of some sort. It wasn't a tree anymore. It was a signpost.

A wave of despair came over me. What was I doing?

I returned to the van and sat in the open door, acutely aware

that *this was not my place*. I had wanted one or two destruction photos in my Alaska coffee table book to balance the dozens of beautiful
shots. But how many trees would be required to make the first press
run of ten thousand books? The sour taste of hypocrisy climbed up my
throat. I was no different from the men who had killed these trees. I
belonged to the same country and culture. I spoke the same language.
I was them and they were me and we were all together.

I drank a beer and sang John Lennon and felt very alone.

Night came quickly and set down too hard for August. I ate a meager meal and wrote in my journal. I climbed into my sleeping bag in
the back of the van and fell asleep with the reading light on. In the
middle of the night I awoke with a jolt. Something outside was rum-
bling loudly and blasting my van with harsh white light. A truck.

I lay absolutely still. Had I locked the doors? Were the keys in
the ignition? The truck revved its engine and hit its high beams, then
inched forward and began to push. I felt the van move. *Shit.*

I was parked in a pullout over a clearcut, three feet from the edge
of a steep drop. My van would roll for certain, with me in it. Nobody
would find me for days, weeks. My heart pounded wildly as I tried to
decide what to do. . . .

Then suddenly the truck backed off, turned away, and sped
down the road out of sight. It was hours before I fell back asleep.

The next day I knew something was wrong. I couldn't say what,
but I knew it. I needed to get back home, back north to the glaciers.

I drove to Hollis and took the ferry to Ketchikan. Every face
around me seemed distant and strange, as if the world had changed
and would never be the same. The ferry docked after nightfall. I
found a phone on the outside wall of the ferry terminal and called
Melanie. She picked it up on the first ring.

"Hi, Sweetie," I said, "it's me."

"Oh Kim," she began to cry, "it's Michio. I'm so sorry. He's
gone, Kim. He was killed by a bear in Kamchatka."

That's when the earth opened up and I felt myself falling,
falling, falling into a blackness I'd never known before.

OLD-GROWTH GUITAR

Chapter Eleven

———

SEVEN DALL SHEEP RAMS waited in their early September dress, horns full and ready for the rut, eyes gleaming. They stood atop Primrose Ridge in Denali National Park and watched as I approached, occasionally grazing. Heads up, heads down, heads up. They'd seen me coming a long way off. Hardly a cunning wolf or a charging bear, I made no attempt to conceal myself. The closer I got the slower I moved until I was within a hundred yards. I stopped and put down my heavy pack, sat next to it, opened my water bottle and took a long drink. They came forward.

Seventy yards away, fifty . . . forty.

We faced each other in that open, borderless space between caution and curiosity. I felt as I always did in such company, transcendental, grateful, a little closer to Heaven. Inside my pack I had a camera and a long wildlife lens. But now, among these animals in their alpine tundra world, photography didn't interest me. I wanted somebody to talk to.

"Did you guys hear?" I said. "Michio's gone."

They took the news better than I had one month earlier.

The first few hours after Melanie told me, I couldn't remember a thing. I moved about not knowing what to do, too stunned to make

sense of the world. I stood hatless in the Ketchikan rain until it
soaked me. I forgot to eat. I bought a ferry ticket to Juneau, lost it,
and bought another. I boarded the ferry and went up to the solarium
(a large covered area on an upper aft deck) where I rolled out my
sleeping bag with a dozen other travelers. A young Asian man saw my
cameras and introduced himself. He said he was from Japan, a new
student at the University of Alaska in Juneau. He had come to
Alaska inspired by the work of a man I may know . . . Michio
Hoshino.

He said the name with such reverence. I thought, *Dear God*.

So I told him. I felt I needed to. I heard my own words tell him
Michio was gone. The young man trembled and fought back tears.
He tried to regain himself, and I told him he didn't need to. He must
have been only twenty or so, the same age as Michio when he first
came to Alaska and lived in the Eskimo village of Shishmaref.

"He was my hero too," I said as I put my arm around this young
man from Japan and tried to comfort him. Michio had been gone
only a few hours and already he had me building a bridge as only
he could do.

I put my van in storage in Juneau and flew home to Gustavus to
begin making preparations to attend Michio's memorial in Fairbanks.
My first night back with Melanie, we held each other for hours and
talked of our loss, of everyone's loss. Our phone rang constantly.
Dozens of e-mails poured in, including two from Richard filled with
sorrow. Rumors ran rampant about what had happened in
Kamchatka.

Near as I could tell, the circumstances of Michio's death went as
follows: Together with a five-man television crew from Tokyo he had
gone to the Kamchatka Peninsula, in the Russian Far East, to photograph brown bears feeding on salmon. The salmon were late, and
the bears, having no other secure source of food, moved about
unpredictably. One bear in particular seemed thin and roguish, and
reason for concern. Michio felt otherwise. He had once told a friend
in Fairbanks that he liked sleeping outside so he could "breathe with
the bears." For several nights he slept in his tent, preferring the

quiet and clean air. The television crew stayed in a small cabin nearby. They got up each morning hoping the salmon had arrived; that bears would be fishing in the river. The salmon finally did arrive, but one day too late. The night before, at about four in the morning, the men in the cabin awoke to the heart-sickening sounds of Michio screaming from his tent. By the time they organized them-selves and got outside, a bear had dragged him into the woods. Russian authorities arrived the next day. The rogue bear was tracked down and killed. Michio Hoshino, age forty-three, was dead.

Sherry Simpson, one of Alaska's finest writers, said in the *Anchorage Daily News* that it was "a betrayal and a benediction" that Michio should be killed by a bear. Celia Hunter, a former WWII pilot and the grand dame of environmental conservation in Alaska, wrote in the *Fairbanks Daily News-Miner* of Michio's "magical ambience." Barry Lopez, author of *Arctic Dreams*, would write a tribute in *Orion* magazine, saying, "Michio's awareness grew direct-ly out of his devotion to the integrity of the animal, the integrity of the place, and the integrity of that unique relationship. You can see in his work a clear regard for what is profound, not cute. . . . What he left us besides stunning images is a call to choose such integrity over material wealth, commercial success, personal image, and the other illusions that have become the stock-in-trade of advertisers and entertainers."

Nick Jans, author of *The Last Light Breaking* and other impor-tant books on Alaska, may have said it best when he wrote, "I for-give the bear that took Michio from us. He must not have known who Michio was."

In late August I flew back to Juneau, caught the ferry to Haines, and drove nine hundred miles from Haines to Denali to have time with my old friends (and Michio's): the Dall sheep of Primrose Ridge.

They stared at me as I gave them the news. I wondered then as I had before if we humans alone share the emotions of sorrow and joy.

Years ago, while hiking in Denali in early June, I had come upon a band of ewes and lambs. Young and frisky on their new, nimble legs, the lambs gamboled about as if gravity didn't apply to them. I

watched one lamb in hot pursuit of another take a shortcut by running right over the back of its mother as she rested on the tundra. A
deep gorge separated me from the sheep; they took little notice of
me. Then something caught my eye. One ewe was off by herself, bedded down at the edge of the gorge, not feeding, hardly moving. It
made no sense until I looked far below and saw at the bottom of a
cliff, deep in the gorge, the lifeless body of a little lamb. Her off-
spring. For two days she stayed right there, high above her lamb.
Holding out hope? A vigil? When I broke camp two days later and
left in a cold, hard rain, she was still there.

The image of her has never left me.

Of course the rams on Primrose Ridge said nothing back to me.
Michio gone? Did I expect a Disneyesque, cartoonish response? No.
I just wanted to know they were still on their mountain, and always
would be, eternal, enduring, unafraid of winter and the darkness.

The next day I drove to Fairbanks with two other photographers, Tom Walker and Dan Cox. Each had a wry, dry sense of
humor, but no one was feeling funny then. We talked about Michio
and what a privilege it had been to know him. He had asked a lot of
the angels over the years, and in the end he asked too much. We
managed a little laughter, the kind that quickly turns to tears.

Two or three hundred people filled Dog Musher's Hall in
Fairbanks on a beautiful September afternoon, faces from around the
world and every corner of Alaska. Michio's framed images graced the
peeled log walls. Celia Hunter welcomed everyone as she brushed
strands of white hair off her face. Kim and Roy Corral showed slides
of Michio's work, and of Michio himself out on the open tundra, asleep
next to his campfire, curled around the coals. Somebody sang a love
song. I sat in the back on a metal chair and felt like a wren with a thorn
in my chest. I didn't intend to say anything. But after Tom Walker
spoke with such sincerity, I walked forward, unprepared for the sea of
faces looking back at me, stoic, strained. Michio's mother and father
sat in the front row, together with Naoko and little Shoma in her arms,
almost two, squiggling, unaware of the depth of his loss and just as well.

Tears filled Naoko's eyes like two dark lakes. Yet no tear spilled down her face. Seated behind Michio's mother and father, a young Japanese man was ready to translate my words quietly into their ears. I froze.

Celia Hunter looked at me as if to say, *You can do this, Kim.*

"Michio," I said, "you always wanted a family. If only you could be here now to see what a very large family you have."

The service ended. I stayed seated in the back reading the small foldout program, *In Celebration of the Life of Michio Hoshino.* Inside was a quote from his *Grizzly Bear Family Book*: "If there wasn't a single bear in all of Alaska, I could hike through the mountains with complete peace of mind. I could camp without worry. But what a dull place Alaska would be! Here people share the land with bears. There is a certain wariness between people and bears. And that wariness forces upon us a valuable sense of humility. People continue to tame and subjugate nature. But when we visit the few remaining scraps of wilderness where bears roam free, we can still feel an instinctive fear. How precious that feeling is. And how precious these places, and these bears, are."

THAT SAME DAY in Bartlett Cove, Melanie sat at her desk thinking about Michio. Hank drove out from Gustavus to comfort her. He walked into her office with two Mason jars stuffed with poppies, her favorite flower.

He said, "I'm taking you home."

They drove to his home on the edge of a meadow, near a singing stream, and played cribbage deep into the night. Melanie knew better than to challenge him at poker. He had a way of making up the rules after he got the cards in his hand. She told him stories about Michio as he made dinner. It was time to "eat the country," he said—venison from Lemesurier Island, potatoes and carrots from his garden, nagoonberry pie from Anya's busy fingers. Word around town was that nobody picked berries like Anya, or made better pies. The wood-burning stove warmed the small space to a toasty glow. Four candles provided just enough light.

Hank no longer worked for the National Park Service. His days as an "expert" were behind him. At thirty, he had finished building his and Anya's home, paid off their land (while Anya finished medical school), and resigned without fanfare from the stress and largess of the federal government. He said he'd get by as a carpenter, grow his own vegetables, shoot his own meat. His point was this: Do you work a job that slowly kills you so you can afford health coverage to pay medical expenses? Or do you live right with the earth and make your own way, keep things simple, and take care of yourself?

He asked Melanie, "How many migraines do you have to have before you make a change?"

She shook her head. She didn't know.

Does anybody?

Altruism is a dangerous thing in a bureaucracy. It eats you up. Melanie would pour her heart into the good people around her as if pouring light into a hole. She listened to division chiefs squabble over money until they asked, "Why are we so divided?" *Division chiefs. Divided.* Did it ever occur to them? Language does more than describe; it directs.

First in the office each morning and often last out each night, she would clean the top of her desk only to see it disappear again. She joked that she had no voltage regulator. At the end of the day she had no battery either. She was exhausted. She had wanted to be a park ranger since she was seven. It was more than a career to her. It was a cause. But here she was multi-tasking through budgets, payrolls, schedules, evaluations, a sea of details. John Muir came to mind, his "seven lost years" picking fruit on his father-in-law's California farm and pretending to be somebody he wasn't until his hands became too rounded and soft. So he sailed for Alaska. Logistics, statistics, policies, politics . . . these were the fruits of Melanie's labor. Her near-life experience. She too needed to sail away.

She had resigned from the NPS once before, in Denali, shortly after receiving a manuscript one day from a guidebook company asking her to edit a section called, "Denali in a Day."

She phoned the publisher and said, "It's a six-million-acre wilderness park. It can't be done in a day."

"We have that section in all our books," the publisher said.

Everywhere in a day?

"You could maybe do Denali in a decade," Melanie said, "but not in a day."

Her supervisor told her to stop making trouble.

She didn't resign so much as she took a leave of absence. I called it a leave of presence. After working a few years as a freelance naturalist and traveling to Antarctica to see what Alaska might have looked like twenty thousand years ago (ice everywhere), she was back in the green and gray in Glacier Bay, once again thinking of resigning.

We talked about building our own home someday, and no longer paying rent; of finding the perfect piece of land where a house might fit on the edge of a forest; and of Melanie working part-time, as needed.

THE SPRING AFTER MICHIO DIED, my Alaska coffee table book came out. Big and glossy, it was more coffee table than book. The publisher refused to use any Prince of Wales Island logging photos.

"But they show what's really happening to Alaska," I said.

"This needs to be a celebration book."

"Just one logging shot?"

In the end he used none. He did, however, let me dedicate the book as I wanted: "To John Muir, who prized trees more than timber, glaciers more than gold, dippers more than dollars."

The publisher made arrangements for me to sail on a twelve-day round-trip cruise from San Francisco to Alaska's Inside Passage (and Glacier Bay) so I could give slide shows and sign copies of the book for passengers. He told me to send a résumé to the ship's cruise director. I didn't have one, so I made one up (with help from Hank). Under *Personal* I wrote "born naked and with no teeth," then deleted it (which I still regret). Under *Employment*, at the very top, I wrote "conservationist," given my exalted position as president of Friends of Glacier Bay.

I mailed it off, grabbed my cameras, and flew to the Arctic National Wildlife Refuge, hoping that in some meager way I could parallel Michio's work. Bill Clinton was president, but the Republicans controlled Congress. It was 1997 and the great oil debate was heating up (like the planet): to drill or not to drill for precious black crude in the middle of the caribou calving grounds. One side called the refuge "an American Serengeti"; the other side, with Alaska's Senator Ted Stevens, Senator Frank Murkowski, and Representative Don Young leading the charge, wasn't so complimentary. They called it many things. One oil executive labeled it "a flat, crummy place." It seemed to me that every honest photograph could make a difference. Camped on the Kongakut River, I awoke one morning to the sound of hooves like castanets on the river bar. I ran to the top of a bluff and for the next fourteen hours watched one hundred thousand caribou braid over the tundra and swim the river ". . . like a procession from a Kipling fantasy," I wrote in my journal. Two days later I flew to Arctic Village, then Fairbanks and Juneau. I dropped my cameras and camping gear at Richard and Luann's home, grabbed a suitcase and flew to Seattle, then to San Francisco where I boarded the ship. Caribou still thundered through my head.

It wasn't *Planet Princess*, but it had many of the same features—keel, hull, bridge, pool, spas, lounges, restaurants, casino, movie theater, ubiquitous waiters, invisible room stewards, standard cruise ship stuff. A note on embossed letterhead welcomed me aboard and asked for my "presence" in the lounge at 8:20 P.M. where the cruise director, Paul, would get to know me (in person) before introducing me (and the rest of the ship's staff) to the passengers. I showered and even combed my hair, and was in the first row of the lounge, stage left, at 8:20. Paul didn't show. The lounge filled with hundreds of people. At 8:30 the lights went down as a deep, resonant voice filled the room and announced our "grand voyage to the last frontier." Lavender light hit the stage and a dance troupe yippee-yehaawed through a cowboy number. Then a singer, a Vegas-style, honey-voiced guy fresh from filming *Braveheart* with

Mel Gibson (so he said), came on stage and crooned, "Hey, did you happen to see the most beautiful girl in the world?"

Then Paul himself hit the stage. "Wow, everybody!" he boomed over the microphone, "We're going to Alaska."

The crowd went wild, cheering, clapping.

Paul introduced the staff, including the "official wine tasters" from the Reagan White House, the art auctioneer from Spain, the dance instructors from . . . I can't remember where, a husband-and-wife team that did a combo mambo, tango, cha-cha, salsa, oh-la-la. Big applause. "Now for our ambassador hosts, come on up, fellows." Four white-haired men walked on stage to shake hands and yuck it up with Paul. These were the guys who would dance with the older single women passengers. Finally, Paul said it was time for our "enrichment lecturers."

Enrichment lecturers? Am I one of them? I began to sweat. Had this Paul guy read my résumé? Did he know what a conservationist was? I closed my eyes and saw caribou in the Arctic, the young calves bounding like springbok over the tundra, the Africa of America.

Did you really think it would stay the way it was?

I thought it might.

Paul introduced a retired geologist from the California Academy of Sciences.

"Tell me, Neil," he asked, "is it true that geologists have their faults?"

Neil laughed. "It sure is, Paul."

Ha, ha, ha, ho, ho, ho . . .

"Now, ladies and gentlemen," Paul said, "it is my honor to introduce to you a young man I've not yet had the pleasure to meet. He lives on an iceberg in Glacier Bay. Please join me in welcoming our very own . . . Jim Peacock, conversationalist."

I crossed the stage in rich lavender light that made my head spin. *Conversationalist? Somebody, help me* . . . Paul stood there, that same light gleaming off his ten-acre forehead, a big smile on his face.

"Welcome aboard, Jim. It's great to have you here."

"Thanks, Paul."

"You're a real Alaskan, is that right?"

"I was born in Idaho and raised in Spokane. I moved to Alaska about twenty years ago."

"Yes, well, tell us a story from Alaska, Jim." He handed me the microphone.

"Uhhh . . . well, I just spent ten days in the Arctic photographing caribou."

Paul grabbed the microphone back. "Wow, Jim. Tell us more."

"Yes . . . well, they crossed the tundra as I imagine they have for ten thousand years or more. The calves were only three weeks old, but they ran like the wind and swam the swift river and bounded up the bank right past me. One hundred thousand caribou. It was incredible."

Paul grabbed the microphone and said breathlessly, "Ladies and gentlemen . . . my goodness. Did you hear that? How would you like to have to clean up after all those caribou?"

Ha, ha, ha, ho, ho, ho . . .

"Great to have you on board, Jim." Paul motioned me off stage and did the same thing two hours later for the second wave of passengers at 10:30 P.M. He introduced the staff with canned jokes, including Jim Peacock, conversationalist. In fact, he called me Jim the entire first half of the cruise until somebody corrected him. Then he called me Kim. "Unusual name for a man," he said.

People lined up to buy my book and have me sign it. I was almost famous. A man wearing a silver bolo tie approached me with the kind of swagger that made me think he came from Texas, where real presidents come from. Could be Mr. Extraction, Mr. EXXON, Mr. Gonna-Set-This-Radical-Straight-on-the-Arctic-Refuge-Debate. He had the book opened to the dedication page.

"I just read this thing here for John Muir," he said, "and I got one question for you."

"Okay."

"What the hell is a dipper?"

"It's a small bird, also called a water ouzel. It was John Muir's favorite bird. It feeds along streams and . . ."

"Oh . . . ," he said excitedly, "I've heard of it. It flies underwater and catches aquatic insects."

"That's right."

"Damnation. That was John Muir's favorite bird?"

"Yes, sir, it sure was."

"Well, don't that beat all."

"Yes, sir, it sure does."

He rocked back on the heels of his kick-ass cowboy boots and said, "Say, do you know that story about John Muir and the little dog?"

"Stickeen?"

"That's right, Stickeen." His eyes glowed. "I heard it years ago and never forgot it. It'd sure be dandy some night during this cruise if you could tell it, you know, as a reading?"

"You bet."

He shook my hand. Nearly crushed it.

"Where you from?" I asked.

"Houston," he said with a big smile. "Houston, Texas."

"I think I've heard of it. Nice place, right?"

"The best."

THE STICKEEN STORY attracted three hundred passengers who sat stone still while I read every word. Outside, the faint ringing of casino slots leaked down the long passageway but seemed to distract no one. When I reached the part where Muir says to Stickeen, "C'mon, little fellow, no right way is easy in this rough world. We must risk our lives in order to save them. . . ." you could have heard snow falling on water. I finished and the audience sat motionless, then burst into applause. People surrounded me afterward to hear more about Muir and the little terrier. I was stunned, and I thought, *Dear God, these people are hungry for stories, for authenticity, for something arduous and real, anything but Fox Television.*

A woman asked me if John Muir was my hero.

"My hero? I suppose he is, in a way. . . . Have you ever heard of Michio Hoshino?"

She had not. Nobody on that ship had.

What was it Fitzgerald said? "Show me a hero and I will write you a tragedy."

The Japanese have no word for wilderness. Places close to it are considered "unkempt." Other places are called "nature," the ones manicured by monks who trim trees and rake stones into garden-like islands surrounded by urban sprawl. Young men by the millions throw coins into Shinto temples and pray for jobs. I dreamed about Michio standing there. He pulls out a coin and when nobody is looking, he walks away and keeps walking until he reaches Alaska.

I can't explain it. Dreams have no logic.

It isn't easy to be different. It isn't easy (at first) to find comfort in the silence, the big nothing that says so much. It's easy to rev up the machine. Climb aboard, join the race. Tune into millionaire players who perform for billionaire owners. Gold coins speckling, spoiling the bed.

Nature and technology have an uneasy relationship, yet each has something to offer. One is where we came from, the other is where we're going. One shrinks as the other grows. One loses in a war, the other wins and determines winners. One makes you feel vulnerable, a subject of the Earth, the other makes you feel powerful, a lord of the Earth. One is Christ in the desert finding clarity, the other is Christmas at Macy's buying Calvin Klein. One explains death and disease while the other attempts to eradicate them. One is accepting what comes your way, the other is hacking DNA. One teaches grace, the other breeds pride. One is about slowing ourselves down, the other is about making things fast. One is words, the other word processing. One is stories, the other statistics.

Wilderness is on the map, but wildness resides in that most wondrous and mysterious chamber, the human heart. You can't measure it any more than you can measure the music of a mountain stream, or the thunder of running caribou.

Toward the end of the cruise I had dinner with an elderly couple who had attended my Stickeen talk. Married for sixty years, they had five grown children, seventeen grandchildren, a summer home in Connecticut, and a winter home in Florida.

The woman said, "Every time we go down to Florida there's more construction and development. It's hard to watch."

"Can you imagine what Florida will look like in another hundred years?" I said casually.

She pulled back. "I can't think about that."

Not until I returned to my spacious stateroom to find a mint on my pillow and the bed turned back (by the invisible room steward) did I consider her comment. Of course she couldn't think about it. If she did . . . if she took to heart every Orwellian, apocalyptic aspect of endless growth on a finite planet, it would turn her world upside down. No, it was easier to slide along and go about one's business knowing things aren't right but that somebody someday will address the problem.

Or maybe things *are* right. Maybe there is no problem. Who said ceaseless growth will one day bring us to a point where we lose more than we gain? All this doomsday stuff is hogwash, an empty cake cooked up by academics and the liberal press. Maybe we were put on this Earth not to use it, but to use it up. Saddle up, boys. Freedom is back. Time to harness and harvest everything, and put America back to work with a million invisible hands lopping off the peaks and valleys of biodiversity.

Some people can do that. I'm not one of them. Dr. Folsom taught me to see the world differently.

One of the costs of having an ecological education, said Aldo Leopold (another pesky academic), is that you live in a world of wounds.

When alone, I thought of Michio. His life and death created many eulogies, and to a degree I joined them. But part of me didn't want him to be my hero. It's a heavy weight. Heroes are made to be broken. He spilled his coffee and sang off-key. He was just a friend, a rare and beautiful friend who slept on the ground and happened to be a brilliant photographer.

It was becoming increasingly clear to me that my dearest friends—Richard, Michio, Melanie, and Hank—all slept on the ground. They slowed down. They listened, and took risks, and won my deep respect. They never really went after the money. It's easy in Alaska to get a state or federal government job and be secure and never accomplish a single daring thing the rest of your life. None of them did it. They moved through their days on the edges of things, taking care of loved ones but dedicated to something larger as well. They belonged to a small but growing corps of Alaskans who understood Aldo Leopold and felt the wounds we inflicted on nature. The Earth, too, was a loved one, and their expression of that love sometimes had them saying daring, unpopular things. They carried the burden of a crisis others refused to recognize, yet they never lost their senses of humor. It was easier to laugh than to cry.

On first meeting Richard and Hank this might not seem apparent. There's Richard careening down the halls of the Juneau middle school where he teaches, daypack filled with books over his shoulder, walking that glacier walk, working with students, coaching track, nurturing his own kids but never boasting about them. Late at night he writes an op-ed on the Arctic Refuge that gets scathing rebuttals. The truth is subversive, he tells me. Write to the center of what you believe, dare to be different.

"The most important writing has always been revolutionary."

Richard's op-ed elicited a response from none other than Lew Williams, Mr. Pro-Growth. What did Richard do? He phoned the guy and invited him to lunch.

"What was that like?" I asked.

"He's a nice man," Richard told me. "It's hard to demonize people once you get to know them."

Then there's Hank, barefoot in the woodpile, axe in one hand and phone in the other as he works to establish a land legacy that will keep one-fourth of Gustavus open and undeveloped *forever*. An hour later he's on the phone again, working to set up a local hospice program.

When Hank and Anya got married in an outdoor ceremony at Eagle Beach, north of Juneau, I wrote a song called "Two Healers," and played it for them on my new Martin D-28, a gift from Melanie. Anya was working as a family physician in a medical clinic in Juneau. Hank split his time between Gustavus and Juneau and healed by caring. While many people become islands as they age, isolating themselves for one reason or another, I could see Hank becoming just the opposite. An ocean. In ways uniquely his own he would touch the shores of everyone around him.

About this time Bob Howe, the former superintendent of Glacier Bay, lost his wife, Doris, after more than fifty years of marriage. They lived summers in Gustavus and winters in the San Juan Islands of Washington State. When Doris's health failed, she asked to come home to die. Gustavus welcomed her. Townsfolk visited day and night while she grew weak. They read to her and held her hand. When she finally slipped away, everyone gathered for a large dinner and farewell. A week afterward, I saw Bob at the Beartrack Mercantile and asked how he was doing.

"I'm okay," he said (loudly, so he could hear himself through his hearing aids). "You know, I moved up here because of the country, the place, the wildness and all that. There's nothing like wild Alaska. But after all my years here making friends, I realize now that it's not the place that makes this place, it's the people that make this place."

I told him about a woman in Juneau who described Gustavus as flat and boring. The mountains were too far away. She said, "There's no there there."

"Maybe so," Bob said with a smile, "but there's plenty of here here."

A YEAR LATER I was riding my bicycle from Gustavus to Bartlett Cove when I met Dan Thorington riding the other way. We stopped and talked as people in a small town do. A quiet man with kind eyes and an easy manner, Dan rode his bike everywhere to avoid driving a car and burning fuel. He put Wesson Oil in his chain saw to lubricate the bar while cutting brush around his home. Less toxic that way, he said. He mentioned a piece of land near his own, kitty-corner and behind, eight acres owned by a man from Japan.

"Could it be that photographer friend of yours?" he asked.

I didn't know. I had forgotten that Michio had land in Gustavus.

That night I phoned Karen Colligan-Taylor in Fairbanks. Yes, she said, the land was Michio's. She had introduced it to him and Naoko the year before, excited that Michio would be her neighbor in Gustavus and Fairbanks. The next day I walked the land with Melanie. What magic it had. What mystery. On still nights we could stand in the hushed forest and hear humpback whales blow in Icy Strait, three miles away. A moose had died along the east boundary. Wolves and ravens fed on the carcass. Paul Barnes, a neighbor, showed me where the wolves bedded down some nights, under dead-fall along the river. Towering Sitka spruce and western hemlock dominated the west side of the land; an open forest of cottonwood, spruce, and shore pine ran to the east. Greg Streveler (we called him Grigori, as he loved to speak Russian) found two mountain hemlocks on the property. Anya found a circle of cottonwoods and said, "This would make a nice house site." Hank had a hop in his step just thinking we might get the land, only a ten-minute walk from his and Anya's place.

I phoned Karen again, for advice.

"Call Naoko and express your interest," she said. "The house in Fairbanks represents her union with Michio and Alaska, the first home of her son. But the land in Gustavus isn't part of their lives yet. I think she would be happy for you to have it. She'll probably also want to consult with Michio's parents."

I called Naoko in Tokyo. I loved hearing her birdlike voice over the phone. She told me all about Shoma, what a little tiger he was, what a joy. I asked her about the land; might she one day sell it? She said she needed to think about it. A week later she called back and said she'd love for us to have it. We agreed on a price and made arrangements.

It took me a year to map a road route to the house site, fitting it with gentle curves that avoided swales and big trees. Rivers don't run straight; neither should roads. I wanted every bend to unveil new visual treasures. I wanted everything as Michio would have wanted it. But he was gone; his ghost had little to say.

A raven landed in a nearby snag and watched.

Melanie took a leave of presence from the National Park Service to be the general contractor. I called her "the general." She bought a pair of Carhartts, a tape measure, and a tool belt. She ordered lumber, hired a crew, and learned the difference between an excavator, a backhoe, and a front-end loader.

"Those big, yellow machines," she called them.

It wasn't easy to watch them tear trees out of the ground.

"You have to break an egg to make an omelet," Hank told her.

"I don't eat omelets," Melanie said.

"You do now."

An architect friend in Juneau helped us design the house. We wanted something cozy for two but comfortable for twelve. We talked about a home that could be an institute someday, a learning center, a place to honor Michio and Glacier Bay, where concerned hearts could gather to talk about the future of wilderness, wildness, endangered places and spaces.

Melanie called it a "Camp David for conservation in Alaska" until she found out that at the real Camp David, people come and go by helicopter, and security guys are in the woods with machine guns.

We had a great construction crew. They got popcorn at break time on cloudy days, popsicles on sunny days. Every other Wednesday was payday and hot lunch (spicy enchiladas). I got bursitis in both elbows from sanding beams. When the second story went up our hearts sank. The house seemed too big and presumptuous. But the cascading roof and covered decks helped to bring it down.

As Mary Oliver once asked, "Do you think the wren ever dreams of a better house?"

During a visit to Gustavus, our friend Richard Nelson, himself a writer and occupier of small spaces (we called him Nels), saw a huge three-story house thrown up in a slash-and-burn clearing and said, "Look at that. Frank Lloyd Wrong."

With the road and house complete, the land lost some mystery but gained familiarity. We learned each tree by its traits and expressions. To let in the light I cut some down. One in particular, a large spruce, was over one hundred years old. I counted the rings in the fresh stump and dated it back to 1890, the year John Muir built his cabin at Muir Point and met Harry Fielding Reid. Grigori pushed the date back ten more years, saying that's how long it would have taken the seedling to reach the height of the stump. That brought us to 1880, the year Muir and Stickeen had their big adventure crossing the crevasse.

In 1880 Gustavus wasn't Gustavus. Except for a few Tlingits fishing in the Salmon River, Gustavus was a townless, treeless, silt-filled glacial outwash plain patterned by dryas and alder. Any spruce seed that succeeded in taking root back then in such a young, harsh place was one in a million, one in ten million. All others failed. Yet this one survived. It prospered. It grew through a hundred winters and a hundred summers, through earthquakes and storms that made it stronger. It added nutrients to the soil and provided protection for younger trees around it. It sired a forest of its own. Then one day a guy with a chain saw cut it down because it made too much shade. Who appointed me executioner? As I sat there thinking about the killing and subjugation of living beings—how the Roman Republic was fed by citizen farmers, but the Roman Empire was fed by slaves—I recalled Thomas Jefferson's own reflection on slavery. Himself a slave-owner, he said it was "like holding a wolf by the ears."

When Meriwether Lewis reported back to him on his and William Clark's remarkable journey up the Missouri River, over the Bitterroot Mountains to the Pacific and back; about the Shoshone, Nez Perce, Blackfeet, Mandans, and Teton Sioux, most of them friendly, a few not, Jefferson was astounded. Historians like to speculate that the two men got on their hands and knees in the Oval Office to look at Clark's map (drawn by dead reckoning, the total miles were off by less than one percent). Such a vast and rugged continent. Jefferson said it would take one hundred generations for Americans to populate it. It took five. Forever restless, often creative, sometimes indulgent, the westward-moving people of a young nation hit the Pacific Ocean and headed north.

"Born often under another sky, placed in the middle of an always moving scene, himself driven by the irresistible torrent which draws about him, the American," wrote Alexis de Tocqueville five years after Jefferson's death, "has no time to tie himself to anything, he grows accustomed only to change, and ends by regarding it as the natural state of man."

A Frenchman, de Tocqueville knew Frederick Chopin and Louis Agassiz. While he irritated some Americans (as only the French can), I found myself drawn to him. I imagined sitting in the fourth grade in France, sneaking sips of wine, distracted by a nature mural filled with the names the French have given us: *glacier, arête, col, serac, moulin, crevasse.* The French don't know everything. Nobody does. But back then they knew rivers of ice better than anybody else.

HANK FOUND ME leaning against the stump, playing my Martin, picking the melody of "While My Guitar Gently Weeps," the descending bass in A minor, the refrain in A major. George Harrison, what a guy. With every mistake could we truly be learning?

Hank nodded that wise nod of his. He preferred Greg Brown.

In his low voice he sang, "It's a messed-up world, but I love it anyway."

I told him the age of the tree and he said, "You can't have intense joy without deep pain."

"Why not?"

"I don't know. That's just the way it is. I don't make the rules."

"You don't follow them either."

"Not if I don't have to."

He studied the guitar, the tight-grained Sitka spruce and Indian rosewood, the perfectly fretted neck, the shiny pegs. He strummed it and hummed.

I said, "This is the land where Michio said all his dreams would come true."

"And they will," Hank said. "Make them your dreams. That's what he would want."

Sometimes it paralyzed me. But Hank was right. I had a chance like no other to honor Michio. He could live on his land through Melanie and me and our intentions. It was a huge gift.

"You need to write about this," Hank said as he patted the stump and looked at the house.

"I know. I think I'll make it a chapter in a book."

"About accountability and finding hope," he said. "Call it 'My Old-Growth Guitar.'"

SNOW

Chapter Twelve

———

TO LIVE in Southeast Alaska is to have a relationship with islands.

"Kim," Michio once asked me, "how many islands are there in Alaska?" He had a large map opened across his lap, its corners stained with brown coffee cup rings.

"I don't know Michio. A lot."

"Just the right number, I think," he said.

It hit me then that the distance between any two islands is as important as the size and shape of the islands themselves. The map calls them archipelagos; Michio called them "families." It was his way of securing the relationships between things. Islands near one another may be separated by high tide but joined at low tide, their shores reaching out to one another. Yet even when the water is high they still touch. We all do at some depth. Go deep enough, we all touch.

Richard's island was Admiralty, so named by Captain George Vancouver of His Majesty's Royal Navy when he poked around Alaska in the 1790s. The Tlingit called it *Kootznoowoo*, "Fortress of the Bears." At seventeen hundred square miles the island has roughly seventeen hundred brown bears, one per square mile, give or take a few. Richard went there every November. Not for the bears, though he liked the idea of being in their neighborhood. He went to hunt deer.

Hank's island was Lemesurier, where he also hunted deer. More than that, though, it was the wildness, the quiet, the hours of soft walking and solitary sitting that attracted him. Both men might see a deer and not shoot. To watch an animal so exquisitely fitted in its world was better than any ballet, they said. And eating venison? It was like eating wisdom and grace. When Hank returned from Lem (short for Lemesurier), Melanie would say he had "clear eyes." The wildness had healed him.

My island, and Melanie's too, is a family called the Beardslees, immediately north of Bartlett Cove. The Pleiades of Glacier Bay, they lie clustered like the seven daughters of Atlas metamorphosed into stars. The Beardslees number more than seven. If any mythology applies to them it is Tlingit, not Greek. Yet the comparison works, I believe. There is no other family like them in Glacier Bay, or in all of Southeast Alaska. The Arabs used the Pleiades to test their vision, looking skyward on clear desert nights to see if they could pick out seven distinct stars.

The Beardslees test our vision, Melanie's and mine. We look for sign of coyotes and moose, river otters and black bears. We read the tides and listen for eagles, kingfishers, and wrens. Without a map on foggy days, it's easy to get lost in the maze of sinuous shores. Once in Europe, I met an old man who told me to go to Venice and spend all night walking the streets without a map.

"Go there and get lost," he said. "It's a beautiful city for that. Sometimes getting lost is the best way to find yourself."

That's how it is in the Beardslees. Easy to get lost.

The largest member of the Beardslee family, Lester Island, lies south of its relatives and faces Bartlett Cove and Glacier Bay Lodge, while Lagoon Island, a smaller cousin, separates the cove from the inner lagoon, home to park headquarters. A perfect crown of spruce and hemlock gives Lagoon Island a nice symmetry. Blue herons feed along the shore, tall and patient. Crows pick up clams, hover high, and drop them on rocks to crack them open. Whimbrels stop by in May, northbound to the Arctic. Moose and bears leave veins of tracks in the soft sand and intertidal mud. Harbor seals glide by just off shore. It's an easy island to look at.

SO I DID. I sat in the superintendent's office and looked out the window at Lagoon Island while he, the superintendent, talked and talked. Hank sat next to me. The chief of resource management sat to his other side. Nobody else. Just the four of us, a summit of sorts. Hank represented his lone wolf self. I represented Friends of Glacier Bay, though just then I couldn't remember why I was there. Since Michio's death my mind worked in a fog, stumbling from one distraction to the next, always hungry for the moment of interruption.

The superintendent was saying something about the new paved road from Gustavus to Bartlett Cove, what an improvement it will be. And the new dock, bigger yes, but stronger and more environmentally sound. The new Native cultural center, the new visitor center, the new employee housing, and all the new signs and exhibits. So many improvements. So many accomplishments. After decades of neglect, progress was finally coming to Glacier Bay National Park.

Hank nudged me. I sat up straight and folded my hands in my lap. My eyes floated across the wall to another distraction. I couldn't believe it. I got up. In the middle of the superintendent's speech I stood up (as if under a spell) and walked to the wall. Hanging there for everybody to see, matted and framed, was a certificate written in bold print: FLEW IN AIR FORCE ONE.

The superintendent had stopped talking.

I turned to him and said, "You flew in Air Force One?"

"Yes, years ago."

"What was that like?"

"Very comfortable. You wouldn't even know you're on a plane. The president was on board and . . ."

"The real president? The one from Arkansas?"

Near the certificate was a handsome plaque, the Harry Yount Award, given once a year to an employee of the National Park Service voted by his (or her) peers as ranger of the year. Harry Yount had been a wrangler and packer in the famous Hayden Expedition to Yellowstone, and later became the park's first "gamekeeper," posted there all by himself to stem a tide of illegal poaching by market hunters. He would go into the mountains for weeks at a time and live by his wits.

The superintendent talked about Air Force One and all the important people he knew. I asked about the Harry Yount Award. "Oh yes," he said . . .

He had won it for reasons too many to list, but mostly for his work in recent years (in Washington, D.C.) to raise the pay of all NPS employees to a professional scale. I wondered what old Harry would think about people in the NPS today making more money in a day or two than he did in a year.

Hank was trying to get the superintendent's attention; trying to get him to protect the wildest coast in Glacier Bay as a "commercial-free zone." Don't let people go there to run businesses and make money. They'll ruin it. Keep it inconvenient. Let people get there on their own, as travelers not tourists, one or two at a time to experience the "transitory enchanted moment" of Fitzgerald's dreams, the last vanishing of America, John Muir's "morning of creation." Let them stand barefoot in the surf, toes deep in the sand, unbothered by any construct of the modern world. Hank didn't say this, but he implied it. He wanted bears to live their entire lives on that coast and never see a single human being. I watched him fidget in his chair.

"I'll get there one day," our friend Nels had said about that coast, "and it won't be easy. I won't want it to be."

Make access easy, and a place dies. The National Park Service in its own environmental impact statements describes the "continuing demand for access" in Alaska. It never ends. Access becomes excess.

Hank fidgeted again. It was a difficult time for a dreamer.

My attention drifted back out the window, beyond the western end of Lagoon Island to Bartlett Cove, where I saw the blow of a humpback whale. The thin, vertical spout caught sunlight in a way that would have excited Michio.

Another blow. Was it another whale? I couldn't tell at that distance. Some years in Bartlett Cove forage fish (herring, sand lance, capelin) are so abundant that the humpbacks stay there all summer, regardless of heavy boat traffic. Killer whales come through as well, off Lester Point, up Sitakaday Narrows, hunting, always hunting. Like many toothed whales, they use sonar to determine the location, size, speed, and direction of travel of other whales (and boats), and may in fact bounce sonar off the internal organs of other whales to determine their disposition, just as we read one another from body postures and facial expressions without saying a word.

Speaking of expressions, if I read him correctly the superintendent wore a satisfied one just then. *Consumer Reports*, the magazine that ranks everything from electric toasters to riding lawn mowers, had just ranked national parks, and by a poll of its readers had listed Glacier Bay "Number One." This was wonderful, he said.

Hank's heart was breaking. I knew him well enough to feel it myself. Yet he didn't give up. Slowly, patiently, as artfully as Michio would approach Dall sheep, he worked the gulf between himself and the superintendent, drawing two islands together, knowing at some depth they would touch.

I became distracted again, my mind thinking other things. When I returned I was astounded to hear the superintendent talking about his childhood, how as a kid he loved all the little wild places on the edge of where he grew up.

"Are they still there?" Hank asked him. "All those little wild places?"

"Nope," the superintendent said, "they're gone, every one of them."

He spoke differently now, his voice softened with reminiscence. I watched him drift back to his youth, when America was younger and wilder too, better somehow. He came from the same place many of us did, a place of loss that couldn't stay the way it was when too many people did to the land what they said they had a right to do. They changed it, tamed it, enslaved it, and in so doing they enslaved themselves. They called it progress and said it was their right. Never mind the children not yet born who would prefer a meadow to a mall. In this new feudalism they would have to make their selections from a glossy, mass-produced menu sanitized for their own protection. They would never know what they didn't know.

"Will there come a time," Hank asked, "when people in America defend their liberties without denying them to others?"

A light came on in the superintendent's eyes. Hank was doing for him what Dr. Folsom had done for me. He was making him *see*.

I felt a bubble of hope. Was that the greatest risk? The journey deep into ourselves? The going in that brings us out?

Years ago on my college field trip, when the Montana ranch woman told Dr. Folsom that God made those landforms, and Folsom said, "Of course He did, but how'd He do it?", the good professor turned a moment of potential conflict into one of mutual curiosity. He could have corrected her, but he complimented her instead. She became his newest student, an enthusiastic one at that, and we gathered in her kitchen for muffins and milk. The best thing Dr. Folsom taught me (though I didn't realize it at the time) was not how to see nature, but how to get along with people who see it differently. It's better to touch a heart than it is to teach a fact.

Risk is reaching out. It's being bigger than your pride. It's John Lennon watching fifteen-year-old Paul McCartney singing and playing guitar, and thinking, *He's good. He may challenge my leadership one day, but I think I need him.* It's a fourth grade teacher catching a student who's distracted by a nature mural, and rather than scold him she tells him she put the mural there for him, and for others like him; it's okay to be distracted by nature, even an artist's rendering of nature. It's Michio breathing with wild bears, giving his life to them. It's Richard calling up Lew Williams and asking him out to lunch. It's Hank sitting in an office, unpaid, and getting the superintendent to say we have to save the wildest coast in North America. It's Melanie loving a man who thinks he can make a living as a writer and photographer, knowing he'll never take photos like Michio Hoshino, or write like F. Scott Fitzgerald.

"Live your dream," she told me. "Take the risk."

I remembered Josie from *Planet Princess*, the old woman who'd been a nurse in France during WWII, and later worked in Africa to restore elephant habitat. She would quote First Lady Eleanor Roosevelt: "Do one thing every day that scares you."

YOU HEAR a lot these days about risk analysis, cost-benefit analysis, the bottom line. In a world of regulatory affairs and environmental law, everything becomes a commodity, even human life. How then do we price the priceless?

I could have said no to Richard when he invited me to go kayaking with him all those years ago. He frightened me a bit with that goofy grin, saying, "I may not know karate, but I know craaaa-zy."

Had I come to Alaska in search of guarantees?

I don't think so.

Security can be anesthetizing. Some people pursue it their entire lives and seem dead on their feet. "The Perils of Safety," Hank called it. Obsessed with comfort, we even pad our coffins. I went kayaking with Richard partly because I was young and naïve and downright stupid, and because I sensed within him something different, illuminating, profound. Raised in Ohio and Indiana, he'd been missing glaciers his whole life, Indians too. He knew his history. He loved literature. He made me laugh. We did everything wrong on that trip, and everything right.

It changed my life.

Now it was Hank's turn to change a life, or at least try.

A popular Juneau photographer, Mark Kelley, was working on a book on Glacier Bay that Sherry Simpson had agreed to write. What pages she didn't fill with words Mark would fill with his beautiful photos. He planned to hike the wildest coast—the one dear to Hank—and include it as a chapter in the book. He met Hank and invited him along, though Hank may have invited himself for the single purpose of convincing Mark to drop the chapter and keep the coast a mystery. Sherry signed on for the hike as well, unaware that it would be one of the most frightening and rewarding adventures of her life. Richard took the final slot, since he and Mark were friends. Like Hank, he knew the coast and was a strong hiker.

I bade them farewell as they boarded a floatplane to fly over the mountains. Richard had a big bag of popcorn in one hand and margarita mix in the other, and a copy of Bukowski stuffed in his pack. Hank looked at me as if to say, *I know I'm crazy, but I think this guy's crazier.*

He was.

They all survived, but not without a close call. While crossing a glacial outwash river, Sherry flipped a small raft and was washed away. Hank threw her a line, but she failed to grasp it, so he plunged into the raging current and caught her before she went through the surf. Richard grabbed the raft, their only means of crossing more rivers and reaching their pickup spot. That night around their campfire they laughed and told stories.

"When you have a big adventure and everybody survives," Richard said, "you talk, talk, talk. And when nobody survives, you get very quiet."

Later, Mark asked them what the title of his Glacier Bay book should be.

"Tides, Turds, and Tourists," Hank said.

"Bugs, Bergs, and Bureaucracy," Richard said.

Mark got the point. He dropped the chapter on the coast and ran a few pictures from the hike, labeling them in a way that obscured their location. He co-published the book with Goldbelt, the Juneau Native Corporation, and called it *Glacier Bay*. It won the Benjamin Franklin Nature Book Award a year later. He phoned me from Juneau, all excited. I congratulated him.

In her text, Sherry wrote, "Some places in this world fill a space larger than their actual geography. . . . I realized the truth of this as our small plane flew over Glacier Bay. . . . It was as if we floated above both the beginning and the end of the world, a world that contained both chaos and serenity."

I WAS OUT by the shed splitting wood when Melanie came to give me the news. A dead humpback whale had been discovered near

Point Gustavus, in the lower bay. Janet Doherty, a whale biologist, found it floating out there, and with help from local boat operators pulled it to shore. It was identified as Whale Number 68, a pregnant female about forty years old, also known as Snow, a name given to her by a researcher who first recorded her in Glacier Bay in 1975, four years before Richard, Michio, and I arrived. The year was now 2001. With help from a veterinarian from California, the National Park Service performed a necropsy and discovered a fractured brain case and crushed neck vertebrae. Everybody in town talked about it. People said a cruise ship hit it. The NPS issued a press release that added nothing to the gossip. They said the Park Service had received a phone call from somebody on board who felt a large thump as the ship left the bay. Behind the scenes, attorneys went to work.

"The crime wasn't in accidentally striking the whale," a park employee told me. "It was in failing to report the strike."

I had no interest in hiking out to Point Gustavus to see Snow's broken body just then. Michio had known her. I needed some time.

Naoko was coming for a visit. Melanie and I wanted the house and land to be ready. She stayed at a lodge in town, saying she didn't want to inconvenience us. She had Shoma with her, and Michio's parents, who had never been to Gustavus or Glacier Bay. We drove out to greet them, and handed them a wrapped gift. They had one for us in exchange. Shoma scampered about like a Dall sheep lamb, or—more appropriate to Glacier Bay—a mountain goat kid. Naoko pulled him to her side and had him shake my hand in greeting. Melanie's too. I loved looking into his bright face and seeing his father. They climbed into our car and I drove them to our house. It was raining hard, but the Hoshinos seemed undaunted. I offered to hold a small piece of roofing over Michio's parents to keep them dry. They declined.

The house site was a mess from the construction, mud everywhere, stacks of pallets and plywood. Shoma took pictures with a little Instamatic camera.

Speaking nervously, I tried to compensate for the mess, to get the

Hoshinos to understand what it would look like someday when the landscaping was finished and the moss came back, when boardwalks flowed through the trees and connected everything and . . . and . . . and . . .

Naoko smiled with deep, dark eyes.

"It's beautiful, Kim," she said. "Thank you."

"It'll look better someday, Naoko, after the . . ."

I stopped as she reached her hand out from under the eave and let the rain pool in it.

She said, "I am grateful."

For a brief moment all I could hear was the rain. Somewhere high in the Fairweather Range, in the birthplace of glaciers, snow was falling. Naoko had lost her husband, yet she had the capacity to be grateful. I had my life, my wife, my friends, and health and home, a purpose, a sense of place. I knew where I belonged. I had a thousand gifts right in front of me. They say gratitude is the most exquisite form of courtesy. For Naoko, though, it was a request.

She wanted me to do the right thing.

A YEAR AFTER Naoko's visit, Hank called.

"You want to hike around the point?" he asked, meaning Point Gustavus, an easy ten-mile walk from Bartlett Cove around the point into town.

"To see Snow, the whale?" I asked. Portions of the large carcass were still there.

"Yep. You ready?"

"Sure."

Anya and Melanie joined us. We ended up laughing most of the way. Everything was just funny that day. It might have been the water, or the sun, or a Greek-like tragedy-comedy thing. Hank said the new dock at Bartlett Cove was big enough to play soccer on. That started it. We threw sticks and chased each other, and wrestled in the sand near Point Gustavus.

Snow was not as large as I expected her to be. Much of her body had rotted away. Wolves had feasted on her, and perhaps a bear or two. Biologists had removed parts of her for research and education. Long strips of baleen were saved for the Gustavus school, where kids would learn whale anatomy, life history, and behavior.

Recently, scientists from SETI, the Search for Extra-Terrestrial Intelligence, had visited Point Adolphus (across Icy Strait from the entrance to Glacier Bay) to make sound recordings of humpback whales. They did this, they said, to better understand the origin, evolution, and distribution of life in the universe; to help determine if we humans were intelligent enough to recognize intelligence in other species right here on Earth. What was intelligence, exactly? SETI said they measured it by language "orders of entropy" and "degrees of complexity."

Huh? We listened for an hour and didn't get it.

"That should tell them something," Hank said.

A kayak guide and friend of ours, John Baston, took the SETI scientists to Point Adolphus so they could do their important work. One night as they stood on shore with their delicate instruments in the water, headphones on, listening for whales, John went down the beach about a hundred yards. He put a tube-like length of bull kelp in the water, and with the other end at his mouth he softly sang, "Louie, Louie, oh baby, we gotta go."

The SETI team didn't think it was funny.

Hank and I thought it was hilarious. We thought it was true intelligence.

That summer, more humpback whales were recorded in Glacier Bay than any summer before, all in waters that didn't exist two hundred and fifty years earlier. They communicated over great distances with sensitive acoustics. They moved with surprising agility, often very near to shore, using their fifteen-foot-long pectoral flippers. And while cruise ships traveled mid-channel at reduced speeds in designated "whale waters," they nonetheless cut through the sea in a manner unparalleled by any predator for fifty million years. Their speed and shape created "sound holes" off their bows that a whale in the wrong place at the wrong time could not hear.

Snow might have been asleep in the middle of the lower bay, or traveling slowly, breaking the surface in a modest way as she carried her unborn calf and dreamed her whale dreams in waters she'd known all her life, her massive heart beating slow and steady. From the bridge of a modern cruise ship, high on the ionosphere deck, she could have been difficult to see. The evidence says she was struck hard and fast. Maybe she never woke up. Or maybe she was seen swimming on an intercept course, and the bridge officers thought they could avoid her, and did not.

Standing beside her remains at Point Gustavus, I tried to imagine what it must have been like in 1750, when Glacier Bay was all glacier and no bay. The great tongue of ice that filled it then was in the earliest stages of catastrophic retreat (after occupying the bay for some two hundred years). Its tidewater face would have been six to eight miles across, and three hundred feet high. Icebergs would have filled Icy Strait from Pleasant Island to Cross Sound.

Since then a bay has been born, a nation too, one founded on unprecedented principles of freedom, democracy, and the pursuit of happiness. We have gone from slaughtering whales to celebrating them, from fearing wilderness to cherishing it. Countless new lives and friendships have come and gone in the cradle of resilience that is Glacier Bay.

If the land can heal and begin anew, can we too?

"Through every vicissitude of heat and cold, calm and storm . . . ," wrote John Muir, "we see that everything in Nature called destruction must be creation—a change from beauty to beauty."

Before she left the house that rainy Gustavus day, Naoko told me that Michio's ashes were in the Hoshino family gravesite at a Buddhist temple in Ichikawa, Japan. Not all of them, though. Some ashes were in his home in Fairbanks, and the rest were scattered on the tundra along the Jago River, his favorite place in the Arctic National Wildlife Refuge.

"I thought you would want to know that," she said.

AS THE LITTLE PLANE flew north over the spine of the Brooks Range, I looked out the window at the patterns below. Everything down there was the Arctic National Wildlife Refuge, and I didn't want to miss any of it.

Years before, Dr. Folsom had told me about rivers that were older than the mountains around them. He called them "antecedent" rivers; that is, they were there first. Over the deep time of millions of years, as the mountains rose, the rivers cut faster and held their original course. Watch for them, he said. It takes a remarkable river to hold its ground and defeat rock. I did watch for them. As far as I could see, though, the mountains had had their way in the Brooks Range for a very long time. They told the rivers where to go.

Melanie sat next to me with my hand in hers. Our friend Annie Griffiths Belt, a *National Geographic* photographer, sat up front and talked by headset with the pilot.

Spokes of sunlight spilled through clouds that wheeled overhead. As we approached the North Slope where green foothills tapered into the Coastal Plain toward the Arctic Ocean, the pilot banked east and I asked him about the Jago River.

"Yes," he said, "it's over there, to the northwest. See, with the sunlight glinting off it? That's the Jago, where the caribou are."

I watched it until it disappeared from view, that silver ribbon of water running to the sea, connecting all things. I watched as if looking back on a childhood, never knowing your life can become what it is, never knowing you can fall so deeply in love with a place.

Melanie squeezed my hand.

"You okay?" she asked.

"I'm fine," I said. "I'm just grateful, that's all."

HOLDING ON

Epilogue

CHRISTMAS MORNING. After breakfast with friends, Melanie and I drove out to Bartlett Cove where everything was quiet. Pan ice lay across the inner lagoon like the first page of winter. Trees stood sleeping in the cold. The air temperature had climbed to fifteen above and stopped, unwilling to go any higher. We found our kayaks under a tarp, frozen to the ground. What to do? We had an old double kayak on a rack nearby, a big yellow plastic thing that was more submarine than kayak, misshapen from the year before when it filled with rain on the rack and got bent like a taco. But it floated, in a way. We hauled it down to the shore and loaded up.

As usual, we said nothing. Through the years Melanie and I had learned to approach our kayaking silently. Glacier Bay had become our holy place. It wasn't just scenery, it was memory.

We got in—Melanie forward, me aft—and pushed off. I saw her take a deep breath and relax. Sitting in a kayak was like yoga for her. The busy, bustling world couldn't get her now. We began to paddle, pulling with one arm while pushing with the other, our paddles rising and falling stroke for stroke. We hit the paper-thin pan ice and listened to the crystals breaking all around us.

The tide was high. We went through the cut between the mainland and Lagoon Island and headed for sunshine far out in the middle of Bartlett Cove, near Lester Point.

Already my fingers and toes were cold. We paddled to stay
warm, working hard, knowing the day wouldn't last long.

We reached the sunshine and looked southwest to see the flat
waters of Glacier Bay open into Icy Strait, the pale sun moving in a
low winter arc over Chichagof Island, bashful, already in descent, full
of light but little warmth. Not a sound. The world was at peace . . .
somewhere, at least. I began to hum "Here Comes the Sun."

Hard to believe, George Harrison had died. After battling cancer, the youngest Beatle, wise beyond his years, slipped away peace-
fully in a friend's home in Los Angeles. People said he had no fear
of death. A day or two later I heard Garrison Keillor on the radio
playing songs from the album *All Things Must Pass*.

"Thank you for your music, George," he said. "Thank you for
your grace."

"He was a beautiful man," Paul McCartney said, ". . . like a
little brother to me."

His magical, mystery tour was over . . . or just beginning.
Everything around me seemed eternal and evanescent just then.
Uncertain if I was supposed to hold on or let go, I sat in a kayak in
Glacier Bay.

Rumor had it that the Ibach cabin was still standing, and last
summer somebody saw a bear on Garforth Island. A robin built its
nest next to the trail to our house, so we detoured around it.

"This is what it all comes down to," Melanie said, "making room
for others."

A famous historian speaking on the radio said that hundreds of
years from now when they write the history of the rise and fall of the
American Republic, they'll compare 1943, when we were told to
conserve for war, to sixty years later, 2003, when we were told to
consume for war. Be a patriot. Shop till you drop.

In Anchorage recently I had seen signs everywhere telling me to
buy, buy, buy so I could save, save, save. So many deals "too good

to pass up." I had no idea I needed to spend money to save it. So much vitriol and polarity on television. So much rant radio. I had to turn it off. I wanted to be informed, not inflamed.

Secretary of the Interior Gale Norton was in the city then, pushing for oil drilling in the Arctic National Wildlife Refuge, a place she called "a white nothingness." She wanted to drill along the Jago River for what she called "homeland defense," as if she were somehow defending the land itself. With people on a first-name basis in Alaska, I called her office to ask her to lunch, just as Richard had done with Lew Williams.

"And who are you?" a staffer asked me.

"Uh . . . Jim," I said. "Jim Peacock, conversationalist."

"And what exactly is it that you do?"

"I work on cruise ships. I . . . talk to people."

I'd seen Secretary Norton on television and figured I could talk to her too, about many things: her childhood and mine, where our values came from, the pioneer's paradox and what it means to take a risk and find a new language, a new definition of wealth.

She was unavailable, her staffer told me.

Miss Norton came from Wyoming, where carved into stone on the state university campus is a credo: STRIVE ON—THE CONTROL OF NATURE IS WON, NOT GIVEN.

Frank Murkowski had become Alaska's new governor (and appointed his daughter to fill his vacated U.S. Senate seat). I imagined that Secretary Norton had lunch with him that day, the two of them crafting a leave-no-lobbyist-behind energy bill, boldly "striving on" toward their mutual vision of a better, more prosperous Alaska.

I doubt they discussed global warming, melting permafrost, or Eskimos hearing thunder on the tundra for the first time in their lives. I doubt they considered the people of Shishmaref, living where the sea always froze, who now faced great uncertainty as winter storm waves eroded the bluffs beneath their homes. I doubt they discussed scientific reports that said ARCTIC PERENNIAL SEA ICE COULD BE GONE BY THE END OF THE CENTURY.

I doubt they discussed the recent prediction that in thirty to fifty years Glacier National Park in northwest Montana would have no glaciers. What would we call it then? Global Warming National Park?

According to glaciologists, more and more tidewater glaciers in Alaska were "going terrestrial." Starved for new snow, they retreated off tidewater and no longer calved ice into the sea. What did that say about glaciers still at tidewater? Were they extraterrestrial?

I liked to think so.

On my Alaska Airlines flight from Anchorage back to Juneau, en route home to Gustavus, the weather was what pilots call "severe clear." Glued to the window, I could see Hubbard Glacier pushing far down Disenchantment Bay, its massive tidewater front threatening again to pinch off Russell Fiord at Gilbert Point. Margerie Glacier looked feisty and well-fed, as did Johns Hopkins, Gilman, and Grand Pacific glaciers, all flowing into Glacier Bay. Deep snow lay in their mountain pantries.

I thought of John Muir, of the glaciers that inspired him; the ice that started a fire. I smiled and remembered his words: "The Master Builder chose for his tool, not the thunder and lightning to rend and split asunder, not the stormy torrent nor the eroding rain, but the tender snowflake, noiselessly falling through unnumbered generations."

Would the glaciers of Glacier Bay grow and merge and again fill the bay? Would yesterday become today? Is that what I wanted?

Hundreds of years ago when glaciers consumed Glacier Bay and climates cooled around the world from Switzerland to Siberia, a glacier marched down from its high perch in the Alps and buried a small Swiss town one home at a time, devastating the lives of the people there. As the glacier approached the little stone chapel and consumed it from back to front, people gathered to pray. The glacier didn't plow through this chapel. It rolled over it, gently wrapping itself around the front. And there it stopped. The wooden door, ornate with frescoes and stained glass, could still be seen through the ice. For many years the glacier stayed like this, holding the chapel in its frozen embrace. When it finally melted away, it returned the chapel to the people unharmed.

Once, yes, I wanted the icy rivers of Glacier Bay to come back. But now . . . I didn't know. If creation and destruction are one and the same, then what about our own moments of doubt and grace, the ones we bring upon ourselves? Does that which nurtures us in turn deserve our nurturing?

Richard asked me once if anything had changed.

"Yes," I said, "I have."

Children change. We know this and accept it. At a very young age they don't want to be scared. But once they get a little older they love it. They squeal in a wonderful mix of fear and glee as you set their faces aglow with surprise. Where does it go, this love of something bigger than any one of us, something wild and unpredictable?

If Glacier Bay has taught me anything, it is the willingness to accept a little fear and uncertainty in my life, in all our lives, from childhood to old age. It's a long and winding road, as Paul McCartney would say, but no worthwhile journey is short, straight, or easy.

We talk about how the world is changing, but what we're really talking about is how we are changing the world. It doesn't have to be. I've yet to see a man improve a tree.

BY NOW the sun had set and my toes were numb with cold. Soon I wouldn't feel them at all. Melanie handed me some Christmas chocolate. I handed her a flask of wine. Five goldeneyes swam by, much nearer to us than if we'd been talking and paddling. Melanie reached for my hand.

A minute later she asked, softly, "What are you thinking about?"

"Nothing." *Everything.*

"Guess what? We're the only kayak."

"Yes . . .," I said, "we probably are."

The silence stretched forever. The land, water, and sky were as still as heaven and earth holding its breath. I knew then that it wasn't the only kayak that gave me hope. It was having someone to share it with, a friend, a true love, a hand across a deep crevasse.

I once lamented to Hank about the rift between humans and nature, and he replied, "It isn't easy to change the world, but it's a good beginning if you can talk to your neighbor."

He and Anya were the new parents of a little girl named Linnea Rain, a huge sign of hope. Richard and Luann had taken Lydia and Laura to Thailand to attend school and become citizens of the world. Naoko would bring Shoma to Alaska every year so he could know what his father knew. Maybe each of them, alone or together, would one day be the only kayak.

I couldn't feel my toes. My nose was as cold as a glass knob. The kayak behaved as if it had shipped water. We needed to get back. We needed to stay. We needed to laugh and cry and sing and fly. We needed to let go and hold on. With only arms and shoulders we'd gotten ourselves out here; with only arms and shoulders we'd get ourselves back.

The sky had turned twilight blue. One stroke at a time we headed home. A seal watched. A raven called. We landed the kayak on Lagoon Island and Melanie walked ashore. She found a clamshell covered in hoarfrost and brought it to me, holding it delicately in her gloved hand. She pointed at the crystals, each a small glacier in itself, filled with light. I stared. She returned the clamshell to where she'd found it. When I looked at her face, rosy-cheeked and radiant, she was biting her lip and fighting back tears. Tears of joy. How good it was to have each other, to have our home and family and friends, this beautiful Earth and perfect day.

It was more than we would have hoped for.

But then, so was this bay.

Bibliography/Suggested Reading

Abbey, Edward. *Beyond the Wall: Essays from the Outside*. New York: Henry Holt & Co., 1984.

———. *One Life at a Time, Please*. New York: Henry Holt & Co., 1988.

Agassiz, Louis. *Études sur les Glaciers*. Neuchatel, 1840; New York: Hafner (reprint edition, translated by A. V. Carozzi), 1967.

Ambrose, Stephen E. *Undaunted Courage: Meriwether Lewis, Thomas Jefferson, and the Opening of the American West*. New York: Simon & Schuster, 1996.

Barnes, Julian. *Flaubert's Parrot*. New York: Vintage International, 1990.

Batin, Chris. "Where Giants Walk." *Outdoor Life*, March 1999.

Berry, Wendell. "Life is a Miracle." *Orion* magazine, Spring 2000.

Bohn, Dave. *Glacier Bay: The Land and the Silence*. San Francisco: Sierra Club-Ballantine Books, 1967.

Bolles, Edmund Blair. *The Ice Finders: How a Poet, a Professor, and a Politician Discovered The Ice Age*. Washington, D.C.: Counterpoint, 1999.

Boorstin, Daniel. *Hidden History*. New York: HarperCollins, 1987.

Brakel, Judith T. "Fishing Versus Majority Ideologies: A Southeast Alaska Case." *Alaska Journal of Anthropology*, Volume One, Number One, 2001.

———. "A Maritime Sense of Place: Southeast Alaska Fishermen and Mainstream Nature." Ideologies. Unpublished Master's Thesis, Department of Anthropology, University of Alaska, Fairbanks, 1999.

Bronowski, Jacob. *The Ascent of Man*. New York: Little, Brown and Company, 1974.

Brown, William E. *Denali: Symbol of the Alaskan Wild*. Virginia Beach, Virginia: The Donning Company, 1993.

Caldwell, Francis. *Land of the Ocean Mists*. Seattle, Washington: Alaska Northwest Books, 1986.

Catton, Theodore. *Land Reborn: A History of Administration and Visitor Use in Glacier Bay National Park And Preserve.* Seattle, Washington: U.S. Government Printing Office, 1995.

Craig, G. Y., and J. H. Hull. *James Hutton—Present and Future.* London: Geological Society of London, 1999.

Davidson, Art. *In the Wake of the* Exxon Valdez: *The Devastating Impact of the Alaska Oil Spill.* San Francisco: Sierra Club Books, 1990.

DeMille, Nelson. *The Charm School.* New York: Warner Books, 1989.

Durbin, Kathie. *Tongass: Pulp Politics and the Fight for the Alaskan Rain Forest.* Corvallis, Oregon: Oregon State University Press, 1999.

Ehrlich, Gretel. *John Muir: Nature's Visionary.* Washington, D.C.: National Geographic Books, 2000.

Fagan, Brian. *The Little Ice Age: How Climate Made History, 1300–1850.* New York: Basic Books, 2001.

Fitzgerald, F. Scott. *The Great Gatsby.* New York: Scribner (reprint edition), 1996.

Fradkin, Philip. *Wildest Alaska: Journeys of Great Peril in Lituya Bay.* Berkeley, California: University of California Press, 2003.

Grun, Bernard. *The Timetables of History: A Horizontal Linkage of People and Events.* New York: Simon & Schuster/Touchstone, 1991.

Hardin, Garrett. "The Tragedy of the Commons." *Science* (162, 1243–1248), 1968.

Haycox, Stephen. *Frigid Embrace: Politics, Economics, and Environment in Alaska.* Corvallis, Oregon: Oregon State University Press, 2002.

Heacox, Kim. *Alaska's Inside Passage.* Portland, Oregon: Graphic Arts Center Publishing Co., 1997.

———. *In Denali.* Santa Barbara, California: Companion Press, 1992.

Hoshino, Michio. *Grizzly* (translated by Karen Colligan-Taylor). San Francisco: Chronicle Books, 1987.

———. *The Grizzly Bear Family Book* (translated by Karen Colligan-Taylor). New York: North-South Books, 1994.

Hutton, James. *Theory of the Earth*, Vol. III (facsimile). London: Geological Society of London (reprint edition), 1997.

Keeble, John. *Out of the Channel: The* Exxon Valdez *Oil Spill in Prince William Sound*. New York: HarperCollins, 1991.

Kerouac, Jack. *The Lonesome Traveler*. Grove Press (reprint edition), 1985.

Kittredge, William, and Allen Morris Jones (editors). *The Best of Montana's Short Fiction*. Guilford, Connecticut: The Lyons Press, 2004.

Kunstler, James Howard. *The Geography of Nowhere: The Rise and Decline of America's Man-Made Landscape*. New York: Simon & Schuster, 1993.

LaPerouse, Jean-Francois, Comte de. *The Voyage of LaPerouse Around the World in the Years 1785, 1786, 1787, & 1788* (translated from French). London: John Stockdale, 1797.

Limerick, Patricia Nelson. *The Legacy of Conquest: The Unbroken Past of the American West*. New York: W. W. Norton, 1987.

Lennon, John, with Paul McCartney, George Harrison, and Ringo Starr. *The Beatles Complete Scores*. Milwaukee, Wisconsin: Hal Leonard Publishing, 1989.

Lentfer, Hank, and Carolyn Servid (editors). *Arctic Refuge: A Circle of Testimony*. Minneapolis, Minnesota: Milkweed Editions, 2001.

Leopold, Aldo. *A Sand County Almanac*. Oxford, England: Oxford University Press (reprint edition), 1987.

Litwin, Tom (editor). *The Harriman Alaska Expedition Retraced: A Century of Change, 1899–2001*. Piscataway, New Jersey: Rutgers University Press, 2004.

Manchester, William. *A World Lit Only by Fire: The Medieval Mind and the Renaissance, Portrait of an Age*. New York: Little, Brown and Company, 1992.

Manning, Richard. *Against the Grain: How Agriculture Has Hijacked Civilization*. New York: North Point Press, 2004.

Marx, Leo. *The Machine in the Garden: Technology and the Pastoral Idea in America*. Oxford, England: Oxford University Press, 1964.

McKibben, Bill. *The End of Nature*. New York: Doubleday (reprint edition), 1999.

McMurtry, Larry. "How the West Was Won or Lost." *The New Republic*, October 22, 1990.

McPhee, John. *Annals of the Former World*. New York: Farrar, Straus and Giroux, 1998.

———. *Coming into the Country*. New York: Farrar, Straus and Giroux, 1976.

Melville, Herman. *Moby-Dick*. New York: Harper Brothers, November 1851. (Originally published under the title *The Whale*, 3 vol.). London: Richard Bentley, October 1851.

Muir, John. *Stickeen: John Muir and the Brave Little Dog*. Heyday Books (reprint edition), 1990.

———. *Travels in Alaska*. New York: Houghton Mifflin, 1915.

Murie, Adolph. *The Wolves of Mount McKinley*. Washington, D.C.: U.S. Government Printing Office, 1944.

Nash, Roderick. *Wilderness and the American Mind*. New Haven, Connecticut: Yale University Press, 1982.

Nelson, Richard K. *Make Prayers to the Raven: A Koyukon View of the Northern Forest*. Chicago: University of Chicago Press, 1983.

———. *The Island Within*. San Francisco: North Point Press, 1989.

Nicholson-Lord, David. "The Politics of Travel: Is Tourism Just Colonialism in Another Guise?" *The Nation*, October 6, 1997.

O'Claire, Rita, with Richard Carstensen and Robert H. Armstrong. *The Nature of Southeast Alaska: A Guide to Plants, Animals, and Habitats*. Portland, Oregon: Alaska Northwest Books, 1992.

Oliver, Mary. *Blue Pastures*. New York: Harcourt Brace & Company, 1991.

Pyle, Robert Michael. "The Rise and Fall of Natural History." *Orion* magazine, Autumn 2001.

Reid, Harry Fielding. "Notebooks and Journals of Expeditions of 1890 and 1892." *Glaciology*, American Geographic Society, 1892.

Schooler, Lynn. *The Blue Bear: A True Story of Friendship, Tragedy, and Survival in the Alaskan Wilderness*. New York: Ecco, 2002.

Scidmore, Eliza R. "Discovery of Glacier Bay," *National Geographic*, April 1896.

Sellars, Richard West. *Preserving Nature in the National Parks: A History.* New Haven, Connecticut: Yale University Press, 1997.

Servid, Carolyn, and Donald Snow (editors). *The Book of the Tongass.* Minneapolis, Minnesota: Milkweed Editions, 1999.

Simpson, Sherry. *Glacier Bay* (photographs by Mark Kelley). Juneau, Alaska: Mark Kelley Photography, 2000.

Smith, Adam. *The Wealth of Nations.* New York: Bantam Classics (reprint edition), 2003.

Smith, Henry Nash. *Virgin Land: The American West as Symbol and Myth.* Cambridge, Massachusetts: Harvard University Press, 1971.

Sontag, Susan. *On Photography.* New York: Farrar, Straus and Giroux, 1977.

Stegner, Wallace. *Where the Bluebird Sings to the Lemonade Springs; Living and Writing in the West.* New York: Random House, 1992.

Streveler, Greg. *The Natural History of Gustavus.* Gustavus, Alaska: Icy Strait Environmental Services, 1992.

Tocqueville, Alexis de. *Democracy in America.* New York: Signet Book (reprint edition), 2001.

Turner, Frederick Jackson. "The Significance of the Frontier in American History." Tucson, Arizona: University of Arizona Press (reprint edition), 1986.

Turner, Jack. *The Abstract Wild.* Tucson, Arizona: University of Arizona Press, 1996.

Weeden, Robert B. *Alaska, Promises to Keep.* New York: Houghton Mifflin, 1978.

Winchester, Simon. *The Map that Changed the World.* New York: HarperCollins, 2001.

Wolfe, Linnie Marsh. *Son of the Wilderness: The Life of John Muir.* New York: Knopf, 1945.

Acknowledgments

The making of this book was something of a glacier, luminous at times, but mostly a long grind, impossible without the help of friends and the kindness of strangers. The idea came into my head more than ten years before publication, but didn't land on paper until I *believed* I could do it.

Where did the belief come from? I think first of Carolyn Servid and Dorik Mechau and their Island Institute in Sitka, creating and hosting twenty years of writing symposia that touched the lives of hundreds, mine included. I think of Richard Steele, Michio Hoshino, and Hank Lentfer, who taught me to laugh. I think of Lynn Schooler, who in his book, *The Blue Bear*, showed me how to write about Michio without making him into something he was not. I hope I've succeeded as well as Lynn did.

I think of Mike Folsom who still teaches at Eastern Washington University; who received my manuscript and wrote back, "I too recall that trip to Montana, that encounter with the lady landowner who wanted to supervise our use of her scenery, [my] driving and semi-poetical invitations to see and look and open your pores and smell and taste and roll around in the glory of the place . . . What a fine encounter with the better parts of what it means to be human . . . Thank you for reaching back and reaching out. This is a good time in my life and you have made it better."

I think of Tomie Patrick Lee, the first woman superintendent of Glacier Bay National Park & Preserve, one of the best in the Service, I believe, because she works from gratitude more than from pride. I think of other Park Service employees past and present who have honored me with their friendship and dedicated themselves to the well-being of Glacier Bay and Denali national parks. Some are ptarmigan who stay year-round. Others are terns who summer in Alaska and winter elsewhere. And still others are watchful ravens who play active roles in Friends of Glacier Bay and Denali Citizens Council. Bless you.

I think of Bruce Black, the first full-time ranger in Glacier Bay (1953–55), who watched icebergs drift into Bartlett Cove, and half a century later, retired in Oregon, gave me permission to use his photograph of Joe and Muz Ibach. I think of Bruce Paige, former chief naturalist in Glacier Bay, who phoned me in Death Valley and offered me a job. He hired Richard and Melanie too, and many other people who became dear friends.

I think of fellow writers, photographers, and musicians who encouraged me in this project and whose vision inspires me to believe that we can turn this machine around: Dave Bohn, Tom Walker, Kathy Moore, Doug Chadwick, Sherry Simpson, Bill Sherwonit, Dean Littlepage, Deborah Williams, Tom Bean, John Baston, Bill McKibben, Jeff Rennicke, Ian Ramsey, Allen Smith, Dan Henry, Libby Roderick, Annie Griffiths Belt, Karen Colligan-Taylor, and Mike Taylor.

I think of my literary agent, Marianne Merola, and my editor, Holly Rubino, who saw in a manuscript a book, and believed in it when others did not, and worked hard to make it the best it could be. I think about my copy editor, Jane Crosen, and her valuable corrections to the manuscript and her praise. Any faults or shortcomings that remain are mine alone.

I think of my elders: Bob Howe, Bill Brown, Greg Streveler, Richard Nelson, Jack Lentfer, Sandy Kogl, and George Wagner, the best erratics Alaska could have.

I think of Melanie, who loves the tundra and the tides, and is always there for me.

"I celebrate your journey," Mike Folsom wrote. "I grieve for your journey. I trust in your heart and in your honesty and in your friends that your journey goes on well."

It will, Mike.

Thank you all.

Author's Biography

Award-winning writer Kim Heacox is the author of several non-fiction books and the novel *Caribou Crossing*. His feature articles have appeared in *Audubon*, *Travel & Leisure*, *Wilderness*, *Islands*, *Orion*, and *National Geographic Traveler*. His opinion-editorials, written for the *Los Angeles Times*, have appeared in many major newspapers across the U.S. When not playing the guitar or doing simple carpentry or writing another novel, he's sea kayaking with Melanie, his wife of nearly twenty years, or watching a winter wren on the woodpile. Learn more about him at www.kimheacox.com.

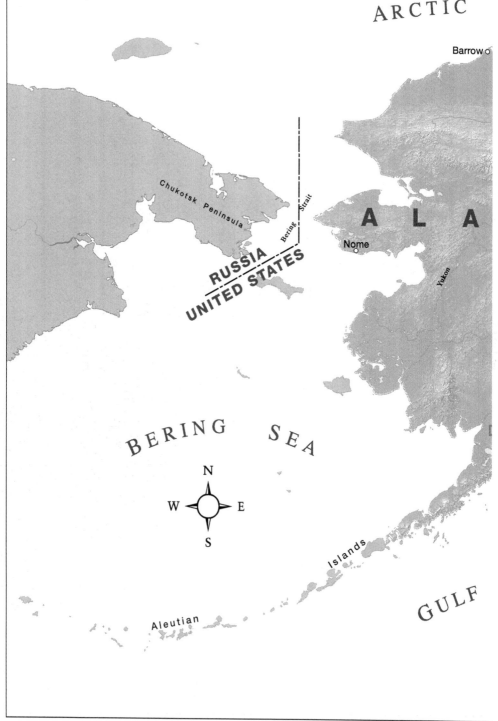

Made in the USA
San Bernardino, CA
23 April 2017